Keith Johnstone, *The Last Bird*

Keith Johnstone was born in 1933 in Devon, England. He is a theatre director, writer and drama professor whose teachings and books have had a major influence on the art of improvisation. He worked from 1956 to 1966 at the Royal Court Theatre as play-reader, drama teacher and director and became Associate Director of the theatre. His unorthodox techniques were aimed at opening his students' imagination and improving their spontaneity. After leaving the Royal Court Theatre in 1966, Johnstone continued to develop important principles of acting and drama. He founded The Theatre Machine, an improvisational group in England which toured in many countries. Keith Johnstone taught at the Royal Academy of Dramatic Art until he left England and moved to Canada in the 1970s, and has taught or given workshops at major European Theatre Schools and Universities. In Canada, he taught at the University of Calgary, of which he is now a professor emeritus, and is a founding Artistic Director of the Loose Moose Theatre at Calgary. Johnstone still lives in Calgary and teaches all over the world.

Keith Johnstone has developed many new forms of improvisation including Theatresports™, Maestro Impro, Gorilla Theatre and The Life Game which (along with his techniques) are now being used worldwide, and has written two books about his work (*Impro: Improvisation and the Theatre* and *Impro for Storytellers*).

www.keithjohnstone.com

Keith Johnstone

The Last Bird

Stories & Plays

Alexander Verlag Berlin | Cologne

Also by Keith Johnstone

· *Impro – Improvisation and the Theatre* (1979)
· *Impro for Storytellers: Theatresports and the Art of Making Things Happen* (1999)

© by Alexander Verlag Berlin | Cologne 2012
Alexander Wewerka, Fredericiastrasse 8, D-14008 Berlin, Germany.
All illustrations are by the author.
Proofreader Nick de Somogy
All rights reserved.
info@alexander-verlag.com
www.alexander-verlag.com
ISBN 978-3-89581-270-5

CONTENTS

Meeting Beckett 7

Stories
Restart 23
Noah 24
The Most Amazing Lion in All the World 25
Educated Fleas 28
Another Fine Mess 31
The Miracle 35
Connibeer's Leg 40
Fitting In 59
My Adventure With the Reverend 80
The Cord (*an adapted play*) 100
Open Season (*an adapted play*) 120
The Wheelchair 134
My Wife's Madness 139

Plays
Frog Wife 148
The Last Bird 186
Moby Dick 277
Crusoe 293

Oliver. *The Word Story* 312

MEETING BECKETT

I was one of a handful of would-be painters who hung around the Battersea Men's Institute. They admired Garbo, whom I'd never seen, and Cézanne, whose achievement I was blind to. They had booked seats for Peter Hall's production of *Waiting For Godot*, a reputedly "difficult" play by someone called Samuel Beckett, so I went along with them.

I regarded the West End Theatre as a kind of placebo, but *Godot* was the real thing. It was about the sort of people we grew up with. Vladimir and Estragon were poor. They had to find work. They had some education, but they had no idea why they existed (and the theory that a "messiah" had "saved" them was ridiculous). Pozzo was the sort of landlord who would enjoy removing the roof from your house, and Lucky was one of those millions of poor wretches who slave away for a few crumbs. I was so thrilled by the play that when the interval came I urged my friends to leave.

"That was perfect!" I said. "It's a complete statement. Anything more will ruin it. Let's walk back."

They refused, so I went back in with them, and we discovered that the second act was a compressed and more upsetting version of the first, nailing it home.

Each evening we took pleasure in the knowledge that *Godot* was being enjoyed by yet another audience.

"The second act must be starting about now!" we'd say, and we'd cheer up.

We were sure that the author must be a young man like ourselves, but he wasn't.

The play seemed so simple – none of us found it obscure – and yet fifty years after the first English production Simon Callow can write that "for no known reason Pozzo is suddenly blind and Lucky suddenly dumb." Pozzo becomes blind and Lucky becomes dumb because time degrades us and takes away what is most precious to us. And why does

Lucky carry sand? Because his work is pointless! It's difficult to see how Beckett could have made it clearer.

Kenneth Tynan, heartless as usual, claimed that *Godot* was "the funniest play in London". Displayed outside the theatre his review added to the confusion, and led to laughter at bizarre moments (as when Lucky gets kicked).

Godot presents us as animals who are tormented by unanswerable questions, and who are aware of their mortality. "They give birth astride of a grave, the light gleams an instant, then it's night once more." What's obscure about that?

***

I saw this first English production eight times (and in those days I had to pay for my tickets). After one performance I enthused about the play to a waitress (Lorenza Mazzetti). We discovered that we were fans of Kafka, and of silent movies. Three weeks later, after seeing the last of the short films that Chaplin made for the Essanay company, she led me to Soho Square, and up a staircase, and up a narrower staircase, and up a narrower and more precipitous staircase to a room that for a split second seemed festooned with black seaweed. The "seaweed" was hundreds of dangling strips of thirty-five millimetre movie film. Among them sat Lindsay Anderson who was editing a movie that she had directed, and which she had somehow neglected to mention.

Tony Richardson and George Devine were directing the Royal Court Theatre (this was in 1956). Anderson, who knew them, accused them of "playing safe" by commissioning established authors. I had just won a prize in a newspaper short-story competition so when they asked, "What unknown should we commission?" he said, "Why not Keith?"

The money they'd paid me soon ran out, so I became their reader of plays. Devine asked me to write a pamphlet about Beckett to help publicize *Endgame*. It wasn't difficult – I just alternated extracts from reviews with suitable comments – but Devine admired it, so, by default, I became their "expert on Beckett".

***

We sat around a table in a small, low-ceilinged room, at Devine's house. This "intimate gathering" had been arranged to honour Roger Blin and Jean Martin (from the French cast of Beckett's *Endgame*). Colin Wilson, John Osborne and myself sat opposite them, and Beckett and Devine sat at either side of the table as "buffers" between the two groups. Beckett was to my left but I couldn't get much response out of him.

The tobacco smoke kept forcing me to exit across the hall to a toilet where I threw up. I kept staggering back, not wanting to miss anything that Beckett might say (this might have been my one chance to be in his company) but for two and a half hours he leant forwards with hands clasped and head bowed while the conversation continued over and around him. Was he ill? Was he praying? Was he praying for the meeting to be over? All evening he hardly said a word. When the party broke up he followed me into the hall.

"Would you have lunch with me tomorrow?" he said.

***

He was not the austere and grim person that was described in print. Journalists saw him that way because he resented being interviewed and/or photographed. Photographers liked to make him look ghoulish, but if you saw him on a bus you'd never think, "Who's that tormented person sitting over there?"

His privacy was so important to him that keeping a record of our conversations, or our correspondence, would have felt like a betrayal. Years later I was astounded when he let Deirdre Bair write a biography. He had told her: "I won't help you but I won't stand in your way," and this was enough to have people cooperate with her.

At that first lunch he expressed indignation at reviewers who had detected a "Christian message" in *Godot,* and at the way that the play had been softened in its first English production: Peter Hall had added a fragment of Bartók's *Dance Suite for Orchestra* when Gogo and Didi listened, the leaves on the tree were obtrusive palm fronds, the lighting romanticized the actors, and so on. I told him that whatever the faults of the production the play had still been an overwhelming experience, that it was why I had accepted the commission to write a play of my own, that it had changed my life forever – but he was unwavering.

He invited me to lunch when the mood took him – or perhaps when no one else was available. We always sat opposite each other, and there was never a third person present (unless I had invited someone). Most of the time we ate in silence. One such silence lasted until he was spooning his dessert. Then he said: "What do you young people think of James Joyce?"

"Irrelevant," I said, and the conversation lapsed until he paid the bill.

He once said, out of the blue: "Joyce walked like a heron in long grass, lifting each leg high and then setting it straight down." (The blind Joyce must have been trying to avoid smashing his shins.) Another time he told me that his aim in writing *Endgame* was to create a play that had no crescendos or decrescendos, that sustained one level of tension from beginning to end. This seemed such a stupid ambition that I hadn't the heart to argue with him, but it turned out to be the path that he was determined to pursue.

Sometimes a more complex bubble of thought would break the surface. I remember him suddenly explaining how he would direct *Hamlet*. The gist of it was that Hamlet would be centre stage the whole time, and the other characters would move only so much as they had "freedom of action".

I invited Ann Jellicoe to have lunch with him. Her extraordinary play *The Sport of My Mad Mother* had just been savaged by the critics, so I was sure that he'd know who she was. He was charming to her; there were no silences at all, even though, as I found out later, he had no idea who she was. She asked him why he had changed from writing in French to writing in English. He said sardonically: "Exchange of boredom."

I was comfortable with his silences, and would never ask fool questions like "Who is Godot?" or "What did you intend when you were writing the play?" But I wasn't the best of companions. I wouldn't drink with him because I was giving up alcohol (and he was appalled when I offered him some marijuana). I'm sure he had a better time with Harold Pinter; they would have talked about cricket, and Pinter would never have dismissed Joyce as "irrelevant". He was far more on Beckett's "wavelength" than I was.

Why did Beckett put up with me? Why did he send me plays personally – his own plays and those of other writers? Almost certainly it was because Devine – whom he trusted – had recommended me, and because he felt it a duty to encourage young writers.

He was a sparse figure, a sometime cricketer, lean, angular, with pale blue eyes and a soft Irish accent. He had some resemblance to an eagle refusing to savage Prometheus. He seemed a bit hunted – but then so do I. There was no sense of being with an academic. He didn't flaunt his learning. He didn't try to impress you any more than the Dalai Lama would try to impress you – this made him feel like a friend that you had known for years.

When I first knew him I never saw him use a wallet. His jacket pocket was stuffed with pound notes. I fantasized that he had a trunk crammed with pound notes and that each morning he took out a handful. He can't have needed money, not with *Godot* being a performed in city after city. He didn't seem to have any respect for money. I couldn't imagine him owning a chateau, or a large yacht.

He decided that he would give the Nobel Prize money to "promising young writers" so he asked John Calder (his publisher) for a list of deserving candidates. Calder was embarrassed because he would have preferred to distribute the money to his own stable of writers but that wouldn't have looked good. It took weeks of torment before he managed to hammer out a reasonable list. And then Beckett apologized, and confessed that the money had already been distributed.

***

I found him sardonic, rather than miserable (except for that first evening at George Devine's). His view of life was pessimistic, but even Buddha teaches that "all life is suffering". Was he any more depressed than, for example, Woody Allen, who says: "Without any question I think that life is tragic. There are oases of comedy within it. But, when the day is done and it's all over, the news is bad. We come to an unpleasant end."*

Beckett had once written to Eisenstein requesting a job as an unpaid assistant director, and yet he had never seen Dovzhenko's *Earth*, a movie that was important to me (mostly because of the hero's walk in the twilight). He agreed to see it until I said: "His universe is just as complete as yours, except that it doesn't deal with physical pain."

"Augh!" he said. "That's easy!" And he lost interest (just as well, because when I invited a group of other playwrights to see it they dismissed it as a propaganda film for Stalin's Collective Farm policy).

Blake wrote that "Contraries do not negate", and I agree. The universe is everything you want to say about it, dazzlingly beautiful and hideously ugly, wonderful and nightmarish, and these opposites don't cancel out, but Beckett would have none of that. For him, future pain diminished pleasure now. He had been an athlete but his body kept letting him down. And, of course, like most great pessimists (Sartre, Camus, Dean Swift, etc.) he had no children.

People were eager to please him to an extent that puzzled me. Actors like Billie Whitelaw or Jack MacGowran were devoted to him – that was understandable – but so were the two young secretaries in the office (one was fifteen years old and the other was sixteen). I discovered that they were learning his plays by heart. Many famous people came through the office but no one else had such an effect on them, yet all he would have done was to be courteous, and to be himself.

***

There were sides to Beckett that I never glimpsed. Kristin Linklater wrote for permission to present an evening of his writings intermingled with Shakespearian sonnets. She received a postcard in which he refused to have his work associated with "Shakespeare outpourings".

---

* *Guardian Weekly*, 6–12 January 2006.

My friend Marc Wilkinson had composed music to the "dry leaves" section in *Godot*. He phoned Beckett and a very old man answered, saying: "Yes? Who is it?" Marc identified himself, and heard the man – perhaps some ancient family retainer – plod away to croak "Sam! Sam!" Marc was invited round to the apartment (which was full of large old dark furniture). After he arrived the phone rang and Beckett answered it in the ancient retainer voice, saying: "Yes, who is it? I'm sorry, Mr. Beckett is not here."

This was before there were answering machines to screen one's calls.

***

I had been astonished when he invited me to lunch, and I was even more astonished when he invited me into his rehearsals. Few directors enjoy being watched by outsiders, but Beckett was open to anyone that he thought was serious about Theatre. From then on I watched him direct as often as possible. (In later years he invited all kinds of people – perhaps I had made a good impression.)

He felt that everything on a stage had to earn it's right to be there. He didn't like "decoration". He explained this to me in a letter, saying that: "A stage should be an area of maximum verbal presence and maximum corporeal presence."* (Hence the rope around Lucky's neck, the garbage bins in *Endgame*, the mud in *Happy Days*, and so on.) The word *corporeal* is far better that the word *visual*. "Corporeal" means fleshly, means solid, means something graspable, whereas "visual" might describe the traditional *Swan Lake* rather than *Endgame*.

Beckett directed the actors (even though Devine was the official director). His manner was reticent, almost self-effacing; he preferred to climb onto the stage to speak quietly to an actor rather than give notes from the auditorium, but he knew exactly what he wanted. He gave the exact inflections and rhythms for the lines – and they were always right. If he'd read the play aloud to the actors they would have absorbed the

---

* This sentence was quoted by William Gaskill in his autobiography.

inflections unconsciously, and I think that when he was older he began to do that.

I never heard him encourage the actors to be emotional. Like most playwrights he thought that emotion distracts from the text. If you stress the verb, respect the noun, and sustain the energy right through to the end of the thought, the words will convey the feeling.

I've directed *Godot* at least five times. One Vladimir told me that he had no idea "what to do" with the great speech that begins: "Was I sleeping while the others suffered? Am I sleeping now? Tomorrow, when I wake, or think I do, what will I say of today? That with Estragon my friend, at this place, until the fall of night, I waited for Godot?"*

I said: "It's a wonderful speech – do nothing. Just say the lines clearly."

He took my advice (perhaps to prove that it was bad advice) and I wept, and the other actors wept, and the stage-manager wept, and even the prompter wept. Vladimir was elated – at last he had experienced himself as a great actor – but from then on he couldn't help asserting his "ownership" of the speech. He kept adding emotion. This became a screen between us and the text, and it never thrilled us again.

That speech mustn't be done for the glorification of the actor or as 'giving the message of the play'.

Beckett's fault as a director – when I knew him – was that he tried to re-achieve in the directing what he had already achieved in the writing. What was grim became even grimmer.

Productions that stress the misery of Beckett's characters encourage theories about the "Theatre of Boredom". I saw twenty minutes of a *Godot* in which the actor playing Vladimir held his face in a mask of grief, but Vladimir is not at a funeral. He's trying to pass the time enjoyably under difficult circumstances. Even in death-camps the prisoners make jokes. Beckett's characters are interesting when they struggle to be happy.

---

* Beckett translated *Godot* into English himself, and wherever I can detect a difference, the English version seems superior to the French. It's sad that when other countries translate *Godot* they use the French version.

I watched him direct *Happy Days* – the play in which Winnie sinks into the earth while trying to stay cheerful (like all those millions of women who are sinking into the sludge of suburbia). He paid little attention to the humour, and his pedantry killed any possibility of playfulness. A week before our opening he flew to Paris for the French premiere. Madeleine Renaud, who played Winnie, was reported to have had a great comic success. I thought that he'd be furious, but he arrived back delighted by the play's reception, and continued directing in exactly the same leaden and humourless way as before. Michelangelo may have been tormented by the infinity of shapes within the uncarved block, but for Beckett there would only have been one shape.

***

When he sent me plays written by his acquaintances they were always imitations of his own plays. The pages of my own work that he praised were the ones most influenced by him.

He passionately resisted any changes to his work. Not for him "director's theatre" – in which the text is just a starting point. Even after his death nothing was to be altered. He saw Max Brod's decision to publish the stories that Kafka had asked him to destroy as a shameful betrayal. Even in the grave the author had to be the one in charge.

There was an element of irrationality about Beckett's stubbornness. I was watching the rehearsals of *Krapp's Last Tape* when Beckett arrived carrying what I thought was a bottle concealed in a paper bag. It was his slippers. He asked Krapp (Pat Magee) to shuffle about the stage wearing them, and was pleased by the sound that they made, the exact sound he had imagined (well, yes – because they were the slippers that he had been shuffling about in while he was writing the play). Magee wore them during the performance but the exact sound was irrelevant to the spectators.

It's not quite true that he never altered his work. Krapp was supposed to slip on a banana skin at the beginning of *Krapp's Last Tape*. When Pat Magee protested that he wasn't a knock-about comedian Beckett cut the effect instantly. There was no discussion, no suggestion that they should hire a gymnastic instructor.

When he directed *Godot* at the Schiller Theatre he cut some lines, including some when Pozzo was fussing with his pipe – "too boring", he said.

He occasionally made minor changes that I regretted. For example, when Estragon asked, "Don't we have any rights?" Vladimir used to say, "We've waived them," but the printed text now says, "We got rid of them." An actor must have complained that it was difficult to get the sense across to the audience, but I admired the way that it took seconds for the audience to comprehend the word "waived", and how the word compelled you to elongate it as you said it.

He had trouble with the Royal Censor (as we all did). For example, the line in *Endgame* about God – "The Bastard! He doesn't exist!" – was found objectionable, not because of the atheism, but because it cast doubt on the chastity of the Virgin Mary.

I remember Devine returning from St. James's Palace, outraged by the Lord Chamberlain's interference with *Krapp's Last Tape*. There's a line that says "Let me in" that occurs in the "reeds sighing beneath the stem" sequence. The Lord Chamberlain (who was an ex-Guards officer) had said: "It means he wants to Roger her, old boy!" – a reference to the chorus of a bawdy song about "Roger the Lodger" that must have been belted out during randy evenings in the barracks.

***

When people asked, "Is Beckett mad?" I used to say, like Dr. Watson describing Holmes, that he was the sanest man I knew. But if they'd asked, "Is Beckett normal?" I'd have had to say that he did not always behave like a normal person – often because of his desire to act fairly and courteously.

He took me to the first night of *Happy Days*. We sat in what were considered the best seats (five rows back and in the exact centre). There was a murmur when people recognized him.

The curtain rose and enough light bounced off of Jocelyn Herbert's light-toned set to make us clearly visible to Winnie (Brenda Bruce), who was sunk to her waist in a mound centre-stage.

Ten minutes into the play Beckett stood up and squeezed his way along the row to vanish behind a curtained exit that led to a toilet. The total silence in the auditorium – not a laugh, not a chuckle during the entire performance – made his exit very noticeable. A "normal" person would have watched the rest of the play from the back of the auditorium, but Beckett – being supersensitive to such things – didn't want Brenda Bruce to think that he had walked out on her, so he edged his way his way back to his seat. Ten minutes later he had to leave again. By the third time this happened I'd had the sense to change places with him so that he had one less person to negotiate. I remember him as traversing out and back about twelve times, but common sense tells me that it can hardly have been more than six. Even so, it was like some sort of avant-garde provocation.

***

Whenever I really tried to persuade Beckett of something I always failed. The first time was when I tried to tell him that Peter Hall's production had not destroyed the power of *Godot*. When he seemed likely to end up like Giaccometti (the minimalist sculptor who "sculpted" the tree for the first production of *Godot*), I argued that "less is not always more!", that one is not responsible for one's inspiration, that the imagination should say what it wants to say, and that *Endgame* reads like an earlier play than *Godot* because *Godot* is more expansive, is richer, is more multifaceted. It was like talking to a wall. I saw his work as going into a decline and I began to lose interest. The genius for language was still there, but there were to be no more *Godot*s. I believe that after the reception of *Godot* he was determined never to be misunderstood ever again, and minimalism offered a way to achieve this.

The last time I tried to influence him was when I adapted *Philoctetes* for Sir Laurence Olivier's Old Vic Theatre. It was to be preceded by the first English performance of Beckett's short play (called *Play*) in which the three actors are trapped in vases with just their heads sticking out (more minimalism). He had directed them to speak in a lunatically fast staccato fashion with the result that they were often unintelligible, especially when their monologues overlapped. Olivier was afraid of Beckett so he fled to Brighton leaving William Gaskill in charge. Gaskill, who hardly knew Beckett, asked me to help.

When you are familiar with a text it's difficult to judge how clearly the actors are speaking it (because your brain fills in the gaps). I solve this by inviting courageous strangers to shout "What!" whenever a word is spoken indistinctly. I hoped that it might be possible to explain this to Beckett – after all, why would he want his text turned into gibberish? But the moment that he realized that we wanted him to slow it down, he reacted quietly, but grimly. Suddenly I was Max Brod betraying the dying Kafka. It was my only unpleasant encounter with him, and one of my last before I moved to Canada. The last time I was with him Tynan brought Sean Connery over to introduce him (Connery had become world-famous as James Bond). Beckett was courteous, but I'm not sure that he knew who Connery was.

***

Years after writing this essay – and weeks after this book first appeared in print – Theresa Dudeck, my literary executor, discovered – among my papers – a couple of trivial notes from Beckett, plus a short letter and a long letter.

The shorter one explained that he had sent a story of mine to an editor of the *Paris Review*, advising him to accept it (when it was rejected he made John Calder publish it). He says that "I do hope they will and that you will not object to my having done this without consulting you… Good luck and always write the Dichtung and the Wahrheit." It would have greatly encouraged me had I been able to read it, but the sloping handwriting defeated me. It took the skills of Theresa Dudeck and Frank Totino – fiftyfour years later – to decipher it.

The longer letter was typed and must have been far more difficult to compose than it is to read. It's an example of a great writer giving advice to an unknown writer (me) in such a way as not to discourage him. He had not liked the second half of my play, *Brixham Regatta* (quite rightly since I'd had no idea how to develop it), so he gave me his own view of writing for the Theatre – expressed in a way that I haven't seen anywhere else. Like the first letter it shows him as a sensitive, modest, caring and gentle person. He wasn't writing for journalists or scholars, but out of a deep concern for me – and yet I was someone he hardly knew. Here are some extracts from it:

"Assessment of writing is not my affair. The more I go to the [word missing – probably Theatre?] the less I know about the whole dreary business...The thought is hateful to me of the distress and harm I may cause a young man like you by my arbitrariness and expression of personal warp. Do not for God's sake take too much to heart what follows... Up to the arrival of the invisible monsters I was quite absorbed. At that point I drifted out and never really got in again."

Then he refers to Ionesco's *The Chairs*:
"The invisible audience of *The Chairs* is acceptable (though to me unsatisfactory) because proceeding from and illuminative of a human situation. In your case the invisibility seems to be above all a technical necessity. Visible listeners in *The Chairs* would kill the play, visible monsters in yours would improve it. Here then you fall out of your vehicle. Not because we don't see the brutes, but because you bring them on and don't show them. Only what is off stage is legitimate matter for evocation. What is on stage never. What is on stage is to be seen, with the greatest possible acuity. [...] A theatre stage is an area of maximum verbal presence and maximum corporeal presence. Any dimming of the one or the other, or of the one by the other, is anti-theatrical. [...] Your play then breaks down for me the moment you invite me to look and deny me vision. The true theatre-goer's eyes are a ravenous organ. Words for the hidden (heart and next door), but not in lieu and place of what is *there* and patent for your players, when there is no or

insufficient psychological ground for the discrimination. Conclusion, your monsters will be much more present, and oppressive, if you don't bring them on (as much roaring off as you like), and not only that, but the writing whereby they are communicated will tend towards a much higher level. [...] The flags on the contrary, are excellent, because they extend the visible. [...]

This is only a small part of what I would try and say, with your help, over a glass of wine. [...]

Our conversation in London gave me the impression that you were not very interested in writing. That is very understandable. But if it did come to matter more to you I am pretty sure, from the little you have shown me, that the results would be considerable."

Beckett was so insistent about his privacy that my loyalty prompted me to destroy all communications from him except for this letter – and I soon misplaced it among my papers – remembering only the "corporeal" sentence. Any other communications from him that survived, survived accidentally.

Both letters can be seen in Theresa Dudeck's forthcoming biography to be published by Methuen.

***

I trusted Beckett. He would never have cheated me. I'm grateful to have had at least one acquaintance who was himself (rather than presenting a "performance" of himself). I've never said this to anyone – but I've always seen him as a man in hell whose revenge against God was to do good. (Someone asked Beckett what Vladimir and Estragon would have done during the war and he said, "Joined the Resistance, of course.")

I hope these notes are of interest to you. I've tried to be accurate, but one of the truth's that Beckett presented so forcefully is that memory is not to be trusted.

Keith Johnstone, October 2012

Stories

RESTART

Heaven was disintegrating. The Angels were creeping about in terror.

"Are you telling me that they're all dead?"

"All but one, Lord!"

"The whole damned lot of them?"

"Yes, Lord, except the child, but no one's alive to feed it. We don't think it'll last another quarter of an hour."

"You mean consciousness is finished? It's all guttered out?"

"Yes, Lord, except for the child."

The domes and palaces and triumphal arches were being replaced by a mass of giant wooden blocks with gaudy colours.

"What's happening?"

"It's the child's building blocks, Lord. It's the best you can expect from such an undeveloped consciousness."

"What about the gorillas? The chimps? The… the… the…"

"Perished…"

"And the whales? The dolphins?"

"We're sorry, Lord."

"What about those squid things on Gallus Five. Weren't they conscious?"

"Wiped out by the supernova, Lord."

"Everything's getting blurry."

"The child's dying, Lord."

"Well, if there's no one left to believe in me I'll just have to create another Universe. Pass me the instruction book."

"It'll be eons before it can generate any consciousness, Lord."

"Will you stop carping!"

The Angels were turning into stuffed toys.

"Let's see now!" said the Lord, leafing through the pages: "Rhubarb… Steeples… Singularities – got it!"

Everything had vanished except his rapidly fading mouth.

"Let there be light!" it said.

NOAH

They laughed at Noah, but one year the rain never stopped and the waters began to cover the earth. The animals tried to line up two by two, but crowds of people were fighting their way to the gangplank.

"Animals only!" cried Noah.

"Who needs them?" roared the crowd. "What rights do they have compared to us?"

"But the animals are without sin!" he cried.

A mother held up her son and shrieked: "My Ronnie is without sin and he's worth a thousand animals!"

They drove off those that were already on board (except those that they planned to eat). The Golden Eagles and the umpteen varieties of Darwin's Finches were the last to go. "And you'll be next," they told Noah, "if you don't pipe down!"

"Life's going to be even better than on shore," they said, as the waves covered the last nipple of Mother Earth. "And what's healthier than a sea-voyage?"

The animals swam about, rolling their eyes, but when night came the roars and groans and squeaks and hisses faded away until the Ark floated like a lantern above a sea of corpses.

After forty days Noah said: "Where's the dove? It's supposed to fly out and come back with an olive branch."

But it had been eaten weeks ago.

Porpoises and whales romped in the waves, and shoals of tiny fish broke the surface pursued by dark shapes, but not one fish ever came near a hook. Battles for food and fresh water raged from deck to deck, and soon even the corpses were being eaten.

A fire started and the Ark burned on the waters, not like a lantern, but like a great torch. And from then on the sun shone on a world that was all ocean, and no matter what horrors were in the depths, there was very little suffering visible on the surface at all.

THE MOST AMAZING LION IN ALL THE WORLD

Mummy was too busy to take Billy to the circus, but when he showed her that he could tie his own shoelaces she said that he was old enough to go by himself so he ran all the way to the field where the big tent had been erected.

The circus was even better than the year before. He cheered the acrobats, and laughed at the clowns, and was thrilled when the lions leapt on their pedestals, but the best part was when the biggest lion – the one with the thick bristly mane – bit the lion-tamer's head off. Billy laughed and laughed until the Ringmaster explained that the head-biting wasn't part of the show and that they needed a volunteer so that the lions could continue.

"Me! Me!" shouted Billy, jumping up and waving his arms, but the Ringmaster ignored him until there were cries of, "Give the wee laddie a chance" and "Here's a brave little fellow". Billy jumped into the ring and said that if he was old enough to come to the circus by himself then he was old enough to tame the lions. And it was true, because as soon as he cracked the whip the lions somersaulted from stool to stool and jumped though flaming hoops better than they ever had before. The Ringmaster was so pleased that he let Billy borrow the big fierce lion to take to school for "show-and-tell".

Billy hoped that Mummy wouldn't mind having a lion in the house if it was just for the one night, but she hit it with the ironing board and it bit her head off. Daddy said, "For goodness sake, what's the matter now!" so it bit his head off as well.

Next day Billy was late for school because the lion kept chasing motorbikes. Mrs. Grimsby was writing on the blackboard as he sneaked into the classroom. "I can see your reflection in my spectacles, Billy!" she said. "And there'll be no lions in my classroom! So you can…" But before she could finish the sentence, the lion had bitten her head off.

The children thought that the lion was the best thing ever for show-and-tell. They threw sticks for it, and rubbed it under the chin until it purred like a motorbike, and stood it against the wall so that they could chalk around its outline. It was three o'clock before Billy remembered that he had promised to return the lion by midday. He jumped onto its back and they galloped to where the circus had been, but there was just a sixty-foot circle of sawdust.

When they arrived home he thawed some meat in the microwave for the lion, and made himself a peanut butter and jelly sandwich. Mummy and Daddy looked untidy, without their heads so he dragged them to the compost heap and covered them with earth and leaves. Back in the house the lion sat in Daddy's saggy old leather armchair and watched a nature programe.

"Come out and play," said Billy, switching off the TV.

It bared its teeth and said: "Do you know what time it is?"

"I haven't learned to tell the time but if it's bed-time you could read me a story."

"Oh no, it's not bed-time!"

It leapt onto the table (where it slithered about until its claws dug into the wood).

"What time is it then?"

"I'll tell you what time it is!" it roared. "It's time to bite *your* head off!"

It chased Billy upstairs and downstairs and out into the garden where it pinned him to the grass beside the lilac bushes.

"Now it's your turn to chase *me*!" it said, and ran off, looking back over its shoulder.

Next morning Billy nailed up a sign that said *The Most Amazing Lion In All The World* and charged admission. So many people wanted to see the lion that it wasn't long before Billy had saved up enough money to have the house and the garden sent to a part of Africa where there were no teachers, and where Billy and his lion lived happily ever after.

***

Mrs. Grimsby compressed her lips into something resembling a smile:

"Very well, class, I've read your stories about visiting the circus, and you all get high marks –" she peered around the classroom – "except for one little boy!"

She made Billy stand on the seat so that the other children could stare at him; then she wrote "Silly Billy" on the blackboard and said: "His name will be 'Silly Billy' from now on, because his story was very, very silly!"

Glass and window frame exploded into the room as a huge long tawny shape with a thick bristly mane crashed through the window, but instead of biting anyone's head off it whimpered and held up a paw that had a sharp piece of glass sticking right through it. Mrs. Grimsby knew exactly what to do. She took a toy-gun from the drawer where she kept the things that she had confiscated. "Stupid lion," she said, and pumped six bullets into its heart. "Those aren't real bullets!" shouted Billy, but his wonderful lion died without a murmur.

EDUCATED FLEAS

Fleas that are to perform in the flea-circus are placed on a tray under a sheet of glass. Every jump smashes them against this invisible surface. After a couple of days they'll never jump again and are then known as "educated" (as in the line from the Cole Porter song – "Bees do it, even educated fleas do it…").

The arm is late and we experience the familiar suffering. The Great Arno, permanently bound to his iron chariot, trundles his immense wheels. Our two Gladiators – swords glued to their shells – lie clasped together, each afraid to release the other. The Mighty Zorgo, condemned to extricate himself thirty times a day from under a glass paperweight, stares with desperate eyes.

The air pulses with vibrations. The walls darken and the arm descends. Metal surfaces seize the Great Arno, together with his chariot, and place him in the feeding position. We frolic between the golden hairs (those of us who are not welded to our apparatus). Our guts tighten, and our mandibles throb with pleasure. Satiated, we drop away one by one, and the arm blurs into invisibility.

Which of us does not remember that bursting loose from earthly confines that could precipitate us into water, or into fire, but that was so exhilarating that we leapt regardless? And which of us does not curse the fate that has condemned us to this dismality? We have mastered undreamt of skills – Caesar thrashes his whip as he rides Arno's chariot, the Mighty Zorgo emerges yet again from under his gigantic paperweight, my treadmill makes the little bulb glow with astounding brilliance – but what sense can be made of all this?

Some youngsters have been added to our number. One was held between the metal surfaces while his starboard legs were trimmed; he is a replacement for dear departed Waltzer whose affliction we had believed congenital. The others leap with passionate intensity, aware of the barrier but determined to overcome it. Ah, the optimism of youth!

The newcomers have accepted their fate. One continued leaping until the third day, and he now seems the most dispirited. He has become Fearless Freddy who at each performance is shot from a cannon through a hoop of fire.

I press my head against the base of the walls and stare into the substance that confines us. Patches of light expand and dissipate but if I stare at them for a long time they form shapes that are like mountains perambulating. Needless to say, the others lack the discipline to penetrate beyond the surface.

"And what of it?" they jeer. "What use all this metaphysics?"

Only Freddy remains at my side. He cannot share my vision, but he looks at me with solemn eyes and does not mock.

I have observed certain smears in the air above us. Freddy confirms their existence, but the others are interested only in the presence or absence of the arm.

"Look!" I cry. "Can you not see that the smears vanish just before we are fed? At such times the barrier is removed to admit the arm! Leap then, and regain your freedom!"

Something unusual is happening. A mauveness is moving back and forth across our sky.

"Look, brothers," I cry. "The smears are being wiped away. Jump now before they can form again!"

The Great Arno sneers – for him there can be no escape – but the younger fleas tremble with excitement. "Show us!" they cry, watching with great intensity as my muscles begin their contraction. Some even cheer as I enter that final agony when one must leap or die, and then – Aaaaaaaah, the joyous release from flatness, the splendid soaring that is at the heart of fleaness. For a split second I believe that I am free, but then I slam into the barrier that does not cushion onethousandth of the force of my hurtling body. When I regain my senses my innards feel ripped loose, and the Great Arno is running his chariot over me in a gesture of contempt.

During the night the metal surfaces seize me and attach my feet to iron bars. Ahead of me, and to either side, are circles of spidery metal.

If I rotate my rearmost legs I can move forwards, and when I jerk my mandible a bell rings, but my jumping days are over as surely as those of the Great Arno.

Freddy is my consolation. He too has begun to study the smears that contaminate our sky. Their numbers increase with time but they disappear when the arm is feeding us.

Something splendid has happened – I call it "splendid" in spite of Arno's scepticism. Today, as we were feasting on the arm, Freddy launched himself into infinity, up, up, and away! And there was no barrier to smash him back! Arno claims to have seen him seized by the metal surfaces but I shall not reject the evidence of my senses. In what universe is Freddy now? I fear I shall not meet his like again.

The new Waltzer has gone quite mad, and it is possible that I too am well on the way. I have become reconciled with the Great Arno, and can almost believe that he is correct when he says that wisdom lies in the curbing of ambition. We stare into the substance that confines us, he with his chariot, and I with my tricycle (naming things is one of our few pleasures).

Why has it never occurred to me that the arena is without walls? I share this idea with the new arrivals (Freddy's departure has given me some reputation among them). "The time to leap," I whisper, "is when you are on stage! Leap then, and you will regain your freedom, all those that are not welded into your apparatus!"

I have finished my part in today's fourteenth performance, and at this very moment the young fleas must be clambering into their gymnastic pyramid. There is no hope for me, glued to my tricycle, but this new generation – may God give them courage!

Days pass and the youngsters are still with us, prisoners of their unbelief. My life has become less arduous – my tricycle has been oiled and its movements begin to feel almost natural – but for how long must I keep on pedalling?

ANOTHER FINE MESS

It had been drizzling all week, but a strip of light on the horizon promised better things. The occasional truck drove past with hooded lights. Strips of sky were reflected in the ruts where the tanks had chewed up the tarmac. Children were making their way to school in the gloom.

I'd been at the Three Bears' house since five a.m. working on Bugs Bunny who had O.D.'d. He was still in bad shape when I left him – whiskers crumpled, and ears like week-old lettuce – but Tigger and Piglet promised to keep an eye on him.

I was kicking a dead Triffid outside the fast-food restaurant when Stan Laurel and Oliver Hardy trudged past. Ropes had been tied around their necks and soldiers were jerking them along. Stan carried two shovels, and each time he was jabbed with a rifle he shouted "Oh, Ollie! Ollie!" but when Ollie was jabbed he just said, "Oh pardon me!" and raised his hat.

There were the usual riff-raff, plus a few children and a couple of photographers. Little Red Riding Hood and Goldilocks were trying not to get their booties soaked, but the Three Little Pigs were splashing through the mud and having a wonderful time (just as well as they were bacon by Saturday). A photographer said that Laurel and Hardy were to be executed as war criminals, so I tagged along.

Stan wanted to go around a large puddle where the drains had backed up, but Ollie said, "What's the use!" and tried to walk through. Halfway across he vanished into a shell-hole and was made to keep repeating it for the photographers. He'd had lost so much weight that he was unrecognizable without his hat so the soldiers made Stan dive in and grope about till he found it. Ollie put it back on and it began to raise and lower by itself until he removed a large frog.

We arrived at the quarry where Humpty Dumpty had been thrown off the cliff ("to see if he bounced" as they joked on the *Late Night Show*). Two graves were paced out and Stan and Ollie were told "start digging". Their shovels clanged on solid rock but the soldiers kept yelling: "Faster! Faster!" Stan kept saying that they should be digging where the soil was deeper. Ollie hit him to shut him up, and Stan kicked Ollie in the shin, and Ollie kicked him back, and the conflict escalated until Stan kicked one of the soldiers.

Goldilocks began to cry and Little Red Riding Hood comforted her. "You'll be late for school," I said, but they shook their heads stubbornly. The soldiers huddled together, trying to protect their cigarettes from the drizzle, as Ollie tried to revive Stan.

"Forget the graves, let the dogs have them," said the Corporal.

Stan's legs slithered in all directions as Olly tried to stand him up. The Corporal lost patience and fired a revolver. Stan leapt to his feet, staring wildly about as if he'd no idea where he was. He was pushed against the rock-wall beside Ollie where he recovered enough to do his famous scratch-the-top-of-his-head routine, but it didn't look right, not with his wet hair plastered down. The soldiers clicked the safety-catches on their rifles, and suddenly the famous duo – idols of millions – were fighting to get behind each other as if the cliff might gape and swallow them up.

A photographer shouted, "Not yet!" and strolled in to hold a light-meter to their face, and then Ollie remembered a speech that he intended to make. He tried to unfold it but the rain turned it into papier-mâché.

They looked more alone than anyone that I'd ever seen. Stan bawled like a child, but Ollie was made of sterner stuff: he abandoned his prepared speech, removed a dent from his hat, gave a last twiddle to his bow-tie and launched into an oration:

"It's all been a terrible misunderstanding…" he said, but the Corporal shouted: "AT THE READY!"

Olly was galvanized.

"We'll tell you!" he shrieked.

"TAKE AIM!"

"Finlayson's in the attic!" he cried (Finlayson was the innkeeper in the movie *Way Out West*). "We dragged the wardrobe in front of his cubby-hole to hide him!"

"FIRE!"

Olly held up his hands to shield him from the bullets (a comedian to the last) and then everything went into slow motion just like in the movies.

I've seen many deaths: King Kong swatting at the airplanes, Harpo trying to catch the bullets in his teeth, Tarzan letting out a scream that went on and on until a truncheon ended it, Buster Keaton running magnificently until flame enveloped him (and even then he kept on running) – but Laurel and Hardy were among the most pathetic.

The sound was shockingly loud. The children covered their ears and went on staring as if it was all happening on TV. Stan collapsed but he kept lifting his head from a puddle to take his last gasp. Ollie sank to his knees, eyes wide with terror as if still seeing the bullets expanding towards him. He began to dab at his face and chest, slowly at first, then faster and faster, but there was no blood, no wounds. The soldiers laughed and the crowd laughed, and even I laughed, although the children seemed disappointed.

The two famous clowns were dragged to their feet. Stan vomited down the front of Ollie's now over-size trousers, but what with the general muck and the rain it didn't seem to matter:

"Oh, Ollie, is this Heaven?"

"Very likely," said Olly through bruised lips.

The fast-food place would have been open by now, but I'd lost my appetite. I leaned against a burned-out Volkswagen and watched them plod back into town. The soldiers kicked Stan to make him do his comical jumps, and Ollie fell into the shell-hole for the umpteenth time. The soldiers began to sing. They were too far away for me to make out the words but I already knew the words:

"Raaaain-drops are hissing on the gun baaarrels
A new day is daaaaawning in the east..."

The children had taken charge of the ropes and were making the famous clowns run zigzag. Stan was doing his famous leaps and Ollie was being used as a sled as they passed from view.

Had Finlayson failed to show proper respect to a policeman? Or was he a member of the Donald Duck club in the years when it was prohibited? Had Goofy reported him as a "suspicious" person? The authorities say that Stan and Ollie were never arrested but I saw them with my own eyes.

At midday the sky began to clear, and by six o'clock Bugs Bunny was out on the street, trying to score.

THE MIRACLE

My earliest memories are of Heaven and Hell, and Hell was marginally the more terrifying. The idea that God might roast me a million times and then start over, sickened me, and yet while most boys wanted to be Engine Drivers or Astronauts, I was determined to be a Priest (because what shall it profit a man if he gain the whole world but lose his immortal soul?).

One day as we sat out on the cliffs watching the sea gnaw into the land we began to discuss the Bible. Colin, the teacher's son, said that the miracles were lies, or magic tricks.

"What about the burning bush that was not consumed?"

"It was natural gas! They'd just escaped from Egypt, for Christ's sake! What did *they* know?"

"And the Ten Commandments?"

"Moses got someone to carve them for him."

"Don't be stupid, Colin!"

"Then why did he smash the first set and have to go back for replacements?"

"Because the people made him angry."

"Those were God's tablets – would you smash God's tablets? I expect there were spelling mistakes. People must have said: '*A dull try* – that's not how you spell *adultery*.'"

We fell about laughing but Colin began rubbing the pads of his fingers together.

"They feel fuzzy," he said.

"Fuzzy?"

"Yes. The ends of my fingers feel fuzzy."

A few days later we heard he had caught polio, and might never again walk unassisted. This convinced us that God really was omnipresent and it became embarrassing even to use the lavatory – it was no good spreading out my shirt to stop him seeing my private parts if he was also staring up from inside the bowl.

***

Father Cashel took charge of my religious instruction. He was a tall, soft-spoken man with the type of baldness attributed to an excess of the male sex hormone.

"Absolution," he said, "followed by Holy Communion, can create the most intense feelings of self-worth imaginable. It's such a sweet experience, my son."

He took me by my shoulders, his eyes agleam in the half-light:

"Persist in your spiritual exercises and you will understand that all creation is an expression of God's will."

Some of Colin's scepticism had rubbed off on me.

"Then why does Dad have emphysema?" I said. "And why are the animals all eating each other? And what about VD?" (There were posters warning about venereal disease in every public lavatory.)

He could have blamed Eve for tempting Adam, but he just ruffled my hair, and said:

"Ah, ye of little faith! Once you ingest the wafer that is His flesh, and sip the wine that is His blood, all doubt will dissipate like smoke. And as for syphilis, is God to blame if men fornicate with sheep?"

He seemed to have no friends, He referred to himself as "the lone eagle of God", and yet a radiance gathered around him, especially at Mass. Already his touch could work miracles, but not when he put his hand into my trousers.

"You're too young," he said, feeding me a peppermint, and showing me how to milk him. The arc of white "urine" that pulsed out amazed me, although it couldn't really have been the pint of ejaculate that my brain remembers.

"I am God's representative," he said. "And if you speak of this you will be damned forever. Anyway, it's of no consequence."

***

Boys (long dead) had carved their names into a table in the vestry. One had died heroically in battle, so it was now "part of our heritage". I had found space for my own name, but the wood was from some far-flung corner of the Empire and so hard that I still had two letters to complete (I had rubbed shoe-polish into the cuts to hide their freshness).

I arrived early on the eve of my first communion, ready to finish the carving so that when I became Pope young boys would read my name and realize that they too could escape from this shit-hole. I was so absorbed that I failed to hear Father Cashel until the door was already opening. He had urgent need of me, so I tightened the blue ribbon about the base of his penis (the knife and the polish were in full view) and applied myself. Usually he was as mute as a giraffe, but he groaned and leaned back against the table for support. "What in Christ's name…" he said as his fingers sank into the polish.

He slapped me repeatedly about the head, forced me against the table, downed my trousers, and rammed into me, using the polish as lubricant. There was some chemical in it that stung horribly. I tried to scream but he pushed his tobaccoey fingers into my mouth and I was too subservient to bite them.

"That's enough penance," he gasped, wiping himself: "Stop snivelling! You enjoyed it too, dirty little sod!" And then, with his handkerchief wadded in my crack to stop the bleeding, he gave me my final instructions, stressing that when he placed the communion wafer on my tongue it must be swallowed intact.

"To even graze the wafer with your teeth would be such a mark of disrespect to our Lord, that it would bleed!"

He was his old self again, but I was racked by guilt.

"Run along," he said, pressing a small silver coin into my palm.

**

I heard sniggers as I knelt at the altar rail. Was fresh blood oozing from my behind? I blushed hotly, convinced that a stain was spreading on my trousers, and that by some Einsteinian bending of light it had become visible even to those casual sightseers at the very rear of the Church.

Why couldn't I bring honour to my family like the boy who died for his country, instead of this degradation?

The tapestry of Father Cashel's costume dangled inches from my face as he placed the light, frail, magical, ever-so-dry wafer on my tongue. "Corpus Christi," he said as I drew the body of Christ into my mouth, but the spirit of God did not enter me. The wafer sat there, big as a canoe, and my demon whispered: "See if it bleeds! What better proof that the universe is sacred?"

I closed my lips against the wine and let it trickle down my chin while the wafer grew firmer and fleshier. My need to experience the magical underpinnings of this universe was irresistible. I moved it between my teeth and clenched them. I must have hit an artery because my cheeks bulged and blood spurted out onto the carved Christ and on to Father Cashel who raised his hand – to strike me? Who knows? – because he slithered and fell, clunking his head. I sprawled backwards, barking like a seal with my urgent need to expel Christ's blood and the blood kept on expanding, even after it had spurted out of me.

I staggered to my feet, my brand new shoes already squelching. I stepped forwards and was up to my knees. The blood swirled, fountained, whirlpooled, surged and resurged as if desperate to find a way out into the world. People clambered onto the pews, or breasted the waves with arms chest-high. Mum was swept into the chapel of St. Beefius, and for a split second I was washed against my father who struck me on the mouth. Cries of lamentation rose and fell as people were slopped against the walls and columns.

What might have happened to us had the doors not burst asunder? Light blasted in as pews, hassocks, hymnals, worshippers, the entire caboodle, surged out into the marketplace. Shop windows shattered. A school bus rolled over and over. I spun like a matchstick in a flushing toilet. I had a vision of no one left alive on earth except the astronauts in their orbiting ark, but I had managed to vomit out the remaining fragments of Christ's flesh and the deluge was beginning to subside. Blood flattened out in the expanse of the car park where the drivers climbed onto their cars, not to save their lives, but to protect their shoes.

Bodies were so broken that it was difficult to tell what sex they'd been. The injured pleaded for help but most seemed beyond saving. I was clutching my guts (in the lunatic hope that some surgeon might sew them back for me) when they began to snake back of their own accord. All around me corpses were resurrecting. Torsos grew fresh limbs, and torn-off limbs extruded new bodies (so that single people became twins, or quadruplets even). My undescended testicle was correcting itself. I had perfect vision in my blind eye. My bum didn't feel ravaged any more.

We stared at each other like souls on Judgement Day and began to dance and praise God from sheer happiness. Colin, minus his wheelchair, was leaping like a Watusi. A cheer went up, together with cries of "God be praised!" and "God bless Father Cashel!" but he was never to be seen again, although he was rumoured to be preaching in another diocese.

***

We have become a second Lourdes but whereas the grotto at Lourdes is hung with crutches, our church is agleam with glass eyes and its ceiling is festooned with artificial limbs. Not one of us that endured that fearful baptism has suffered a day's illness. Dad's emphysema is in remission, and our ninety-year-olds gallop up hills and across country like frisky young teenagers. The pilgrims call us Lazaruses after the man Christ brought back from the dead.

Droplets of Christ's blood are sold at immense prices. I've nibbled the "host" many times, seeking for instant riches, gingerly of course, but to no effect. Perhaps Father Cashel has to bugger me first.*

NOTE: Priests in Canada have propagated the syphilis/sheep theory. Catholics in Canada and in Germany confirm that their priests told them that the wafer would bleed if they bit into it.

CONNIBEER'S LEG

I was convalescing at a fishing town in the West Country, and had settled into a routine of walks on the cliffs (not too strenuous), meals in a restaurant that overlooked the harbour (making sure I had the correct amount of roughage), and then early to bed. My rented cottage was an excellent haven to recuperate in, and there were few mornings when I did not wake up without at least a trace of my old vigour.

The locals were said to resent "grockles" (their name for the tourists that invade the town each summer) but those I met were friendly enough. One was Alan Connibeer whose dog had bounded over to me as I was sunning myself out on the cliffs. He was a younger man, in his mid-thirties, and yet his hair was already streaked with grey.

There can be an awkwardness when people learn that I am a psychologist (as if their innermost secrets were suddenly visible), but Connibeer was unperturbed. He had confessed to being a "bit of a recluse", yet he was soon visiting me in my cottage, where we engaged in a titanic struggle which had ended in my being mated when I least expected it.

I scooped the chess pieces into their box and the sound woke him.

"It's almost night!" he said, astounded.

The lights of Torquay glimmered from across the bay.

"You fell asleep," I said. "Perhaps the effect of your excellent wine!"

His narrow face turned pale, and he was already pulling a sock over his stump preparatory to strapping on his artificial leg (which he had not been at all reticent about removing). His dog thumped its tail, eager to be off.

"You have an appointment?"

"I hope not!" he said, with a bitter laugh, and then: "Will you accompany me?"

He was owner of a photography shop which was a dozen steps or so above the far side of the harbour and I didn't relish walking him there only to have to trudge back.

"I have night-blindness," he said. "Can't see a damn thing once the sun goes down."

"Nothing simpler," I said, putting a bold face on it. "But shouldn't we finish the wine?"

The bottle glistened in the light from the darkening sky.

"I can't be here after dark!" he cried, angrily, and then apologized. "Put it down as my foolishness," he said, "but I can't be out at night alone."

***

He clutched my arm as we hurried down the steep alleys and precipitous steps. He seemed anxious that we not be followed.

"Are you afraid of someone?"

He turned sharply, and the dog growled – the fur on its neck bristled.

"Is anyone there?" I called.

"For God's sake be quiet!" he muttered.

We scrambled down the last steps to the harbour, clinging hand-over-hand to the cold iron banisters. Noise and light were streaming from one of the many pubs.

"In here," he said, and we were soon crushed into a corner and huddled over our Devon ciders.

"Did you see what was pursuing us?"

"Hardly pursuing," I said, "but I did hear an animal, perhaps a cat."

"It was a woman!" he said. "Do you think the dog would bristle at a cat?"

Some of his acquaintances joined us and for a couple of hours he was the amiable Connibeer that I had first encountered: his tic disappeared, and his glass no longer clattered as he placed it on the table, but at closing time he reverted to stark terror. He arranged to spend the night in one of the guest rooms – inviting me to share it at his expense.

"Imagine the scandal!" I laughed: "Connibeer and the 'London Gentleman' sleeping in the same room, when neither of us live more than a quarter of an hour away."

"As a personal favour?"

"I won't do it," I said. "It's ridiculous!"

He stared as if I were going to my execution.

"It's not safe for you to be alone!"

"Nothing will happen," I said.

"At least take my stick!"

"You need it more than me!"

"Take the bloody thing!" he said.

When I reached the crest of the hill some animal was scratching about in the brambles. Connibeer had so unsettled me that it was difficult to walk past, and whatever it was – "woman", Connibeer had said – seemed to keep pace with me on the other side of the fence. At one point I wheeled round with the stick raised, but there were only dark shapes that did not move, and a faint smell of Devon violets.

***

Connibeer's shop-window displayed photos of gnarled pieces of driftwood and storm-battered cliffs, plus the usual wedding portraits and the subsequent babies. A bell jingled as I entered. To my right was a till, and a counter, and displays of cameras and technical magazines, but the space to my left had been arranged as a photographic studio. A high-backed chair stood between light-reflecting "umbrellas", and a "poetic landscape" was pinned to the wall behind it. I saw a shelf of wigs and a rack of Victorian costumes.

"A way to drum up trade," said Connibeer. "Instant ancestors. Dress them up like their great-grandparents, and sell them sepia prints – I could kit you up as the Mona Lisa in about thirty seconds."

"Actually, I came to return your stick."

He ushered me into a room with a barred window that overlooked the harbour.

The house had been built for a fisherman's family, so the rooms were small (the shop was two rooms that had been knocked into one). I saw a sink covered by a board, and some photographic equipment. He settled me on a ancient couch that had horsehair bursting from the seams, and shooed the dog from a tattered armchair.

"Midweek", he said, settling himself down. "Not much business!"

"Much call for the art photos?"

"I'm afraid not."

Shelves stacked with fat yellow envelopes lined the walls. I remarked on the bars that covered the window.

"To stop break-ins," he said.

"But suppose there was a fire?"

"There's worse than fire."

I told him about the "presence" that I had imagined following me.

"Don't joke!" he said. "Don't make light of it!" He leaned closer and I smelt his whisky breath. "You're sure she followed you?"

Then he hummed and harred and until he launched out with:

"You may know that I have a reputation as a 'ladies man'…"

"I don't hear the local gossip."

"That was before this, of course," he said, slapping his wooden leg. The dog whined and made eyes at him.

"I used to think of myself as a bohemian, an artist," he said. "I cared only for cameras, and light, and the making of the perfect print. I despised people who were not in search of at least some vestige of immortality." He laughed and repeated the word "immortality" as if it disgusted him.

I stared out at the harbour while he attended to a customer. A tiny child was "sculling" a boat with an oar twice his length; a seagull stood one-legged on a buoy; a welder was at work in a shed on the South Quay. There were some books beside the window: Dostoevsky, Von Kleist, and a history of the vampire myth by Ostereich. The dog growled when I tried to pick one up.

Connibeer returned and spoke sharply to it: "So Lucy followed you," he said, settling back into the worn leather armchair. "Lucy – my nemesis. So beautiful. Her skin seemed bursting with life; it made you long to touch it, to stroke it, to rub your cheek against it. She had a smile for everyone – she was too young to know that life must be lived behind a mask. I made myself agreeable but her Dad owned a couple of holiday camps and they thought I was a 'fortune hunter'."

Sometimes he whispered so quietly that he was difficult to follow, and at other times he was loud enough to be heard out in the street.

"One day I found her gathering hazelnuts. I tried to pull her down into the long grass. She ran off, leaving her basket, but I'd kissed her mouth, I'd had my hand on her, and from then on, if I glimpsed any woman, just for a split second, I thought it was her."

"I know the feeling!" I said, and he looked at me as if I said that molten lava was really quite warm.

"One day her brothers saw me following her so they threw me into the harbour. I was stuck waist-deep in the mud. Planks and ropes had to be used to haul me out. The grockles were taking bets on whether the tide would drown me. You heard about that?"

"I'm just a visitor here."

He stared out at a forest of masts.

"You've never been married?" I said.

"I pity the woman who'd marry me!"

He bent over to pat the haunches of the dog.

"One May morning they found her stiff as a board. 'Apoplexy,' said the Doctor. I wanted to take a last look at her before they sealed her coffin, but I was afraid of the brothers."

There was a long silence until the shop-bell rang. The transaction took a while so I slid some prints out of one of the yellow envelopes, just idle curiosity, and the dog had no objection. I saw the image of a naked woman who was using the neck of a bottle in an unusual manner. There were more prints but I replaced them quickly without looking at them. Connibeer obviously had a profitable sideline.

"To cut a long story short", he said, startling me, "I had dragged myself out of an adulterous bed, and was taking a short-cut through the old churchyard when I saw a woman who reminded me of Lucy. I lost sight of her – this was just before sun-up – and when I reached the spot where I'd seen her I found Lucy's 'mausoleum' (if that's the word?). Generations of her family had been laid to rest there."

He laughed, for no reason that I could see, and there was a pause that my professional training advised me not to break.

"Lucy's 'resting place'," he said, at last. "The iron gate had an expensive padlock. I lit some paper and pushed it through the bars, and as it flared up I could see marble shelves with shadowy coffins stacked on them."

"But was it?" I said.

"Was it what?"

"Was it where you had seen the woman?"

"Close enough. I imagined that she'd just crouched down among the graves to relieve herself, and that she hadn't even looked like Lucy. But from then on I began to have dreams in which Lucy was alive and doing any erotic thing you might care to imagine."

"It must be good to talk about it," I said, "if it helps you get in touch with your feelings."

"I am in touch with my feelings, Mr. Psychologist! Would you like to see her?"

He picked up that same yellow envelope, and passed one of the prints to me. I was looking at the face of the woman in the obscene photograph.

"Ah, yes," I said, outwardly calm.

"You know what a succubus is?" he said, leaning towards to me. "A succubus is a female spirit who comes to men at night and drains them of their vitality. Well, it was like being possessed by a succubus. And when I had sex with other women, who did I think of? Only of her! Can you imagine the effect that has?"

"Not really…"

"It's like you're bonding closer and closer with a corpse. So I took a cure."

"You went for counselling?"

A harsh laugh:

"A do-it-yourself cure. I wanted to see her in her coffin. I wanted my mind to accept that she was dead. My 'unconscious' mind," he added, giving me a sardonic glance. "Plus there was always the chance of some interesting photos. I was poking around inside that padlock with a screwdriver when I realized that a strong man might lift the gate straight off its hinges. It came loose with a rush. It hardly took a moment before I was inside. It was obvious which was Lucy's coffin – it looked so much cleaner than the others. I waited there for a long time, and I enjoyed being close to her (about the last emotion that I had expected). Birds were squabbling, and sometimes there were voices. It was strange to wait so quietly in there, and feel her close to me."

"But supposing someone had seen you?"

"I'd put the gate back onto it's hinges."

"You were shut in with her?"

"It seemed reasonable at the time."

An unpleasant thought occurred to me. I tried to speak…

"Let me finish!" he said, angrily. "I've told these things to no one. And I can't hardly believe that I'm telling them to you. Anyway, I had to see her."

"You opened the coffin?"

"How could I not have opened it? You would have opened it!"

"I think not."

"If you had the courage you would! Rossetti exhumed his mistress so he could take back the poems that he'd thrown in with her. And my need was a lot greater than his! The screws were only finger-tight which surprised me, and the lid seemed unnaturally heavy as if something was holding it down from the inside – my groin felt pretty undefended I can tell you – but when I got the lid up past my eyes, I was so astonished that I almost let it crash to the ground."

He was reliving the experience.

"And…?"

"Her flesh was cool, but soft and malleable. I could open her eyes or close them. I could do anything I wished with her."

"You touched her?"

"I did more than that!"

"No decay?"

"Nothing."

"How long after the funeral?"
"Months!"
"She was mummified?"
"Mummified!" He thrust the photo at me. "Is that mummified!"
Lucy's image stared at me, lips frozen in a faint smile.
"Look here!" he said, pointing. "You see the edge of the coffin?"
What I had though to be part of a wooden frame might indeed have been something rather different. He showed me more photographs:
"You took these months after the funeral!"
"Every one of them!"
"But she's naked!"
"Do you blame me?"
"You stripped her?"
"Do you think I wasn't interested?"
Lucy's image looked brimming with life. In some of the pictures she was wearing long woollen underwear.
"What's that for?"
"How would I know. I'm not a mortician!"
None of the photographs was pornographic, but he was keeping half the pile back from me.
"There was something very erotic about having Lucy absolutely under my power."
"You wanted to have intercourse with her?"
"Well now that's a crime, Mr. Psychologist, but tell me, who would be the victim? You can be sure of one thing – there's few that would have dared!"
He was panting as if he'd been running up-hill:
"You're not supposed to look at me like that," he growled. "Don't they train you to be objective?"
Reflected light crawled over the ceiling. There was the occasional whine of a saw. Someone was trying to start an outboard motor. Gulls were shrieking. The room stank of his sweat and his tobacco.
"It's not what you think," he said. "She was moist! She wanted me as much as I wanted her! And inside, in the centre of her, it was like a

hand grasping me. And I took good care of her! I rouged her. I rubbed expensive creams into her. And she liked it. She would turn her neck for me to blow on, and if I lifted her arms up around me she'd hold me as if she never wanted to let me go."

The woman in the photographs was surely some prostitute paid for her services, but if Connibeer *had* violated a corpse then he might well have personified his guilt as a female demon that was pursuing him.

"You… repeated the experience?"

"It was as if I was pumping life back into her. I can tell you", he grinned, "that's one woman who didn't fake her orgasms!"

He sat there, apparently in complete rapport with me, and yet utterly deluded. I knew I would have to get him into therapy.

"You must have felt very isolated."

He sighed, and moved closer until I could see every pore. "I'd decide to pack it in sometimes – necrophilia is bad for the self-image – but then I'd get to thinking of her, and one thing would lead to another. What the hell did it matter anyway?" he shouted, in sudden rage. "The milk was spilt! It became a normality like all love-affairs, until one day I removed the lid and saw…"

He stopped talking, and I waited with fifty ideas running through my mind. Had he seen that the corpse was really a mass of putrefaction?

"Yes?" I said, gently.

"I had lain her clothes beside her in the coffin but now she was fully dressed! Someone had used her, and for some reason he'd felt impelled to dress her."

"Rather a coincidence?"

I regretted my flippancy, but it didn't faze him.

"He could have been spying on us! God knows it wasn't always quiet as the grave in there!"

"And she was the same as always?"

"I tell you she was dressed."

"I mean, her condition. Hadn't she deteriorated after you'd let the air in?"

"I keep telling you that she wasn't a corpse. Don't they call them the *undead*? She used to murmur things as if half-asleep, but it was difficult to make any sense of them."

I was supposed to be on holiday, recuperating, but this was like being back in the locked wards.

I toyed with the photographs. In one of them she had her legs splayed over the side of the coffin and Connibeer's hand was…

"Not that one!" he said sharply, and opened another envelope.

"Try this one!" he said, handing me a picture of a closed coffin with 'KUM WEN DARK' scrawled on it.

"I found it on my next visit – someone had been in there writing me messages. I got the lid off and saw that she had been dressed for a second time. It can't have been easy to cram her legs into that stupid underwear or to get that dress to sit properly on her. I examined her for scratch marks, or fresh bruises, but there was nothing that I couldn't account for. And the message, 'KUM WEN DARK' – was this intended to scare me off? Or did the swine really think we could come to some sort of an arrangement? And was anyone really that illiterate? Was it some sort of schoolboy prank?"

Connibeer was a persuasive talker – one could understand that this ugly man might have success with women. The dog was asleep, but its back leg was twitching. I hoped its universe was simpler than mine.

"You kept the appointment?"

"I had to put a face on that swine, I had to know him. I pedalled up to the churchyard long before sunset and hid myself with a good view of the gate, and as it got darker, so I crept closer, until finally I squeezed myself under the branches of a yew-tree (they used to plant them in churchyards for the long-bows). I was less than thirty feet away from the gate of wrought iron."

"You weren't afraid?"

"Of course I was afraid! I'm lying there, with the dry leaves crackling, and things stirring in the grass. Suddenly there's this rasping noise. God, it was right in my ear – some old fool choking on his own mucus. He went into the church for a few minutes, and then he locked it and walked past me, jingling the keys. I heard the wooden gates scraping on the gravel and I knew that he was locking the churchyard."

"You were locked in?"

"Oh, the walls are only four feet high. They don't think the corpses are going anywhere. Nothing happened until the clock struck the quarter. Then the wind dropped long enough for me to hear a screech of metal. It came from the wrought-iron gate. 'The pig!' I thought. 'He's been in there all the time!' I was mad with jealousy, but it was still only dusk, and even if he was raising the gate from the inside, why couldn't I see him? I was groping for my flashlight when I realized that the gate was lifting by itself!"

"By magic?"

"Shut up! I saw the gate ease itself open and hang on the chain. There was a sound – wood scraping against wood – and a few moments later I saw Lucy cloaked in shadow. She stood motionless for a whole minute perhaps, and then she slipped silently out into the twilight. She leapt on to a granite obelisk and wrapped it with her legs, and pressed herself against it. She leaned back so that her hair was sweeping the ground, and then she spun over backwards and landed delicately on all fours.

"I had been so used to her as quiescent, as gently yielding, that for a moment I thought I was seeing some other woman, but then I felt – I can't really describe this – I felt her mind seeking me out. It was like a tongue flickering in my brain. She was crouching like a sphinx, but her head was ratcheting very gradually in my direction. I tried to make my mind a blank. I stared down at the grass and at a rubber ring from a disintegrated condom, and I kept repeating 'Grass! Grass!' because I had the feeling that she could see out of my eyes, and that I needed to stare down at the grass in order to give her no clue where I was. God knows how long I lay there, but when I looked up she was gone, and it was night.

"I slithered back out from under the branches with you can't imagine how much stealth, and legged it around the church, keeping off the gravel paths so as to make less noise. I was terrified that she might have run round the other side to forestall me. The vision of her had been so weird that I could imagine her compelling me to run into her arms by sheer force of will. She could have leap-frogged over the church for all I knew!

"I tumbled over the wall onto my bike and pedalled away, all downhill thank God, but I felt something pulling the bike back, imagination I suppose. I looked over my shoulder, lost control, and hit the ground, skidding with the bike across the road. Some people ran over to help, but all I could say was: 'Can you see anything?' and 'Keep her away from me!' and they thought I had been knocked silly. It took me weeks before I got my courage back."

"*Was* anything following you?"

"Probably not."

"And who wrote the message?"

He looked at me with contempt.

"Why, she did of course. And I knew what she was after. She wanted us to hunt together – Alan and Lucy, the Demon Lovers!"

Now that he'd shared his secret he could relax a little. Part of his mind had split away, almost certainly as a result of abuse in early childhood. This second personality had dressed the corpse, and written the message (the misspelling suggested the age when the split had first occurred).

"Vampirism," I said, as if I might be taking it seriously.

"The same stories occur all over the world," he said. "Why should we be immune? And where better to be a vampire than among people who don't even know that you exist?"

"And she was going into houses to suck people's blood?" (I suppressed any trace of a smile.)

"There's some sort of amnesia involved. People feel weak and disoriented but they've no idea what's happened to them. They used to be diagnosed with leukaemia. A farmer slept in that churchyard for a bet in the 1800s, and was found stark mad and with his hair turned white – so they say."

"Yet she died only recently."

"You think she's the only one?"

"No one ever discovered you there?"

"Not the way you mean."

He rubbed the dog's stomach with his foot, and its leg started twitching again.

"One day I fell asleep in her arms, and I woke up to find that she was awake. I mean AWAKE! Shuddering with power, her great eyes luminous, her lips drawing back from her long teeth (I think the gums had receded a little). She leeched onto me as the coffins began to groan. The screws were rotating by themselves. The nails were punching out of the wood with sharp little explosions. I got my hands under her chin and tried to push her face away. Her breath stank of dead crabs and I *saw* that the sun was slipping below the horizon as surely as if the solid marble had turned to glass.

"I rolled off of the slab and she sprawled on top of me. The fall loosened her arms and I tried to crawl out from under her but she was clamped onto me like a bitch in heat. Somehow I wrenched loose, but the gate was jammed. I thought *she* was doing it! Someone was screaming! I heard her voice calling to me, muffled like a mouth full of phlegm, and I realized that I'd been pushing against the gate instead of heaving it up. I was out of there like a bat out of hell."

"Who was screaming?"

"Me! It was me! You can't imagine that kind of terror! I don't know why I'm still sane. I bounded over the graves, shitting myself with fear, and crashed stark-naked into a woman who had been rubbing a brass inscription by flashlight. Someone shouted from the tap where they get the water for the flowers, but I had the hounds of hell after me and I was up and over that wall into the orchard like a winged creature."

I wondered where to draw the line between the reality he was describing, and an overdose of vampire movies. I wished I could take notes, and I would have been grateful for a medical attendant in the vicinity.

"I lay in a shed gasping and retching, but I couldn't stay there, not with the sky still darkening, so I wrapped a length of filthy tarpaulin around my middle and ran barefoot to the cottage of a married woman of my acquaintance. Her father was there, skinning rabbits, so I gabbled some rigmarole about being set upon by gypsies, and next morning, when I went back…"

"You went back!"

"She had my clothes in there, and my camera. I was safe so long as the sun was up. I thought of blasting them to pieces with gelignite stolen from the quarry…"

"Not a stake to hammer through her chest?" I said, trying to lighten the atmosphere.

"Too personal! But I knew I'd have to put an end to this… this… sickness. 'Pour in gasoline and burn them to ashes,' I thought. God knows what was biding its time in the other coffins – and then it occurred to me to take one last photograph."

He seemed suddenly very tired. I had a vision of strong-limbed male corpses seizing hold of Connibeer. His air of absolute conviction was making my flesh creep.

"And?"

"The coffin was empty, even her clothes were gone. Had she been trapped out in the open? Had she taken refuge in some culvert? In the shed, perhaps? Had she crawled into some ditch and burrowed down into the mud and leaves? Was she about to grope her way down the steps, blinded by the sun, and with her skin bursting with ulcers? I got out of there pretty fast, I can tell you, but when I looked back it all seemed so tranquil. A tablecloth was spread over one of the stone slabs where some children were having a dolls' tea-party. Lucy's tomb looked smaller in the bright sunlight, the church dwarfing it. I felt the little secret tingling that told me that she was reading my mind. I stared up at the clock where the pigeons were circling. 'That's where she is,' I thought. 'Up there in the tower.'"

The dog stretched, and yawned, and put its chin on his good knee so that its head could be scratched. Six o'clock struck, and Connibeer locked the shop and unstrapped his prosthesis. He had sometimes seemed on the edge of violence, as if the telling of his story was enraging him, but he seemed to have exhausted himself.

"And that's how it ended?" I said.

"Ended, Mr. Psychologist?"

"I have to be going," I said, stretching a little.

"Hear me out!"

"As you wish."

"That night I got drunk, not stinking drunk, but enough to get tiddly. I came home about quarter past eleven, put the kettle on, sank back in this chair, and thought how much courage it had taken. There's not many would have had the guts to make love to a vampire while she was asleep during the day."

He massaged the inflamed stump. "Gives me gyp," he said, wincing. He was becoming emotional again.

"Have you been alone in a house at night," he said, "when some vibration tinkles a glass, or when a tray that's set against the wall suddenly slides onto the linoleum? Have you been about to climb into bed when you hear just one footstep up in the attic?"

"Of course."

"As I sat waiting for that kettle to boil, I heard a movement out in the shop – just the one sound, like a chair being shifted about half an inch. The silence swelled up to a great buzzing. Lucy was in my mind but it's a three-mile walk to the old church, and the shop had been locked all evening. The drink had gone to my head and I told myself it was just my imagination. I had my foot ready to brace the door so that I could open it just a slit to peer in, when something exploded. One of the new bulbs had overheated – I had screwed the damn thing into the wrong socket, and I must have forgotten to turn it off. They cost eighteen pounds each, and I was so sure that I knew the source of the sound that I entered the shop without a trace of fear.

"I was confronted by a surrealist nightmare which resolved itself into a dress thrown over an easel. It was wet and I stupidly thought that the tank in the roof might have sprung a leak. Then I realized that this was Lucy's dress.

"At that moment I knew with absolute clarity that the shop had been pitch-black when I'd walked through a few minutes earlier, yet now every light was ablaze!

"I heard a rustle of silk, and turned to see Lucy, all dolled up in one of my Victorian costumes, and with a wig that was set askew (wigs were strewn about the floor like garbage). She was posing in the chair and twirling a paper sunshade. We stared at each other: 'The photographer and his model' – a tableau. Then the kettle began a whistle that grew louder and louder.

"'Tilt your head to the left', I said, inspired. There must have still been some human reflexes left in her because she obeyed, unresistingly.

"'I'd like to take a test-shot. Don't move!'

"I had done this so often that the words came automatically. Then in one sudden movement she ripped the front of her dress as if it were tissue-paper (a button hit me with stinging force). She was like Diana the Huntress, or some other Greek nemesis.

"'Smile', I said, releasing the shutter. Then I ran in here and wedged a chair under the handle – actually it's a replacement door. I could have leapt straight through the glass – this was before I had the bars put in – but I'd probably have bled to death. I ran up those stairs three at a time – the door splintering behind me. I was in the bathroom with some thought of locking myself in and crawling out the window. I'd have crashed head first, but I'd have done it if I hadn't thought of the attic – the ATTIC! I heaved the chest of drawers under the trapdoor and was dragging myself up through the ceiling when she came screeching up the stairs. I slammed the trapdoor and pulled a crate of books across it and heard her running from room to room like a dog looking for a gap in a fence. I tiptoed across to a patch of sky, and was halfway out into the drizzle when the crate tipped over and light flooded up.

"I'd straddled the roof ridge, intending to clamber onto the next building, when Lucy's fist punched up beside me. I began slithering. I was screaming for help – there were lights in the house opposite, some sort of party was going on. There was another explosion of slate and she grabbed my leg and started pulling it into the attic. I was sprawling, trying to clutch as large an area of roof as possible. My shoe was filling with blood – hot water it felt like – and her hand was sliding up the inside of my trouser leg. I hacked at it with a sharp slate, yet if she'd let go I'll have fallen thirty feet. The party-goers were on their balcony, shouting at me, and someone was hammering at the shop-door: 'Mr. Connibeer! Mr. Connibeer!', but it was too late. It was like being born in reverse. My fingers clutched at moss, at remnants of sun-baked bird-shit, and then I was being hauled into that terrible grinding womb like a peeled egg being sucked into a bottle (if you've seen that trick)."

***

Connibeer had recuperated in Exeter, and spent some time in the Midlands. At one time he'd been to Stoke Mandeville for alterations to his prosthesis. In each place he would feel safe for days, or weeks even, but then Lucy's mind would start "licking" at him, and he would know that it was time to move on. Once, when he was closing a curtain he had glimpsed her standing in the dark in torrential rain.

"I could have spent my life trying to stay ahead of her," he said. "But it made more sense to come back here, put in good locks, strengthen the roof, fortify the windows, buy a shotgun, keep a dog, and never be out after sunset."

"But when they found you – what did they see?"

"Just poor Mr. Connibeer who had been attacked by some carnivore. They gave a circus over at Paignton a hard time, but it soon blew over."

He held eye-contact with me.

"They must have known, you know – her family."

I stood up to leave.

"Well, it's been most interesting."

"You don't believe a word I've said!"

"I believe you're describing an experience that seems real to you."

"You're the one she's following now, Mr. Psychologist!"

"The other night? I saw nothing."

"Didn't you smell her?"

"What do you mean?"

"Devon violets. I used to leave bottles of perfume up there for her."

I hadn't mentioned the smell of violets.

"Don't you believe me just a little?"

The dog paced around the base of the walls, sniffing and growling.

"Does he always do that?"

"He's my protector, isn't you, my handsome?"

***

I sat up late into the night and wrote a full account of Connibeer's narrative. Next morning I went in search of Lucy's last "resting place". Three very worn steps led down to an iron gate, a design that positively invited flooding, but there might have been a drain, or perhaps the shelves were placed sufficiently high above the floor. I did not peer inside as Connibeer had done.

His missing leg was famous in the town.

"I blame that circus over to Paignton," said the fishmonger. "They swore blind that they had no animal missing but I reckon it ran back to 'em and they stuck it in its cage and said nothing."

His wife showed me a yellowing article from the local paper: "DANGEROUS BEAST LOOSE", I read, and "LOCAL PHOTOGRAPHER INJURED". There was a stock picture of Connibeer being awarded a plaque at some photographic exhibition. The hole in the roof was viewed from both inside and out.

"Awful thing to happen!" she said. "He be a changed man you know!"

The idea that some carnivore had pursued Connibeer through his house (and had then torn a hole in his roof to seize hold of him) made no sense. Had he attacked his own leg in a fit of self-hatred? Had he hallucinated that it was some enemy that he was killing?

I was perplexed as to how to get Connibeer into psychiatric care. I inquired after his relatives and learned of a brother in America, and an aunt with Alzheimer's, but by then he had disappeared.

He was found by a Mr. Neil Bell who was walking out on the headland. He was curious about a stench coming from the gorse and was shocked to see the body of Alan Connibeer, who was known to him personally.

The newspaper was careful not to offend the susceptibilities of its readers and it was some time before I learned the nature of Connibeer's injury.

***

I am once more ensconced in my flat at Hampstead, and at work on a chapter on "suggestibility", inspired by my own recent experiences (during those last days the cottage had never seemed entirely free of a faint odour of violets, and there have been other "coincidences").

Thumping against my feet as I write, is the tail of Connibeer's dog. When I collected him I was able to slip the two envelopes of Lucy's photographs under my coat – these at least will not be used to add fuel to the scandal.

Connibeer's death was self-inflicted. Our conversation had opened a crack in his unconscious defences, confronting him with the full horror of his actions; the mode of death is in itself significant (there are many accounts of self-castration in the literature, including that of entire religious sects). I imagine Connibeer crawling through the gorse until weakness overtook him. The rain had no doubt obliterated his trail which might otherwise have led investigators to the knife which was never found, and perhaps even to a hastily scribbled "testament".

Lucy is staring at me from my harpsichord. Her eyes express eagerness rather than vengeance. The shutter has frozen her just at the moment that she ripped open her Victorian costume. Her fists hold flaps of material, and her lips are draw back to disclose longish teeth. She is naked under the torn costume, except for her soiled woollen underwear. I am at a loss to account for the curious erotic power of this image.

The good news is that my tests are within normal limits, and my proctologist says there is only a small chance that the malignancy will recur.

FITTING IN

Edward swung effortlessly out of bed and did some stretching exercises, and some isometric exercises (pushing at the top and sides of the doorframe). Then he emptied his bladder and stepped rapidly on and off of a small box to work up a sweat. After a quick shower, he massaged his skin with a rough towel and studied his nakedness. His body was in excellent condition and he intended to keep it that way.

The TV was lecturing about medieval Japan where young men had been forced to shave their heads in an imitation of middle-aged baldness.

"What rubbish you do watch."

"I'm not watching it," said Mum, setting the table with amazing deftness (considering the crude hooks that had replaced her hands). "That programme came on when I was in the kitchen. I wouldn't give it the time of day."

She flicked the dial onto a news-channel, and he watched excerpts from the latest religious war as he gobbled his breakfast.

"You'll get indigestion," she said, but Edward had an "iron constitution". He put the dishes in the sink and went into the hall to put on his coat and his scarf. Mum hurried after him with the cheek-piece she had just washed.

"It rubs the gums," he said. "And it's stretching my face out of shape."

"Faces don't stretch, silly."

"Yes they do. What about trumpet players, or glass blowers?"

"Wear it in one cheek one day and in the other the next."

"Don't you think someone might notice?" he said, lifting her off of the ground and giving her a kiss.

"I expect you're right, dear," she said. "But you got to wear it!"

She popped the cheek-piece into his mouth, and helped his arm into its sling.

"And here's your walking stick."

"Yes, Mum."

"And remember to lean on it! Heaven only knows the consequences if you go prancing about."

"Yesss, Mum."

It was a lot to put up with, but he knew that she was right. She would do anything in the world for him.

"I love you Mum," he said, giving her a kiss.

"I know, dear. It would be the death of me if anything bad happened to you."

She stood at the window, and watched him cross the road. She hoped he would turn and wave but the bus arrived and he was hidden by it. Still it was a relief to know he'd caught it, instead of having to wait for the next one.

***

At midday she went downstairs to do the shopping, but a scabby old man met her on the landing.

"Morning, Mrs. Tuber," he said. "What was that thump-thump-thump this morning? Nearly brought my ceiling down."

"Thumping?"

"It's beginning to crack the plaster. Come in and take a look."

He edged back a few inches, holding his withered arm as if to disguise it.

"Oh, I don't think…"

"No, no, best to see for yourself. You're only going to the shops, aren't you, same as every morning? Look for yourself – it won't take a moment."

She squeezed past him into a room that was smaller than the room above. It smelt musty and everything needed dusting – the windows couldn't have been cleaned for years. He shut the door and she became fully alert.

"Oh, for goodness sake!" he said. "I'm old enough to be your father. No one's going to molest you, Mrs. Tuber – just go on through."

She entered another room and saw flakes of plaster on the unmade bed, and cracks that ran across the ceiling. She had warned Edward about his exercising. If they lived in a basement he could have exercised all day, but living in an attic…

"All that bumping. What the hell does that boy of yours do up there?"

"It's my loom," she lied. "It's the treadles. I'm so sorry."

"Your what?"

"Loom. I'll move it."

"Oh you'll move it."

"I didn't mean to cause any trouble."

The kettle whistled.

"I do make a nice cup of tea," he said, "though I say it myself! Do you take sugar?"

"It's very kind, but…"

"I expect your son likes sugar. Does Edward like sugar, Mrs. Tuber? Or may I call you Margaret. I expect he's got a sweet tooth, your Edward."

He knew her name, and Edward's name, and yet he'd only moved in the week before.

"You've met my son?"

"Only on the stairs. Quite an athlete when he thinks he's unobserved. One lump or two?"

He was holding the sugar between his fingers.

"One lump, please."

There was a portable radio with food-stains on it – perhaps he listened to it when he was in the kitchen. She tried to make conversation.

"You live by yourself, do you?"

"It's a real treat to have company. Perhaps you'd like to fetch your tea?" He glanced at her hooks. "Oh, I'm sorry, what am I thinking?"

"I manage perfectly well without hands," she laughed.

"I can see that you're a woman of accomplishment."

"Well at least I don't burn my fingers."

He had added milk to her cup without asking.

"Widger's the name. There are freshwater ducks called widges, so perhaps the ancestral Widgers bred freshwater ducks."

She noticed his surgical boot.

"One of my legs was shortened. And they did a few adjustments to my brain – that's when my arm seized up. I don't think they intended to paralyze it. That came as a bonus."

He flashed his ruined teeth at her.

"I admire you, Margaret – you must have been through hell."

"I don't know what nonsense you've got into your head…" she said, moving to the door.

"I was a clerk in the Department of Adjustments before I retired. There's not much I don't know about young Edward."

She put on a bold face.

"Then you know he's incurable."

"Just who do you think you're dealing with? They screwed up some of my wiring," he said, tapping his thinning hair, "but they left me my intelligence!"

"I've got to get to the shops…" she said, trying to open the door, but the knob was so smooth that her hooks slid about on it.

"Sit down!"

He waited for her to obey. Then he placed a porcelain pig on the table, removed its head, and took out four biscuits, two for him, two for her.

"No thank you."

"Oh, but I insist."

He pushed two of them over to her.

"I've been checking up on your Edward," he said. "He's everything a law-abiding mother might wish for – according to his file."

She was filled with the most tremendous agitation.

"I can't imagine what you're on about."

He dunked a biscuit and pushed it towards her mouth.

"Eat!"

"I don't want it."

"I know what's good for you, Margaret."

"Stop it!"

"Humour an old man!"

She opened her mouth to prevent the wet biscuit being smeared across her face. He laid it on her tongue and it was like having a foul tongue lying on her own tongue. She spat it out.

"You'll clean that up later on," he said.

She tried not to show that she was trembling.

"I have money," she mumbled.

"Attempting to bribe a retired public official? I'm surprised at you, Margaret. In fact I'm amazed your Edward has survived this long. You might as well publish your confession in the *Bone Breakers' Bulletin!*"

He was enjoying himself. She felt she would suffocate if she stayed a moment longer.

"Why should I listen to this rigmarole?"

"You tell me."

He took off his jacket, and removed the cloth that he had tucked inside the neck of his thick shirt.

"Take off your hooks."

"What?"

"Are you deaf? Don't you know I've been watching you every time you passed my door? You think I like living here all alone? This is sensory deprivation compared to the life I've led!"

He groped at her. She threw the tea in his face and twisted away. He fell, and knelt panting, trying to recover himself:

"You've got tea on my shirt," he said. "You'll wash that for me later."

"You're mad!"

"Oh, quite possibly."

There was shouting in the street. Dust was in constant motion in a wedge of sunlight.

"It's your own fault, my dear. Your feminine odours are affecting me quite against my will."

He stood up, grasping the table. The back of his skull was exposed to her. Should she drive a hook into it before it was too late?

"You don't have to listen to my foolishness," he said. "You can go on living up there under the roof, you and your Edward, and you can think of me down here, listening to the floorboards creak as you walk about (when that son of yours isn't bringing down the ceiling). But who knows – some afternoon, or night, or next week I might start raging at the unfairness of it all, getting drunker with each passing hour, and brooding on how you rejected my advances, and who knows but what I might become vindictive? 'Good morning, Mrs. Tuber,' I shall say, 'Good morning Edward,' as they drag him down the stairs, his head banging uncomfortably on each step…" Suddenly he screamed with all the power of his lungs: "…That is if they don't throw you both straight over the fucking banisters!"

She shrank back. She had known this would happen one day, she just hadn't known what form it would take. The man pushed his face at her, hairs thrusting out of his nose as if anger was expelling them. He seemed about to strike her, but he calmed himself.

"Mustn't get tetchy, must we, Margaret? No need to get the neighbours involved."

"My money is in certificates. It'll take me a while to get it all together, but…"

"I don't want your money – well, perhaps a little now and again – but that's not what I want. Oh no! I want you to take off your hooks!"

"Don't be stupid!"

"You'll do it for Edward's sake, won't you? God knows what you've done for him in the past! Why begrudge him a little bit extra?"

She loosened one hook and he leaned forwards to grasp it. The back of his skull was vulnerable to her again.

"I need help with the second one," she said.

He unstrapped it and laid it beside the first. Her stumps embarrassed her, but he kissed the callused ends.

"Don't…" she said, softly, tears trickling down her cheeks.

"You'll thank me eventually," he said.

She sat as if made of stone as he unbuttoned her dress.

"You are really something, my dear! Oh, what an enchantress!"

He lifted her breasts out of her brassiere and cupped them in his hands.

"You wouldn't believe the women I've had! Colonialism, that's the ticket! The girls used to line up for me! You could get a woman for a bar of chocolate!"

He dried her eyes but the tears kept coming.

***

The bus disgorged Edward into a street full of handicapped people. There was some sort of confusion – a sedan-chair had tipped over, and a Chinese woman was screeching as she tottering about on her bound feet. He crossed the road and helped the blind lottery-salesman extricate himself from the new street furniture.

"There you go, Mikey!"

"You're a good Samaritan, Edward! You wouldn't believe the people that have passed by without helping me."

"We got to look out for each other, Mikey."

"If only I had eyes like you. You got good eyes, haven't you, Edward?"

"Think yourself lucky. Mum had to use the hoist to get me out of bed this morning."

"No malingering," said Mikey.

"No malingering," laughed Edward.

He hurried across the waste land where the flea-market was held each Saturday, and for a few yards he forgot to limp, so he limped more than usual (as if the burst of speed had overtaxed him).

The elevator was out of order. He had to clamber up the stairs, left foot up, right foot up beside it. It must have taken him ten minutes.

Joan was in reception.

"Any messages?" he said, patting her hump for "luck".

"Mr. Liddel said to give you these." She handed over a stack of papers.

"Thank you, Joan."

She stared at him.

"Excuse me, Sir, but I wish you wouldn't do that."

Edward boggled in amazement.

"Patting my hump. I find it humiliating."

"I'm sorry, Joan, I'd no idea."

"Even hunchbacks have feelings!"

"But there's nothing wrong with a hump, is there? It's a rather pleasant affliction. If you had what I have…"

"I'd rather not discuss it, Sir!"

What was wrong with her? Oh well, it was probably her time of the month. He scanned the newspapers in search of any items with legal implications: a shipment of artificial scars had been seized; a mother had refused to register her new-born – nothing unusual. About mid-morning he went to the wash-room. The wall above the urinal was scrawled with the usual stupidities, and then, just as he was turning away, he saw the words:

Edward Tuber is a Dr. Jekyll.

A "Dr. Jekyll" is a fake cripple who becomes normal when unobserved. He tried to obliterate the insult using a wet paper-towel, but it had been written with indelible ink. He scratched at the surface with his door-key, but then he decided to leave it to show that he wasn't insecure.

Hoskins entered. His hands and feet had been interchanged. Edward had to help him with his fly.

"Old Liddel's in a foul mood."

"What's wrong."

"His innards again. Some sort of blockage."

"I say!" said Edward, nonchalantly. "Look what some fool has written!"

"Good Lord!" said Hoskins. "Someone doesn't like you."

"Oh well, it doesn't matter. Pretty stupid though."

He returned to his office and leafed through a brief that he was preparing, but the accusation niggled at him: *Edward Tuber is a Dr. Jekyll.* The others must have seen it! Why had no one told him?

Miss Pringle lurched in with the weekly horoscopes. She was as dried-up and bitter as Joan was plump and fresh.

"Goodness! Whatever happened to your arm?"

He had been so preoccupied that he'd forgotten to put his arm back in the sling.

"Paralyzed," he said. "They may have to amputate."

She looked at him curiously. "It looked as if it was moving."

"Just swaying. It's been stiff ever since I woke up."

"Perhaps you slept in a funny position." She looked at him doubtfully. "You're not going to physical therapy, are you?"

"Therapy! Me!" Was he laughing too loudly?

"Some people do, you know."

"I wouldn't know where to start."

He cursed himself for his stupidity. Now he'd have to remember to hold his arm stiff all day.

"Er… Miss Pringle!" he said, as she was about to leave.

"Sir?"

"I'd prefer it if you didn't come in here without knocking."

"But I did knock, Sir."

"Well, please wait for an answer."

"Something to hide have you, Mr. Tuber?"

He heard her giggling with Hoskins in the next office. Were they talking about him? *Edward Tuber is a Dr. Jekyll* – if only he could catch the swine who had written it. He spoke aloud: "But of course!"

He typed a password and within ten seconds he had access to the security tapes. He watched his colleagues enter and leave the washroom at breakneck speed. There was a pause and suddenly, there it was! So fast that he had almost missed it – Miss Pringle in the men's washroom scribbling on the wall! Why had he thought that it would be a man – wasn't she usually last out of the office? He froze her image and expanded it until her blurred face filled the screen. It expressed a mixture of anger and savage glee.

"A woman scorned," he thought. She'd dropped enough hints, but how could a fake cripple accept anyone's sexual invitation? And Miss

67

Pringle was no catch – always tight-lipped and proud, as if she was the only one who suffered.

***

It was twelve o'clock and the elevator was functioning again. He bought a falafel at the delicatessen and ate it as he sat by the fountain. A family of flipper children were splashing about, unsupervised.

Joan shuffled up to him, disturbing the pigeons.

"I'm sorry about this morning," she said.

"Oh, that's all right."

"You can rub my hump any time." She turned away, presenting it to him. He hesitated, and gave it a couple of discreet pats.

"I said it because… Well, it was for someone else's ears. I didn't want them to think that just anyone could pat my hump – not that you're just anyone – and I knew I could explain to you afterwards."

He noticed some teenagers looking at her. Even with the hump she was quite attractive.

"Your arm's not in a sling any more. Miss Pringle said it was getting better."

"I'm afraid it isn't. I'm letting it hang loose because it's too painful to bend."

"You ought to tell Miss Pringle to mind her own business. She keeps mouthing off about you."

She touched his arm and his scream shocked her.

"I'm sorry!"

"I'm used to it," he said, secretly pleased – his response must have been pretty convincing.

"I hope the old cow doesn't get you called in for inspection."

Scalpel! Had things gone as far as that?

She looked at the water bubbling out of the fountain.

"Well, why shouldn't I?" she said.

"What?"

"Just thinking aloud. A habit of mine. Come on!"

"What?"

"Don't argue! There's no time!"

She helped him lever himself to his feet.

"Hurry!" she said.

She skirted the beggar in the iron mask (who was prone to lash out at people) and waited for him in the alley beside Kaye's surgical store.

"We've got to talk," she said. "It's a matter of life and death."

"But…"

"In here!"

She entered a doorway and clambered up a narrow flight of stairs. He followed, perhaps faster than was wise, but she was too busy unlocking a door to notice.

"Go in," she said.

The room was in darkness.

"I'll turn the light on," she said.

He groped his way forwards and heard her locking the door behind them. The darkness was impenetrable. There were flashes from inside his eyeballs as he moved them. She blundered into him.

"What's wrong?"

"Nothing's wrong, silly. We've got half an hour!"

She moved away and he saw the dial of her watch jerking about in the darkness. There were swishing sounds and luminosities as silky material rubbed against itself.

"Who's in here?" he said, alarmed.

"No one but us, silly!"

She was trying to unbutton his clothing.

"I've got to be back at work!" he said, but her hands were everywhere. There was an acrid smell.

"Tell me what you want," she whispered. "I'll do anything. We don't have to be in love with each other."

"I want to keep my clothes on," he said.

"Of course you do!" (What did that mean?) "Oh, where is it!" she said, fumbling at his groin. A faint bar of light showed the base of the invisible door, but he had no wish to escape.

"Oh it's big!"

She embraced his neck and swung up onto to him. He staggered.

"I knew you'd be strong!" she said. Her lips were softer and more cushiony than he could have imagined. She was naked except for some strapping around her torso. He responded and she slid down moistly onto him. How could anything so bizarre seem so natural? He swayed against an invisible shelf. Small objects scattered. "Never mind," she whispered, and suddenly he had to do it, had to do it, had to do it, had to do it…

A layer of soft leather covered her hump. He slid his hands lower and cupped them under her buttocks to help her keep time, not that she needed help. It was as if they'd been doing this ever since they were little furry things under the feet of the dinosaurs. He spurted into her, gritting his teeth so as not to cry out. She wrapped tighter around him. He staggered and his heels connected with something solid. He kept his balance by clutching at some coarse cloth that tore loose from a window and allowed daylight to flood in.

She broke away and pulled a blanket from the narrow bed to cover herself, but not before he'd seen her breasts.

"Thank you," he said, politely.

"Oh shit," she said, and then: "Oh, what's it matter?" She dropped the blanket and started to loosen the straps that cut into her ribs.

"I love you!" he said. It was strange to be saying it to someone who was not his mother.

"Dr. Jekyll," she laughed.

He was stricken with terror.

"Don't panic! I was hoping you might be. And, oh God! – you certainly are!"

He cursed himself. He'd been holding her in mid-air with his "paralyzed" arm!

"Calm down, Edward! No one's going to tell on you!"

The leather cover was loosening; what would her hump look like? Brain coral? A giant fungus? The cover fell to the floor, absurdly heavy.

"Look," she said, dancing around the room. He could see her wisp of hair and her swinging breasts. She seemed luminous. There was no trace of a hump.

"You're a…"

"I'm a Mrs. Jekyll!" She giggled, pushing him on the bed and straddling him as she undid his shirt-front.

"It's late," he said.

"Only twelve-thirty!" she said. "We've got fifteen minutes!"

He'd had no idea what the time was.

"We can come here in the evenings," she said. "We can do it in ways that those cripples can't even imagine!"

She thrashed above him and he lifted himself on his elbows to suck her nipples – he hoped she didn't think it forward of him. Miss Pringle's image kept intruding, but he remembered a movie where someone was flayed alive and this elevated him to a second ejaculation.

"They can't break people for ever," she said, strapping on her "hump". "There'll be a whole generation of people like us! Then all the cripples will die off and we can be what we want to be."

His trousers were stained around the crotch. Where had all the liquid come from? He dabbed water on the stain from the washbasin but that made it worse.

"Everyone will know," he said, aghast.

"It'll dry!"

When they reached the foot of the stairs she tried to kiss him, but he pulled away.

"Not here!"

He was angry that she thought his wet crotch was nothing to worry about. She skipped on ahead of him, and he collided with Miss Pringle at the entrance of the alley. She was carrying a bag of shopping.

"Was that Joan?" she said.

"Where?"

"She seemed in an awful hurry."

He walked beside her so that she couldn't see the dampness. He met Hoskins in the corridor and pretended to study the notice board. Then he sidled into his office and dabbed himself with paper handkerchiefs, pushing some inside his trousers. Once his panic was over he felt smug – so that was what love was all about!

At about three forty-five he phoned her at her desk.

"Can I meet you again?"

"Of course! Tomorrow night after work!"

"I'll try," he said, exhilarated.

"Did you get my message?"

An envelope had arrived though the internal mail. It had contained an illegal pamphlet issued by an organization of Dr. Jekylls: "Walk tall!" said the headline.

"Make a hundred and fifty copies," she said. "You have access to the machine."

"Careful what you say on the phone!"

He was terrified that someone might challenge him as he used the copier, but no one paid him any attention. He sealed the pages in an envelope and took them down to her. She touched his crotch. "Almost dry," she murmured, and leaned forwards to blow hot air through the material.

"We're going to fuck our brains out," she said.

He was clearing his desk-top when Miss Pringle presented him with some proofs to be corrected.

"Mr. Liddel said that they had to be done before you leave."

"What's the point?" he groaned. "Even if I do them tonight he won't get them till the morning."

"He's coming in early," she said. "Lock up when you go."

"Oh, er, Miss Pringle. There's something I'd like you to see."

They watched his colleagues flicker in and out of the washroom like life seen by a snail.

"Here's the interesting part," he said, slowing the tape down.

Miss Pringle watched herself scribble on the washroom wall.

"I intend to show this to Mr. Liddel in the morning."

"You wouldn't dare."

He could see the doubt in her eyes.

"Scribbling obscenities about a colleague hardly shows you in a commendable light."

"Well, it really doesn't matter, does it? Not any more!" she said, and clicked away on her sharp little heels.

"Let her sleep on it," he thought. He had called her bluff all right. Tomorrow she'd be begging for his forgiveness.

***

It was almost dark when he took his usual short-cut across the waste land. His body felt strong and well used. Was it possible that all women were as eager as Joan? Could his mother ever have been so… so… enthusiastic? Unimaginable!

A deformed dwarf, and other homeless cripples were cooking a hunk of flesh. A No-Face was waved a bottle invitingly.

"Won't you join us, Sir?"

Edward suppressed an impulse to run.

"No thank you."

"You'll never regret it, Sir."

"I've a bus to catch."

They were spreading out as if to prevent his escape. Hadn't they seen how crippled he was? No-Face intercepted him.

"Just a quick word, Sir, if you'd be so kind."

"Look! I'm late! I have to be somewhere!"

They were all around him, dabbing at him, clutching at him. His right leg was being hugged by the dwarf.

"Leaving work a bit late, aren't you, Sir?"

"What's that to you?"

Had they been spying on him? No-Face grabbed him by the lapels.

"Hold him tight! This one will probably run like a hare!"

"How can I run with this leg?"

Powerful arms seized Edward from behind. He twisted his neck and saw a No-Brain who'd had the top of his skull stapled back on. The dwarf kept chanting: "Nothing will happen. Don't be afraid! Nothing will happen…"

"The thing is, Sir," said No-Face, "that we have it on good authority that sometimes you limp with one leg and sometimes with the other."

They'd never dare treat him like this unless someone had informed on him.

"It's a lie."

"And sometimes your spine's all twisted, and sometimes it isn't!"

"You're confusing me with someone else."

"Nothing will happen! Nothing will happen!" chanted the dwarf.

"Are you a Jekyll?"

"How dare you ask that! I had ten men at my breaking!"

"Where were you broken?"

"In church!"

"What church?"

"All Saints!" he cried, gesticulating towards the church that was silhouetted against the afterglow. "You can look me up in the church register!"

"Someone's ripped out the relevant page!"

"Well, it wasn't me," gasped Edward, panic-stricken. "I haven't been in there for years!"

"No, but your mum has!"

"Look at him," jeered a Stump-Man. "He's getting more crippled every second. He wants to convince us!"

Edward groped into an inside pocket. "I have certificates!"

"Anyone can have certificates."

"Here's my exemption! My categorization! My socialization!"

They dragged him over to the fire. The cook who had been attending to the hunk of flesh examined the papers. It was Mikey, blind Mikey!

"Mikey! It's me, Edward! Edward Tuber! Tell them who I am!"

"These documents are garbage!"

"Not garbage, Mikey, they got the official stamps!"

And then, realizing, the absurdity of this, he said: "What are you giving them to him for? Give them to someone who can see!"

But Mikey was looking at him with intelligent eyes.

"You're not blind!"

"Someone has to keep an eye on things," said Mikey, and they laughed as if it were the best joke in the world.

"Nothing will happen! Nothing will happen!"

"These papers are useless!" said Mikey. "No watermarks!"

They were thrown into the flames. Some fluttered skyward. Edward reached up for them – they were his most precious possession.

"You're no cripple!"

No-Brain hit him so hard that a rib tore loose.

"Scalpel, that hurts!"

"I was sealed inside a jar at birth!" screeched the Dwarf. "What do you know about pain!"

They pressed him face-down into a mulch of rotten vegetables and broken gramophone records. Mikey crouched over him, roaring at him.

"Doesn't each citizen have to be crippled as his parents were crippled! Doesn't every generation have to be broken so as not to outstrip the last? You coward. You were scared of the breaking. You thought the real cripples wouldn't know the difference!"

"I'll go to another country! I'll never come back!"

A kick to his jaw sent the cheek-piece tumbling.

The dwarf grabbed it. "Lookie here!" he cried.

They twisted Edward's head around until his face caught the light.

"Good-looking lad, isn't he!"

Edward slithered through mud and broken crockery. It was too much agony for his mind to correlate. The pain was like bursts of electricity. He kept thinking: "They've done enough! They'll stop now!" He didn't faint when his leg snapped but he did when they twisted it.

When he regained consciousness they were crossing the street and singing the old song:

"*Every man is faaated.*
To be educaaated!
You must be,
Same as me,

That's why we're creaaaaated!"

It was early morning before the collectors found him.

***

Edward switched off the alarm before it rang, and heaved himself out of bed, using the pulleys that Mr. Widger had installed. Once he was upright he could negotiate his own way to the bathroom. Mum heard the taps running.

"Are you up, Edward?"

"Yes, Mum."

"That's a good boy."

He gripped his "Zimmer frame" and crept into the kitchen where Mr. Widger was watching a Give-Away show.

"Morning, Edward, first day back at work! Great day for all of us, isn't it, Mother! Look at that poor bugger on TV. He just won a fortune and now he's bankrupted himself. More tea, Mother, if you would be so kind."

"It was nice of them to keep Edward's job open for him," said Mum, lifting the tea-cosy. "They wouldn't do that for just anyone."

The teapot slipped out of her hooks and she began to weep.

"All over the table-cloth," said Mr. Widger in a cheerful tone.

"I'll soak it in the sink," said Edward. "Then it won't be stained."

"Mother will see to that, won't you, Mother?"

"It's not the table-cloth," she said. "It's just that I can't bear to see him like this."

Widger put his arm around her waist.

"He's happier this way, aren't you, Edward? Who wants to be a misfit? Not me, that's for sure."

He dried Mum's eyes.

"I don't know what I'd do without my Mr. Widger," she said, lifting the pig's head and taking out a biscuit.

"The bus won't wait for ever, Edward," said Widger, nuzzling her neck.

She broke away to butter some more toast, each stroke of the knife making an enormous rasping sound.

Edward finished his breakfast.

"Goodbye Mum! Goodbye, Mr. Widger!"

They listened in silence as he bumped his way down the stairs.

***

Mikey was selling lottery tickets to a Crab-Thing that hardly came up to his knees.

"Are you of age?" he said, waggling a finger at it as it scuttled away.

"Morning, Edward – no hard feelings?"

"All for the best, as they say."

"I'm glad you're taking it so well."

"Well, it's life isn't it! All part of being a good citizen!"

"Isn't that the truth!"

"Tell me, Mikey – how come you still got eyes?"

"Put your hand here!"

Mikey indicated his crotch and pressed Edward's hand against it.

"Go on, have a feel. There's nothing there is there? I have to pee through a straw."

"I had no idea."

"I'm not proud. Still, I'm useful. I keep a sharp look-out. They'll take my eyes one of these days, just to keep the books straight, but I don't tell them everything – I didn't report you for instance."

"Who did?"

"Someone phoned it in."

"Man or woman?"

"Official secret."

"Ah, well. No malingering!"

The lights changed and he began a desperate struggle to cross the street before the cars surged forwards.

"No malingering," shouted Mikey, but Edward was gasping too much to answer.

The elevator was out of order and he was carried up by a couple of resentful mutants from the archives. At the top of the stairs was a "Welcome Back Edward" banner, and people were cheering him as if he were some sort of hero. Everyone wanted to shake his hand.

"I'd like a word with you, Edward," said Mr. Liddel, leading him into the sanctum of sanctums, and pouring him a brandy. "We've missed you, you know."

"Thank you, Sir."

"Whatever was that mother of yours thinking?"

"Well, you know – mothers," said Edward, rather embarrassed. He glanced at the glass case that contained Mr. Liddel's intestine. Some sort of peristalsis was going on. Mr. Liddel strolled over to the huge window, perhaps anticipating a release of flatus, the glass case trundling faithfully behind him. They sipped their brandy – it was a long time since Edward had tasted alcohol.

Mr. Liddel stared down at the congested pavements. "So many people in this world," he said. "And yet so few genuinely of the first rank. I regard you as a first-ranker, Edward, and now that all that… er…sordidness is in the past, never again to be spoken of within these walls let us hope, ha! ha! I might venture to say that some sort of partnership may well be forthcoming in the not too unforeseeable future, circumstances permitting."

"Thank you for your confidence in me, Sir."

"We've planned a small wine and cheese party in celebration at five o'clock today."

"I'm most honoured, Sir. Er… Thank you for the brandy."

"Only the very best for the likes of us, Edward my boy."

By mid-morning Edward had settled back into his usual routine. He saw Joan.

"Can we have dinner some time?" he said. "Or see a movie?"

"I've a boy-friend now," she said. "We're engaged."

"But we could still have dinner."

"What's the point?"

Later that morning he used the washroom. It took him a lot longer than it had in the past. The words *Edward Tuber is a Jekyll* had been sanded out along with all the other graffiti. Outside, in the corridor, Pringle and Hoskins were huddled suspiciously together.

"We're getting married," she said.

"So congratulations are in order," he chuckled, kissing her cheek and shaking Hoskins's proffered foot.

After lunch he found an excuse to dial Joan's desk. She talked to him as if he was a stranger. Later on when he limped past her desk on the way to the washroom she wouldn't acknowledge him. She seemed frightened of him.

"They didn't castrate me!"

"I'm not interested."

"I'm still the same person!" he hissed, angrily.

As he emerged from the toilet cubicle, he saw the retarded office-boy assisting Hoskins to pee. Hoskins was staring at the wall, indignantly. "Look at this!" he said. "Look what someone's written about poor Joan! 'Joan is a Mrs. Jekyll!'"

"Who'd write a thing like that?" said Edward, washing out his bag, but as soon as he was alone he began scrubbing furiously at the wall. Then he leaned forwards, his forehead pressing against the spot where he had written the offensive words. He stayed cantilevered like that for a long time until someone entered and he had to be cheerful again.

MY ADVENTURE WITH THE REVEREND

A tall, balding, thinnish man ran towards me through the rain.

"You must be the Reverend Best," I said, as he squeezed himself into the passenger seat.

"Most awfully good of you," he gasped. "My bicycle's being repaired. Usually I cycle everywhere."

"I couldn't let you trudge home on a night like this."

I had trouble backing out of the driveway; the elderberry wine had been stronger than I expected, and it didn't help that the Reverend was distracting me.

"I don't think I've seen you at any of the services?" he said, using his churchy voice.

"I'm not a believer."

"An agnostic!" he chortled, seemingly in the best of spirits. "Not an atheist, of course – far too educated a man for that. But wherein lies the basis of your unbelief? Fire away! You shan't offend!"

Some fool honked angrily as I reversed into the traffic.

"Actually, I think atheist describes me rather well."

"You teach biology I believe? Theory of evolution? Sex education?"

"Miss Glebe handles the sex-education end – look, I'm happy to drive you home, Reverend, but…"

"As a biologist, you will of course accept that God is revealed through his works?"

"As a biologist I find it more comforting to believe in the workings of blind chance."

"Ah, the theories of Mr. Charles Darwin," he said, as if referring to some outdated fad. I edged onto the hard shoulder to let a tailgater roar past. Dozens of cars followed him, all well over the speed limit. I accelerated to catch up with them.

"I'm told that you regard blasphemy as a civic duty?"

"I do?"

"I have it from a reliable source."

"Miss Glebe?"

"That information I am not at liberty to divulge."

He was beginning to annoy me. "The point is, Reverend," I said, skidding on wet leaves as I turned a sharp corner, "that if beliefs can't be mocked we may end up burning books, and then their authors. And being forced into church umpteen times every Sunday."

That shut him up, but it was the elderberry wine that was talking. We maintained an awkward silence as the lane-dividers pulsed beneath us. The Reverend was on the School Board so I tried to lighten the atmosphere. "Think about it, Reverend – if we kept the Holy days of every religion we'd never get any work done."

"Young Partridge had a good innings on Saturday," he said, with forced politeness. He was referring to cricket, but then he made a choking sound as a cement truck expanded to fill our entire universe.

***

We stood like ghosts in the gleam from the street lamp.

"Reverend!" I said, hugging him. "We're still here!" (I could smell his aftershave).

"Have you taken leave of your senses?"

"We can talk! We can still think!"

"Let go of me!"

I dragged him over to where our bodies were tangled in the metal.

"That can't possibly be us!"

"Who else would it be? There's your 'dog-collar'. We're finished! Dead! Defunct! Kaput! And yet we still exist!"

"But… but I'm breathing."

"Try holding your breath. We could swim the Atlantic underwater."

Flares and reflective triangles were being set out along the road – probably by the driver of the cement truck. It seemed undamaged.

"The resurrection of the flesh," he murmured, and then: "But we're not naked!"

"True."

I rummaged through my pockets; everything was still there – wallet, handkerchief, packet of chewing gum.

He peered into the darkness beyond the street lamps. "Lord knows what we're in for."

"I'm sure God has more to worry about than a couple of dead apes."

He glanced around as if expecting road-kill but then he understood.

"Men are not apes!" he said, rather loudly. "And earth is a spiritual battlefield where our every action may have contributed to our redemption, or to our… our…"

"Damnation?"

"Yes, since you say it so plainly!"

"Well at least you won't have to give any more boring sermons!"

"My sermons are not boring!"

"How would I know?"

He hit his forehead as if slapping a mosquito. "But who on earth will escort the scouts to the Jamboree on Saturday!"

"Somebody will!"

Cars were disgorging our would-be rescuers. Several people ran right through us – rather a shocking experience – so we retreated up a grassy slope where I stumbled through a cow.

***

We looked back and saw that an ambulance was trying to zigzag through a jam of cars.

"My poor wife," he said, sniffing back a tear. (And if tears, why not blood? Why not sperm?) I moved my tongue – certainly I had saliva. "Do you know," he said, "that in another month I would have been married for twenty-seven years?"

People would mourn for me too, would dispose of my books and the jade axe-head that I treasured. In fifty years, who would remember me? Yet my continuing existence annihilated all grief.

"No marriages in Heaven."

"Indeed there are not." He raised his chin and assumed a stoical expression. "Cut off in the prime of life with so much still to be achieved!"

"We'll be back in forty-nine days, according to the Tibetans."

"I have no interest in primitive superstition!"

"All the same, they'd advise us to stay away from pregnant donkeys."

"I see no cause for levity!" A disturbing thought occurred to him. "Are you a Buddhist?"

"I'm not anything."

"You must believe in something!"

"If I did I'd try to disprove it."

The sound of grass being ripped up made him grip my arm.

"It's the cow," I said.

"Ah yes… most probably."

He snapped into his "I'm in charge" mode: "Well, it's no use standing here. It behooves us to use our time constructively."

He began to pray.

"Are you sure you want to attract God's attention? What if he's a crocodile? Or a lemming?"

"If you won't join me," he said, icily, "at least allow me some moments of quietude!"

He muttered about "the things he had done, and the things he ought not to have done" (like stealing books from religious book-stores), while I became happier and happier: my back didn't hurt, my feet didn't ache, each movement had a wonderful fluidity. What a burden my earthly body had been.

I stared at some whorls and spirals that were shifting about in a gap between the clouds. It was unusual to see the Northern Lights so far south.

"Reverend!"

"Leave me alone."

"We're ascending!"

The whorls and spirals had shaped themselves into the tunnel reported by people who have survived their clinical deaths. I had a fleeting memory of having to choose between two similar tunnels (only one

83

of which contained an egg) but already we were being sucked in to a dark vortex.

The Reverend was overwhelmed: "I'm going to Heaven!" he cried. "Hallelujah! Hallelujah! I'm saved! I'm saved!"

***

We floated at what seemed a constant acceleration. The tunnel was dark but we were faintly luminous. The Reverend sang hymns in a rather syncopated fashion and then paused to gloat.

"What does your science have to say about this tunnel?"

"Precious little."

"Exactly! Your knowledge is a candle guttering in the wind, and the greater the flame the greater the darkness!" He sounded as if he was quoting from some pamphlet.

He strove to be solicitous (after his fashion): "All the same," he said, "this might be a suitable time to change your attitude before we meet our maker."

"The mad molecule?"

The mask of politeness disappeared. He gestured to his scrawny neck as if we were floating vertically (as perhaps we were). "I've had it about up to here with your flippancy!" he snarled. "Miss Glebe was right! You're not fit to be in charge of children! You teach evolution as if it was the cat's whiskers… and… and…" He boggled as he searched for more accusations. "And you're a terrible driver!"

"I was drunk!"

"Just let's not talk, shall we?" he said, through clenched teeth.

"Just let's not sing, shall we?"

We floated Heavenward in silence. My continuing existence gnawed at me like a Zen koan. Did I possess a spiritual brain that was an exact copy of my physical one? The idea seemed laughable and yet my clothes and the contents of my pockets felt as real as they had in life.

The Reverend seemed to regret his anger: "I'm sorry for the discourtesy," he said, "but you really do know how to get my goat."

We were approaching the end of the tunnel.

"I'll put in a good word for you, of course," he said quietly, "but your spiritual condition is quite deplorable."

***

There was no dazzling light, no Jesus, or Zoroaster, or Claudius the God waiting to receive us – only a greyness. The Reverend refused to look.

"What's out there?"

"Fog."

I helped him step onto a black and white mosaic that repeated itself endlessly.

"No welcoming committee," I said. "None of that 'Christians to the right, pagans to the left,' death-camp stuff."

I experienced a wave of irritation that was quite alien to me. Was I sharing his emotions? I thought his name.

"What now?" he sighed.

"Are my lips moving?"

He stared at me.

"How are you doing that?"

"I'm just thinking the words!"

"Well don't. I find it most disquieting."

We clapped our hands but there was no echo. We shouted but no one came. Minutes passed – or was it hours? Years perhaps!

"Sorry about the accident."

He forced a smile. "You were doing me a kindness after all."

The fog had soaked into my clothes, but as soon as I noticed this they became warm and dry and I was dressed in doublet and hose. This was fun! I extruded a costume of golden spikes that was quite dazzling. I had tried out dozens of garments and bodily arrangements before I noticed that the Reverend was almost mad with terror. It wasn't easy to calm him down.

"Sorry about that," I said, willing myself into a tuxedo with a wine-red cummerbund. "It seems that we can be whatever we want to be up here."

"I shall remain in God's image!" He stared hard at me. "Are you making yourself more attractive?"

"Absolutely not!"

"Well, don't – it doesn't suit you."

I saw nothing but fog in all directions. "Where's the exit from the tunnel?"

We wandered about, searching for it, but it seemed gone forever.

"God will not desert us," he said, hesitantly.

"Could this be the place they call limbo?"

He turned pale. "Oh no. All the millions of unbaptized children would be here – not to mention all those unfortunates who died before the coming of Christ."

What were we supposed to do? Wander forever through the nothingness? Invent games? Philosophize? Discover mathematical formulas?

We set off through the fog with no way to judge the passing of time: there were no bodily functions, no possibility of exhaustion.

He became reflective. "Whatever one says about earthly life one wouldn't have missed it. My only regret is that I wasn't able to do more."

"Me too."

"What do you most regret?"

"All those women I never had sex with."

"Oh, for goodness sake!"

"Isn't that what God wants? Go forth and multiply?"

"Not indiscriminately."

"Well it hardly matters now."

"It may matter very much indeed."

We walked on, clapping our hands to test for echoes, and shouting as the mood took us.

"Tell me, Reverend, do you really believe that God spoke to those Jews out in the desert?"

"God speaks to those who open their hearts to him. He spoke to me."

"You had a vision?"

"There was a light," he said, defensively.

"Were you really expecting God to be sitting on a golden throne like a Babylonian despot?"

I took his silence for a rebuke, but then he said: "Man needs symbols to describe the ineffable."

He began to pray, and I slid into his mind as casually as taking a book from a shelf. I explored the dank vicarage with its leaky roof and peeling wallpaper. I saw his wife's resentment at his being unable to afford a car. I watched his congregation diminish year after year in spite of the school rock-group that he'd persuaded to play at some of the services. I shared his rage when she stuffed her schnauzer with chocolate which led to horrendous veterinary bills. I burrowed deeper into his memory and saw Jesus "mooning" him from around the shower-curtain (just as God had "mooned" Moses on Mount Sinai).

I sprawled headlong.

"Get out of my mind!" he shrieked, as he towered above me.

"Calm down!"

"I expect you read people's private diaries. I suppose you spy on people when they're about their ablutions! Dear God! Why couldn't I have died with some decent Christian person!"

We wandered on at some distance from each other, but each dreading to be alone. His consciousness probed at the "firewall"' that I had erected. I threw a thread of thought back and encountered an equal resistance.

"Naughty!" he said.

We clapped for the umpteenth time and heard an echo. We emerged from the fog and saw a mile-high wall of unscalable black marble. Directly in front of us were huge doors covered in mother-of-pearl. And far above us the word HEAVE was spelt out in freestanding letters along the battlements.

The Reverend began to cooee and shout his name as if they should have been expecting him.

"Where's the gate-keeper?" he said. "And where are all the dead souls? There should be dozens arriving every second."

A massive "N" lay half buried in the mosaic. He began to explain that it must have fallen from the end of the "HEAVE" sign.

"So God speaks English?"

He swivelled his head towards me (his neck had acquired the flexibility of an owl). "Now you listen to me! If you don't knuckle under and express some sort of repentance, I would say your chances of getting through these doors are just about zero!"

I leaned against one of them and felt it move. "Help me!"

"Waste of effort. They wouldn't let just anyone in."

"God helps those who help themselves!"

It yielded enough to let us squeeze through. The sky of Heaven was the colour that medieval painters achieved by grinding up lapis lazuli. We scrambled over twisted girders and broken concrete to reach a squashed immigration-booth.

"They don't maintain the place very well."

The Reverend was distraught. "It's all smashed up! There's been a war, or a terrible plague. I'm too late! There's no one to worship!"

"Is that what you thought Heaven was? A place where you could praise God until the end of time?"

"Of course!"

"Can't you see how bizarre that is? If I created a shrimp I wouldn't ask it to worship me."

I let him sob for a while before passing him a handkerchief that I conjured out of thin air. He used it with some vigour and handed it back:

"Now what are you doing?" he said, irritatedly.

I was smoothing out some of the ruts by sheer force of will.

"Try it. Start small. Choose a pot-hole and imagine it being filled in."

His face screwed up as he grunted and strained. Nothing happened for a moment, but then a black finger thrust up and became a fountain of molten asphalt. We ran for our lives (old habits die slowly) until I thought of soaring into the air. The Reverend was being overtaken by a wave of steaming black sludge as I scooped him up.

"Don't drop me!" he gasped as I placed him on the remaining leg of a triumphal arch. Smashed domes, and shattered monuments stretched to the horizon. We were awestruck by the devastation.

"Seventy-two virgins for the Islamies," I said. "I wonder if their Heaven is still functioning!"

"There is only one true religion."

"Oh come off it! If you'd been born in India you'd have been worshipping Krishna."

"And I would have been seriously deluded."

"And Christians aren't?"

"Christ was the one perfect man in the history of this Universe, and I have always tried to follow his example."

"By stealing books from religious bookshops?"

He might have punched me if I hadn't found a distraction. "Look over there!" I cried.

A radiance was approaching from the far distance. It resolved into a red carpet that was being unrolled by speeded-up Angels. In a few moments they were staring up at us and singing the Reverend's praises. He shot me a look, half of pride, half of fear.

"They want us to join them," I said.

"But I... er..."

"Come on!"

He would have preferred to argue but I yanked him off-balance. We floated gently down.

"You see how easy it is?"

The largest Angel embraced him in a cascade of feathers. "Welcome, welcome," it said. "We've been so looking forward to your arrival. I'm sure everything will go splendidly now that you're here."

The Reverend's face expressed shock and dismay. I sneaked a thought around his firewall. 'Have courage! They expect you to say something!'

"This is really m... m... most tremendously gratifying," he stuttered: "But I'm hardly de... deserving of this honour... that is to say... I mean... er..."

It was the Reverend's moment, not mine, so I stood aside, and barely managed to claw my way onto the carpet as it shrank back the way it had come.

"What price your unbelief now?" he smirked, as I crouched, gasping.

"This could be the last spasm of our dying brains."

"Boring, boring, boring."

We passed through the suburbs of garden cities where crowds waved banners that said "God bless the Reverend Best" and "The Reverend Best – he is the best!" Every major building displayed his animated portrait, and boy-scouts struggled to control vast balloons constructed in his image. He began to wave, tentatively at first, but he was soon acknowledging the cheers as if he were a football hero.

We entered an office-block-cum-cathedral where the Angels stepped aside and the carpet ascended a grand staircase (rather bumpily I thought). It stopped in front of bronze doors – exact replicas of the famous ones that I'd admired in Florence. A puff of smoke resolved itself into a Las Vegas "welcomer" with cute little breasts who said "Howdy folks!" The Reverend blanched but in the flick of an eye she was clad in a Nun's habit and bereft of all make-up.

"The Almighty is expecting you," she said, bowing respectfully to the Reverend. "He can talk of nothing else."

"Surely there has been some error?" he said, trembling visibly.

"Oh no! He's your biggest fan!"

The doors yielded to the most delicate touch of her fingers, and we entered a space that seemed far larger than the structure that enclosed it. I stood beside her, rather conscious of her warmth (she had reverted to her Las Vegas persona). The Reverend had moved nervously into a pool of light. He gasped and sprawled headlong as he realized that he was at the feet of a gigantic statue.

He was burbling his "I have done the things I ought not to have done" rigmarole, when I materialized beside him, crouching in mid-air.

"Leave me alone!" he hissed.

"Don't you recognize it?" I said, lifting his chin and pointing upwards. "It's even dressed like you!"

"It's not possible!" he gasped. "A statue of me? Here? In the Holy of Holies!"

"They love you here. Didn't you see your picture everywhere? And all those cheering crowds?"

"Some of the women were flaunting their breasts at me."

"They'll wear burkas if that's what you want. This is obviously your Heaven."

"Then why are you in it?"

There was a clap of thunder and the idol spoke in a wonderfully deep and resonant voice: "Reverend Best, as you have observed, all is not well in Heaven. Entire suburbs have fallen into disrepair, and many of the new arrivals are conducting themselves in ways that are only marginally of a spiritual nature. Dancing around a golden calf is perhaps the least of their sins. We need a disciplinarian who will inspire the Angels, and force the blessed to their knees in everlasting prayer. God is therefore abdicating in your favour."

One of its house-sized feet lifted and crashed to the floor in front of our noses. The Reverend would have fled if I hadn't wrestled with him. A slit of light in the big toe widened to reveal an upwards escalator.

"You can't back out now! This is the chance of a lifetime!"

"But I can't possibly become God. I'm not qualified!"

For some reason we were talking in frantic whispers.

"Isn't this what you've always wanted? Well, isn't it?"

He pulled himself up to his full height (actually to rather more than his full height). "In that case," he said, "I'd advise you to start praying until I decide what to do with you."

I was about to follow him into the big toe when a gentle pressure on my arm dissuaded me.

***

The Reverend's shoe was prodding into my backside. "We are not here to rut like animals! You don't even know this woman!"

"Not now," I groaned, but it was too late – the "welcomer" had vaporized into wisps of pink smoke.

I hinged up from my toes and became arrayed like a Chinese Emperor. "Is there a problem?"

He gestured towards the gigantic idol. "We're in Hell! I met my identical self up there behind those eyes and he made homosexual advances!"

"Perhaps that's normal courtesy up here," I said, still miffed at being interrupted. "In some primate species the dominant ape makes a few symbolic thrusts and…"

"Men are not apes!" he whispered, looking every which way.

"Didn't Jesus offer his bum to you?"

"Stay out of my mind, you prying bastard!"

He might have hit me had not a tremendous wind swept us across Heaven and out into the fog again. Cherubs ran towards him from all directions. "Be off with you!" he cried, as they waved copies of his collected sermons for him to autograph. "You're all figments! This is all a device to torment me!"

"Oh, have it your own way," I said, and gestured them into nothingness.

I could almost see a light bulb go on inside his head. I've never seen a man more astounded. He staggered as he groped for something to hold on to, so I created a banister rail.

"Is this your doing?" he shrieked. "Did you create that… that…"

He was almost fainting with rage and horror.

"I thought you'd enjoy it."

"That squashed immigration-booth? Those lascivious crowds? That whore of Babylon? That hideous statue? Were they all your doing?"

"What's the point of just wandering about in the fog bitching at each other? How about a nice sunset?"

Indigo clouds archipelagoed across a crimson sky.

"What are you?" he gasped, crossing his index fingers to fend me off.

"I'm just a biology teacher."

I willed braziers with roasted chestnuts to appear. A Father Christmas rang a bell and shouted "Ho! Ho! Ho!" Scarves wrapped around our necks as snow began to fall.

"Stop it! Stop it!"

"Or how about a trip to the seaside!"

Waves exploded all around us.

"I can't swim!"

I hovered above him, shouting encouragement: "Fly! Think yourself into the air! You can do it!"

"Blithering idiot!"

He rocketed towards me, screaming abuse, but kept tilting to one side and zooming into the distance.

"The physical laws don't apply any more!" I shouted. "We can make our own Heaven!"

"Don't leave me! Don't leave me here! Come back! Bastard! Double bastard! Come back! Come baaaaack!"

He shrank into insignificance as I rose through level after level of spiritual knowledge. Soon I was creating orchards, and grottos, and palaces of infinite variety filled with chimeras and unicorns and other marvellous beings. Libraries sprang into existence together with movie-houses and nude bowling alleys. All needs were supplied instantly or after prolonged struggle (as the mood took me). Each morning Beethoven woke up stone-deaf so that he could have the joy of getting his hearing back. Stephen Hawking pole-vaulted his way to Olympic glory. Serial-rapists copulated with inflatable women and never knew the difference.

One golden dawn I tossed a question to the multi-mouth that shared my bed: "If I was the only conscious being in the universe and all other creatures were just robots, would old ladies still make tea? Would rabbits still scream as the weasels cornered them?"

"Of course."

"Then what need is there for consciousness?"

It sprouted eyebrows so that it could express astonishment: "You want to get rid of your consciousness?"

"Of course not! But what about all those eons of time before life started to evolve? And what happens when the last consciousness has guttered out? How can a universe exist unless there is an intelligence to observe it?"

I felt as if I was on the edge of some thrilling abyss.

"That clergyman really got to you," it chorused, rolling its eyes in disbelief.

It was as if a door had slammed shut.

"Ah, yes," I said, "I wonder how the old chap's getting along."

***

Cathedrals reared against angry clouds. Sounds of worship came from all directions. Somewhere, deep in the earth, heretics were being persuaded to accept Jesus Christ as their saviour.

Paving stones shrapnelled as the Reverend burst out of the ground. He was dressed in black robes and was affecting a monocle.

"How very fortuitous!" he said.

The subterranean lash of whips was louder now.

"Why don't you just *think* them into Christians?"

"I persecute, therefore I am!" (Was he developing a sense of humour?)

"I suppose you realize that you are being tried in absentia?"

He snapped his fingers and a Palace of Justice solidified around me. I was suspended in a cage above a seething multitude. I looked up into a magnificent dome where a painted Christ was consigning souls to eternal bliss or to the other place. I would have congratulated the Reverend, but he had been replaced by an Archbishop of unpleasant aspect who was lording it over a panel of lesser ecclesiasticals. My cage floated towards them so that they could condemn me. This promised to be entertaining so I extruded an armchair for myself plus a cold beer.

A Saint Sebastian – still bristling with arrows – asked me to swear to tell the truth, the whole truth, and nothing but the truth.

"But will you let me tell the whole truth? Will you let me say that I don't know why the Universe exists? Or how consciousness can operate without a brain?"

A Jesus clone looked up from the clay tablets on which he was recording this event. "The words are a just a formality; no one else has ever objected!" he said (his voice rang with miraculous clarity though the massed cries of outrage).

Squads of masked executioners uncovered torture devices.

"Why not let God do her own dirty work?"

There were roars of "God is not female!" and "Burn the heretic!"

"I'm not a believer!" I said. "You have no jurisdiction over me."

There was a shocked silence.

A line of Angels held up individual letters that formed the sentence: YOUR SOUL BELONGS TO US AND WE CANNOT ALLOW YOU TO TARNISH IT.

"All that we need…" said a lobster that was wigged-out as a lawyer. "…is the answer to one question …"

"I'll handle this," snarled the Archbishop, who for a split second looked exactly like the Reverend. "Does the prisoner consider blasphemy to be his civic duty?"

My judges craned forwards, eager to catch every word.

"I told you that when we were in the car."

"You must answer!" gasped St. Teresa, groaning in ecstasy as Angels floated her towards the painted Christ.

I had wanted to tease them, but I couldn't help remembering all those millions of freethinkers forced into destitution, or exile, or "killed as mercifully as possible without the spilling of blood" (to quote the Inquisition's euphemism for boiling in oil or burning alive). "Of course it's our civic duty!" I said. "Because unless we can ridicule people's most cherished beliefs we may end up on a hill waiting for the end of the world, or forbidden to fart unless we face Jerusalem."

"By his own words he is condemned!" cried the Archbishop.

"I don't have time for this," I said, and willed them all into non-existence. The Palace of Justice wavered, became transparent, elevated a foot from its foundations – and crashed back as solid as before.

I panicked and tried again – no effect. I used all my power and this time the dome cracked like an egg. Tons of masonry crashed down but I was already somewhere else. I was lying on an unmade bed in a cheap motel with the Groucho Marx quiz show on the television. "Alone at last!" I thought, but a movement caught my eye – the Reverend was staring out at the rain as he pulled on his trousers.

It was time for an apology.

"I'm sorry about all that 'God abdicating in your favour' stuff!' My unconscious got a little out of hand. Let's be friends. Live and let live. How about a hug?"

He stared, aghast.

"But how will I know who I am unless I'm persecuting someone."

"Persecute someone else."

"But you're the only thing I know that's real!"

I'd had enough of the Reverend and his lust for power, but there was no way to be free of him. We played duets on exploding pianos. We slid down banisters that turned into razor blades. We jousted with harpoons on galloping walruses. "Believe or Burn!" was scrawled in crimson letters across storm-wracked skies, and onto milk cartons, and onto the bodies of dead Jewish children.

Our battles continued until time reversed itself and we endured the events of our afterlife in contrary order. I glimpsed the HEAVE sign and was almost instantly sucked back through the tunnel and into the molten lava of my shattered body. My adventure with the Reverend had lasted for eight desperate minutes while the paramedics struggled to get my heart beating again.

***

A tube distended my throat, pumping air rather slower than I might have wished. A nurse drifted into focus. I tried to communicate my distress but fainted with the effort.

My shattered pelvis was slow to mend, and the damaged nerves made me incontinent and without feeling except for explosions of pain that took me to the edge of madness.

'I'm in Hell,' I scrawled on the pad that the Reverend held up to me (he had received only minor injuries).

"God loves you," he said, pressing his lips to my forehead. Each day he held my hand, and anointed me, and prayed over me – never ceasing to strengthen my spirit.

My damaged leg was beyond saving and due to some mix-up the surgeons amputated the healthy one. During the repeat operation the anaesthetic ran out and the muscle relaxant paralyzed me so I was compelled to experience each slit, snip, slice, wrench, saw-thrust and cauterization while fully conscious. Halfway through they stopped to share a cigarette and than the nightmare continued.

The Reverend protested so vehemently at their incompetence that he was denied visitor privileges for several weeks. When he returned I told him that his selfless example had convinced me to attend his church as soon as I was ambulatory, even though I was still unable to share his beliefs.

"The road to Heaven is not smooth," he said. "But many have travelled it. Why, in my own youth the Universe made no sense until God revealed himself."

I remembered Jesus mooning him from behind the showercurtain. How could anyone give credence to such lunacy?

"It's just that…" I struggled to find words that would not offend him, "the idea that revelation rather than scientific investigation can lead to truth seems so contrary to reason."

"My dear fellow, look at the Mormons – if faith made sense, where would be the struggle?"

"Like solving a Zen koan?"

He placed a finger on my lips. "Don't talk Buddhism."

I was wheeled into court to face a charge of driving while intoxicated. The Reverend gave glowing witness as to my reformed character but I was condemned to "durance vile" and thrown into an oubliette together with stinging insects and other noxious creatures. I licked the walls to obtain moisture, and chewed such pieces of stale bread as the Reverend contrived to push through a small grille. He was shouting verses from the Book of Job for me to memorize when I realized that a sentence of "durance vile" was a flagrant anachronism, and that my adventures since the Hall of Justice had been as delusional as my ten years as an Eskimo sled dog. New legs shot out of my stumps, and the walls exploded with such violence that a reinforcing bar careened through his skull, so confusing him that I was able to shrink him to the size of my thumb and seal him into a green glass bottle.

***

As always, the weather outside the window expresses my mood. I flick grapes for the pleasure of seeing my toucan catch them so effortlessly. Helen of Troy murmurs softly as she oils her body in the next room. I glance out at the yachts in the estuary and see nothing that needs changing.

The green glass bottle serves me as a paperweight. I stare into it (as is my custom) and watch the Reverend as he becomes a toad, a bus-ticket, a small atomic bomb, a pterodactyl, a mass of squirming nuns – to no avail.

He has resumed his human form – but what is he holding? A green glass bottle! And who is crouched over a tiny desk inside that bottle? Can it be myself? And is the Reverend trapped in an even smaller bottle, ad infinitum? The yachts that scud over the choppy waters are replaced by his enormous eyes as he watches me though thick green glass. Will we never be free of each other? Even a donkey's foetus would be welcome now.

My Master beats me without mercy. "Atheist!" he screams, smashing his stick on my delicate snout. "Unbeliever!" he cries, swiping me between my legs. "Hee-haw, hee-haw," I snort, kicking out with my hooves. This so enrages him that he curses me, using my own name, and I remember that I was human once – or how could I understand English? No sooner has the thought entered my mind than the Reverend is in the passenger seat and I am reversing out into the traffic.

"I don't think I've seen you in church lately?"

"Get out of the car!"

"Into this torrential rain?"

"Will you get out!"

I see him dwindle in the rearview mirror as I pull into a lay-by (to avoid the truck – no fool me!). Here it comes, just as before, but at the last second it swerves and heads straight at me. I gun the motor and roar forwards, scattering gravel. It skids in a halfcircle. The Reverend is running alongside it like a professional sprinter. I roar under a bridge that is too low for anything but cars, but the truck leaps high in the air and slams down just ahead of me – SCREECH! CRASH! RIP! TEAR! THUMP! I wriggle through the shattered windscreen and set out across the fields, running zigzag. It hops after me like a gigantic frog. I "will" it to become a toolbox, or all fourteen volumes of Marcel Proust, or a chocolatepudding, but the Universe won't obey me any more.

I take refuge in small wood where the Reverend catches up with me and humps my leg. The truck hoots and grinds its gears, uprooting trees that existed before I was born.

Bolts of lightning illuminate the interior of its cab as it smashes its way into me, but why can't I see anyone at the wheel?

THE CORD

"John?"

The voice was female, complaining, hard done-by, tyrannical. He gave a frightened glance towards the door that was open just enough to admit the thick, purple-veined, insult-to-nature umbilical cord that disappeared into the top of his trousers.

"John?"

He was wearing his school tie, school pullover, short grey flannel trousers, knee-high socks, and the tight black shoes that he could never get shiny enough to please her. Boys of his age should have been in long trousers but who had ever been able to reason with her? (Certainly not the staff at the maternity hospital.)

"John! I'm not standing out here all day!"

"Just a minute, Mum."

He was lying on the floor with his arm stretched under the bath but his fingers could feel nothing but strings of cobweb and chunks of damp plaster.

"I thought you went in there to use the lavatory."

"Well, I'm constipated."

"I don't hear you straining or anything. Have you taken your laxative pills? You need a good clean out."

"No, I don't, Mum."

He pressed his ear to the floor, trying to see the thing he needed. Had he moved it somewhere else and forgotten? Perhaps he really was a useless, forgetful, thoughtless, stupid boy like she kept telling him.

"John! I know what you'm up to in there!"

Her words paralyzed him.

"Book-reading!" she said: "You'm in there reading books while I'm stuck out here on the landing."

"No, I'm not, Mum!"

The door swung open as he was brushing shreds of under-the-bath cobweb from his sleeve.

"Ah! Caught you, en't I!" she said.

The other end of the cord vanished up her skirt. It was lumpy, with veins like tree roots, and it was long enough to coil around her shoulder when they went shopping, forcing him to "lock step" with her.

"Oh Mum, you said you'd never come into the bathroom without knocking."

"I thought you come in here to use the lavatory but I ain't heard it flush though…" She lifted the lid. "… and I don't see nuffin' in there! Oh no – you was coming in here to look for something you've hidden!"

"Don't be silly, Mum."

It was terrible to have a son who was such a liar. He was standing there like butter wouldn't melt in his mouth.

"Silly am I? What you call this then?" She yanked something from the top of her dress. It was the axe that had disappeared from the woodpile. "Stuffed under the bath where you thought I wouldn't find it!"

She began waving it around.

"Careful, Mum, that's sharp!"

"Sneaking in here to play with your father's chopper! To think of a son of mine wanting to cut off his own umbilical!"

"I'm not a baby any more."

"Your father would turn in his grave if he knew how you do talk to me!"

"He was cremated!"

She went berserk. Why did he never know beforehand what she would find unforgivable? He scrambled over the lavatory, the washbasin, the bath, the cupboard – but the cord prevented all escape. He slid down between the lavatory and the wall, shielding his head with his hands, but what use were hands against a blade that could split wood? Seconds passed and he was still alive. He opened his eyes cautiously. She was backing away, almost tripping over the cord.

"I'll swing for you one of these days!" she said (meaning she'd hang for his murder).

She pressed the cool blade against her brow and assumed her long-suffering look.

"Now see what you've done, wicked boy! You've brought on one of my migraines!"

He knew what that meant.

"Oh no, Mum!"

"I shall have to lie down in the bedroom with the curtains drawn! Come on!" she said, flicking a wave along the cord that jerked him to his feet.

"I have to use the lavatory," he said desperately.

She looped the cord over her shoulder and became almost flirtatious. "Well, you'll have to use the po'."

The chamber pot was so noisy, but he locked step with her (desperate to protect the sore place on his stomach from any more jerking).

***

Her needles clicked as she swayed in her rocking chair. The axe lay across her knitting-basket – a reminder of past treachery.

Click, click, click.

"John?"

He was squatting as far away as the cord would permit.

Click, click, click.

"John?"

He stared at the psychotic wallpaper. One day he'd ram those knitting needles into his ears and silence her forever. Flies buzzed daringly around the twisted ribbon of fly-paper. Three o'clock. It would be at least an hour before they could have tea and buttered crumpets.

"John!" she hissed, tugging at the thick, raw, meaty umbilical cord.

"Don't!" he said, angrily.

"Answer me then."

"I am answering."

"Don't you cheek me! I'm the only mother you'll ever have and don't you forget it!"

Click. Click. Click.

She smirked. He'd grown too big to beat into submission, but she could still give him a tongue-lashing.

"What are you thinking, John?"

"I'm not thinking anything, Mum."

"Don't sulk then."

"I'm not sulking, Mum."

Children's voices drifted in from another universe. He could see a scab that he would hinge off when she wasn't looking.

"Jumping out that elevator, hoping the doors would snap it when it closed!"

"Don't go on, Mum."

A fly landed on his knee and began to rub its back legs together. He'd been told that they took-off backwards but he was never quick enough to catch them.

Click, click, click.

"If I hadn't hit that emergency button I don't know what would have happened."

"It was an accident."

"Yes," she said, smugly. "Like the time you ran over it with the lawn-mower…"

Click, click, click.

"Not to mention running across in front of that ship-launching!"

"Well…" he said, goaded into defending himself, "it's…"

The fly evaded him.

"Well, what?" She needed an answer so that she could prove how selfish he was "You might as well tell me, John. I always know when something's upsetting you."

An aeroplane droned overhead. Perhaps it would cross the sliver of sky that he could see through the window.

"Why can't I be like the other boys?" he said softly.

"I don't want you like the other boys – I want you to be a credit to your family."

"Well, it's awkward having to drag behind you everywhere."

"You don't normally complain. You was always on at me to go out in the street so you could play skipping games." She glowered at him: "What do you want to do you can't do when I'm here?"

Achieve world peace? Find a cure for the cancer that killed his father?

"Oh, lots of things."

"You want to hang around street corners getting young girls into trouble."

"No, I don't, Mum!"

Her needles clicked furiously. Hadn't she slogged her guts out for him? Hadn't she changed his diapers a thousand times even though it smelt awful? He didn't have no gratitude!

"We had that nice Jennifer Lorum over for tea the other day," she said, slyly, using her polite voice.

"She's silly."

"She do better at school than you do!"

"She's all spotty – and people keep coming up to pat her hump."

"She can't help that, poor girl. No, you want one of they fancy women. You don't want the sort of girl you can bring home to me."

The worm turned, sufficiently provoked.

"Well, I'm fed up. You know how it itches in hot weather, and everyone laughs at that stupid lagging you knit for it in the winter."

"You'd be the first to complain if we caught a chill in it."

She examined her knitting. She was using up all her leftover bits of wool. It was beginning to look quite festive.

"Can't I ever have a life of my own?"

It was as if the toilet had objected to being shat into. She'd soon put the Kibosh on that!

"A life of your own! Didn't I suffer horribly for you? Wasn't I sick day after day after day? Didn't I lie in the most appalling agony? We had bucket after bucket of hot water. The Nurse helped push. The Doctor used his forceps. They could hear me screaming right up Fore Street –" she struggled to regain her composure – "and that was just your conception!"

The goldfish was swimming around its suffocating little bowl – did it really think it was getting anywhere?

"Grrrrrr… grrrrr… grrrr…"

What was that sound? Was it John grinding his teeth? She would have told him to insert the plastic "retainer" that he'd got from the dentist but spotty, hump-backed, good-natured Jennifer Lorum had opened the door and stuck her head into the room.

"Anybody home?" she said, although they were in full view.

"We was just talking about you, Jennifer."

"I thought my ears were burning. Would John like to play dominoes?"

"All right," he said. (Anything was better than sitting there with Mum nagging him.)

Jennifer clattered the pieces onto the linoleum.

"Would you like to play, Mrs. Podger?"

"You go ahead, Jennifer. I'm going to take one of my catnaps. You may have to keep shaking John awake. He does tend to nod off when I do."

He hated her to refer to the cord when they were in company.

"Now don't scowl, John. It's very nice of Jennifer to come round to play dominoes. It's not every young girl would be so thoughtful."

She lay back with a handkerchief draped over her face and was soon giving very quiet and regular snores.

All day Jennifer had been unable to sit still. If her father had said "Stop wriggling on that chair!" once, he'd said it a dozen times. The cord crossed the floor in front of her. She stared at it and saw it pulse slightly.

"Can I touch it?" she whispered.

"What?"

"I mean she won't wake up or anything?"

He shook his head. "Oh, no."

It was unexpectedly warm.

"It's all right," he said. "You won't hurt it. It's not very sensitive."

She stroked it and said: "It's all silky."

"It's your turn," he said, meaning the dominoes.

She wondered if he'd noticed her new blouse. She stretched her arms towards the ceiling and pretended to yawn. If he could see her breasts he'd know that not all of her was ugly.

"Why aren't you nicer to me, John?"

He studied his dominoes.

"Tell me," she said, edging closer. "If you really liked me you'd tell me."

"I can't." (Was he blushing?)

She fingered the black ribbon around her neck that a magazine claimed to be the height of fashion.

"I won't play with you any more," she said, teasingly.

"Well it's…" He made a helpless gesture. "It's just that you're so horrible. All the boys laugh at me because I see you."

"They laugh at you anyway," she said, matter-of-factly.

"That's what I mean!" he said, not looking at her, and then – as if angry with her – "Are we playing dominoes or not?"

She whispered her reply: "Cut yourself off!"

He shot a quick look at Mum. The silk handkerchief swelled and collapsed in time with her breathing. Was she really asleep?

"Mum says I won't survive on my own."

"Other boys do!"

"She says I'm no good at anything practical."

She stared at him, wide eyed. "We could get married."

His lack of response seemed all part of his shyness (it took a lot to depress Jennifer). "I may not be much to look at," she said, "but I'm all right round the house."

Their faces were so close that they blurred. They kissed, protruding their lips because their noses were in the way.

"She'll wake up," he said, torn between terror and desire.

"We could go out in the passage and cuddle." It was half a statement, half a question.

"All right."

They moved in slow motion (to be as quiet as possible). The cord was a bit short so he lifted it from between Mum's ankles and draped it over her thigh. Now it was long enough.

A factory hooted. A bird cawed as if it had heard a coarse joke. Flies buzzed in a holding-pattern.

The rocking chair creaked as the cord began to pull at it. Mum, in mid-dream, reached across a spiked railing for a sprig of pure white hawthorn blossom. Her foot slipped and a spike stabbed into her armpit, suspending her in mid-air. She felt no surprise that the ambulance was a boat rowed by shirtless men whose rowlocks creaked louder and louder as the storm mounted.

"John!" she screeched as she always did when she woke up, but this time her skirt was rucked around her waist, and the chair was bucking violently as the cord tugged at her insides.

She screeched again as she struggled to extricate herself.

"Just coming, Mum!"

"You get in here this instant!"

She heaved him into the room as he was adjusting his trousers. The door exposed Jennifer in disarray.

"Oh you nasty boy! You've made me all hot and sticky!"

She thought he would attack her, but he just wanted the axe.

"Let go! Let it go!" she cried, wresting it away from him. "I won't be left here on my own. You won't be rid of me till my funeral!"

She placed it on the cushion of the rocking chair and began to straighten her dress.

"You see what you do, Jennifer Lorum! You turn my own son against me! You better make yourself decent and go on home! I'll have a word with your father and won't he just know what to do!"

John tried to back away but she wound him in with the cord. Big or not, she'd have to knock some sense into him. Jennifer pushed between them.

"It's not fair, Mrs. Podger! The doctors should have cut him off years ago."

Mum slapped her.

"Don't you hit me! I'm not your child!"

"You'm not fit to be my child, Jennifer Lorum! Don't you dare set foot in this house!"

Jennifer burst into tears. The front door slammed behind her. They heard her weeping as she ran past the window. They stared at the psychotic wallpaper, reluctant to look at each other. The five-thirty bus laboured painfully up the hill.

Finally Mum said: "Tuck your shirt in!"

He ignored her.

"I said 'Tuck your shirt in!'"

He covered his ears.

"Dumb insolence," she thought. His father had been tied to a gun-carriage for dumb insolence. She began to pick up the dominoes.

"That door stays locked from now on," she said, briskly. "We can't have just anyone flouncing in here. Mr. Lorum can collect this rubbish!" (She meant the dominoes.) "And won't I just know what to say to him! Tuck your shirt in."

John spoke slowly and deliberately:

"I don't want to go on living with you till I'm old!"

"Do you think I scraped and cringed to the grown-ups without expecting my turn? Tuck your shirt in, wicked boy!"

"I'm different than you are!"

"Are you going mental? People who talk like you, John, are mental people! Now take hold of yourself and act sensible! I don't fancy sitting outside your padded cell all day! And tuck your shirt in. What would people say if they saw you with your shirt hanging out?"

"I'm going to masturbate!"

"I'll lay my hand to you!"

"Into the tea-cosy!"

She clutched it to her bosom. She had never imagined such horror.

"Well, what am I supposed to do? How can I help getting excited with all the hormones from your menopause?"

"Don't you dare touch my tea-cosy!"

He grabbed something yellow from the fruit bowl and tried to cram it into the toaster. "All right! I'll warm up a grapefruit!"

"You'll electrocute me!" she shrieked.

He threw it aside and began rubbing himself against the furniture.

"That's enough, John!" she hissed, exerting an icy self-control. She was rummaging for her bottle of pills. "You'll have to take some of my tranquillizers, you're not well!"

"I feel particularly well!" he said, rearing up from the armchair.

"No, no! You're ill! You're ill!"

"Perhaps I could masturbate into you!"

He had the same Saturday-night determination that she remembered from his father. She ran to the window but he hauled her back. They crashed against the table sending the goldfish bowl flying. Flop, flop, flop went the fish.

"Don't you dare touch me – I'm your mother!"

He pushed her down and twisted the cord around her neck, amazed at how easy it was to murder her. He lay sprawled across her for a long time. They had never touched unless they had to, but now they were like spent lovers.

He felt no exhilaration – only a confusing numbness. Her false teeth lay on her tongue so he put them in the glass of water that always stood on the mantelpiece. A framed photograph showed him paddling while she waited on the shore. He laid it face down. He straightened the furniture and put the squashed grapefruit back into the fruitbowl. The goldfish was beyond help. He used Mum's knitting to mop up some of the spilt water. Then he heard voices. Workers were coming home from the factory. He stood behind the net-curtains and watched them as they chatted and called out cheerfully to each other.

The street lamps came on so he closed the inner curtains and switched on the light. He took a log from beside the fire, laid the cord across it, closed his eyes (expecting terrible pain) and swung the axe savagely. The splatter of hot blood surprised him but it hadn't hurt. He opened his eyes and saw that he had made a deep gash in the cord. He cut through the remaining thickness with the bread knife, wiped his end (the shorter end) clean, and stuffed it into his trousers. They bulged, but if he wore his raincoat and leant forwards at an angle, who would notice?

He was dragging her towards the kitchen when she released a series of terrifying farts. For a long time he stared at her, daring her to move. Then he thought: "Why not walk up to the cinema? See what movie's playing. Put her in the refrigerator later on."

He flinched as he stole money from her purse. She seemed to be watching him. He could have put coins on her eyelids half an hour ago but now he was afraid to touch her.

He ran into the hall but the money sprayed from his hand as he was spun around and jerked back. He was sprawled across her like before! What had happened? He tried again, and the same force wrenched him back into the room, but this time he noticed that she spasmed as he rebounded (as through an invisible cord still linked them). He waved his hands in front of his stomach but felt nothing. He slashed at the space in front of him with the axe but he couldn't chop empty air. He kept on leaping away, desperate to be free, but it was too painful. He fell onto all fours, and was sick with horror as the dead mouth laughed at him.

"You won't get rid of me that easily, John!"

"You're dead! You're dead!"

"Dead I may be," it said, lisping slightly because its teeth were on the mantelpiece, "but I'll make sure everyone knows what sort of a son I had! Murder! Murder!"

"I have to live my own life!" he cried, trying to crawl away but held back by the invisible tether.

"You can't, can you! That's how weak you are!"

"You did this to me!"

"You should thank God for my bringing you into this world! Murder! Murder! I've been murdered!" There was a violent knocking at the door. Time stood still until the letterbox clanked open and a voice said:

"Are you all right, Mrs. Podger?"

The thing that had been his mother sat up, and straightened its clothing.

"Yes, thank you," it said. "Everything's as it should be."

"We thought someone was being murdered in there."

"Oh no! There's nothing the matter with our family. I've brought my son up clean and respectable!"

***

The poet crouched on the woman's shoulders with arms extended (a padded club dangled from one wrist). He roared fragments of verse to the desert air:

"*There is a flame in every living soul,
That must aspire toward a higher goal.*"

What joy to feel her so responsive to the slightest pressure of his thighs! They'd put so much distance behind them, and yet ahead lay such vastnesses, such promises of infinite progression.

"This is the life!" he cried as lizards zigzagged out of their way, and tall cactuses slid solemnly past. The ground levelled out and she broke into a steady mile-consuming trot, fast enough to create a pleasant breeze. What stamina she had! What a tribute to the benefits of fresh air and regular exercise! And if he could keep her going until dark, and then ever onwards, eagerly, at each new dawn, there'd be no time for recriminations.

The rhythm of her pounding legs made verse float into his brain. He began to chant: "*Give me power, at this hour! Give me power, at this hour!*" The words both inspired and enraged him. All those massacres with him on the winning side, but where were his fast cars and obliging mistresses?

"Stupid bitch!" he cried, striking her with the club. She had strayed towards a wilderness of thorns where they'd have been entangled like those poor sods who had howled on the barbed wire. She limped back onto the track and began to pick up speed. One blow had been enough. Last week he'd nearly crippled her, and then what would have happened? But by Christ she'd deserved it! And hadn't he served it!

"*The human spirit can't be crushed,
It soars eternal from the dust!*"

He tangled his hands into her hair and was soon dreaming of rape, sodomy, and the women who had eluded him.

***

"John!"

"Just a little further till we find some shade, Mother."

"The way you lug me about. I might just as well be a sack of potatoes!"

He staggered through the hot sand until he could prop her up against some huge boulders.

"I don't know what gets into you sometimes," she said: "You lug me about like a sack of potatoes!"

"You just said that, Mother."

"Well, you don't half shake me about!"

Click, click, click. The wool had been used up ages ago, but she still clicked her needles.

"Got to pee!" he said, dragging her sideways until the invisible cord allowed him to face into a discreet gap between two boulders, but he couldn't urinate.

"I used to think I could do anything," he said, "but now I can't even pee."

The view was like the pictures in *National Geographic* magazines, but no camera could capture such torrents of unearthly light. He stared up at the soaring vultures. "Death Valley," he said. "Who'd have thought that we'd end up here!"

Mum glowered at him. "What *do* you look like!"

His tie was missing, and his toupee had vanished in the last windstorm. Other boys took care of their appearance. "Tuck your shirt in."

"It's too hot for that, Mother."

She had given up expecting obedience but she was sure that he'd never leave her.

"Well at least comb your hair!"

"I don't have any hair."

"You've still got some at the sides. Lay it across the bald bit. You'll look ever so much nicer."

"Someone's coming!" he said.

A tallness lumbered towards them through the convoluted air. It resolved into a naked man who was crouched on a woman's shoulders. She was caked with shit as if her rider was a permanent fixture. The snakes that seemed to thrash about their heads became ropes of clotted hair. "Must keep going! Must keep going!" she gasped in time to the blows of a big red padded club that rose and fell with the regularity of a steam engine.

"I am the master of my fate!" screeched the man, "I am the captain of my soul!" and gave a terrible cry as they sprawled headlong, his legs still clasping her.

Mum turned her back on them. "Let they stew in their own juice, John. They in't our family."

John ignored her. "Are you all right?"

The man looked away, but the woman seemed quite friendly. "I'll be fine once I've rested," she gasped. "Just have to catch my breath."

The man pushed at the ground with the club until the woman achieved a sitting position. For a while the only sound was the clicking of Mum's needles and the woman's wheezing.

"Does anyone have an aspirin?"

"We don't mix with your sort, Jennifer."

"I know that voice! Is that you, Mrs. Podger? Are you John? Is it really you, John?"

"Yes," he said, helplessly. "We've changed."

He knew her by the black ribbon.

"Fancy meeting you all the way out here," she said. "We had such good times together. You was going to be a concert pianist, and I was going to be the first female astronaut."

"Why doesn't your father get off and let you rest?"

"Oh, our dad died donkey's years ago! I don't even dream of him any more."

"He's on your shoulders! He was hitting you with a big club!"

As if on cue her father began to beat her.

"Must be on my way!" she gasped, lurching to her feet. "It's my arthritis. The pain gets worse and worse until I start moving. Must keep on until the fall of night!"

Mum cackled her demon laugh. "She don't want you, John! She got more sense!"

John was desperate: "It's your father! He's hitting you! He got his legs wrapped around you! It's why you can't breathe!"

"No! No! It's my asthma!"

"What are these!" he said, prodding at the father's knees.

"They're my breasts!" she said, slapping his hand away. "Stop tormenting me, John!"

"It's his knees! He's living up there! It's why you stink of shit all the time!"

He began wrenching at the father's thighs. "Let her breathe! Let her have air!"

The club smashed down at him and he seized it, snapping the string. The man cringed, expecting retribution, but Jennifer was backing away.

"Where did you get that club!" she cried. "Father used to beat us with that club!"

"I told you! He's on your shoulders! He's riding on you!"

He ran to Mum. "Where's your mirror?"

"Lost it!"

"Liar!"

He upended her bag, spilling out a bottle of aspirin, a postcard that he'd crayoned for her at age ten, and a shard of mirror. "My wedding ring!" she shrieked as a snake wriggled away with it.

He showed Jennifer her reflection.

"Yes, we've aged."

He changed the angle. "Look again!"

"No! No! No!" she cried. "It can't be! We buried him. We dragged a huge stone up over him so he couldn't get back at us! Beat him with the club! Beat him with the club!"

She spun in circles like a bucking horse. Her father began to slide sideways – CLUNK! His head had smashed against a wall of rock, stunning him. John peeled him off and rolled him into a gully amid a slither of rock fragments.

Jennifer wept. "He was on my shoulders!" she moaned. "He was living on me! His hands were all over me!"

How long did she shudder in John's arms?

Mr. Lorum came scrabbling back up the scree. "Jenny my love! Who's Daddy's sweetheart? Come to Daddy and give Daddy his special kiss that makes him love you!"

He hopped around them with his knees up to his chin.

"You stay away from her," shouted John, kicking sand at him. "Find someone else to ride on.

"Someone else? You hear that, Jenny? Isn't he a silly bugger? We've passed thousands, but they'm all mounted, mounted since infancy! They got teachers, politicians, priests, God knows what riding on 'em."

John tried to pull her away but she resisted.

"He needs me!"

John slapped her face. He began to apologize, but she stared about as if seeing the desert for the first tim.:

"Run free," he cried, sensing the change in her. "Follow your own path!"

She kissed him (warm soft lips on his) and ran off into the warped air.

"Never come back!" he shouted.

"What's left for me now?" despaired her father, stumbling after her.

John and his mum were alone in the desert again. It was years since he'd thought of Jennifer. How strange to meet her all the way out here. Oh well, in a few more miles it would be as if she had never existed.

He tried to help Mum sift through the sand for her possessions but she pushed him away: "Stupid boy!" she said. "You'm no son of mine! You can call me Aunty from now on!"

He began turning over rocks, looking for the snake that had stolen her wedding ring. Mum shrieked a warning, but it was too late! A huge weight had slammed onto his shoulders. It clamped on to him as if it had suckers.

"Yee-haaa," cried Mr. Lorum, triumphant on his new steed.

"Get off of me! Let me go!"

John struggled to unloose the wiry legs.

"I'll gouge your eyes out, boy, you don't behave! What you need eyes for? I can tell 'e which way to go!"

John trembled and snorted as slimy fingers blinkered his precious eyes.

Mr. Lorum addressed Mum with old-fashioned politeness: "I wonder would you be so good as to pass me that club, Mrs. Podger?"

Mum picked up the club and seemed about to pass it up to him, but then she screamed, "He's mine! He's mine!" and began to beat him with a strength that amazed John. Bruised and howling, Mr. Lorum slithered off and rolled out of beating range. Mum turned her savagery onto John, lashing at him until he was able to grab the club and hurl it far away. All three of them watched its trajectory. Mr. Lorum flapped his arms helplessly and burst into tears.

Mum straightened herself out and adjusted her hair. "We'd hardly have known your Jennifer, Mr. Lorum," she said, using her polite voice. "She's grown into such a big girl."

"Arseholes," he said, and thrashed his way through the sage bushes, looking for the club.

Mum smirked at John. "You'd have been carrying him to Kingdom Come if it weren't for me, you maze coon! You have to remember which side your bread is buttered on."

The wind was rising. There was going to be one of those storms that can sandblast the paint off of cars. Strips of paper fluttered around them. One said "Bingo cancelled" so he gave it to Mum. Another said: "My face between her…" He slipped that one into his pocket. A third said. "Tower of Pisa – collapsed!" – that was also for Mum. One had writing on both sides: "One electron…" it said. He turned it over: "…weaving a universe…"

Mum laughed: "Don't you waste your time on that quantum rubbish. I don't know what they'm on about half the time!"

They had to find shelter.

"How you do maul me about!" she said, as he struggled to lift her. "Our John was worth ten of you."

"But I am John!" he gasped.

"Oh no, our John was a far more considerate boy."

"For goodness sake! Don't you know your own son any more?"

A strip of paper stuck to a patch of sand where Mum had relieved herself: "What's it all about?" it said: "Ask your dog for details."

***

Many travellers had died of thirst within sight of those snow-covered mountains. Jennifer had a good view of them from the top of a low hill. How far were they? Fifty miles? A hundred? It might take days to get there.

She remembered her reflection in the broken mirror. What had happened to her glory days when the world was her oyster? She remembered how her mother had slowly become transparent, and how – long after the vanishment – the washing-up would still be done, and the floors scrubbed. The need to gallop had blocked out such memories. If it weren't for John she'd have gone to her grave believing that being a beast of burden was the best that life had to offer.

Strips of paper drifted past. One said, "Let go the lead lifebelt". Perhaps it had blown in from some ship far out at sea. A lizard skidded up and arched its head back to expose the words "Carpe diem" on its T-shirt. "Must be an advert for a carpet shop," she thought. From horizon to horizon furious clouds formed words that said: "Drive your cart and your plough over the bones of the dead." Someone must be advertising graveyards for agricultural purposes.

A movement caught her eye. John was carrying his mother towards a dried-up ocean that offered only the illusion of lakes and cities. Ah well, it couldn't be helped, but then – as if her legs had made the decision – she found herself running towards them and shouting: "Not that way! There's nothing there but salt and bones."

"Not so loud," he said. "She needs her beauty sleep."

"You told me to live my own life, but what about your life? What about your dreams?"

"That's all over with now. We just have to hunker down and hope nothing terrible happens."

"It already has happened! What's life worth if you won't take risks?"

Mum shrieked "John!" as she always did when she woke up. "Mr. Lorum! Come quick! Come quick!" she cried, and began tooting on a whistle that dangled from her neck.

Peeeeep! Peeeeep!

John would have stumbled on but Jennifer clutched his shirt.

"There's more to life than uninhabited desert," she cried. "There's snow on those mountains! There's water! There's greenery! We don't have to live in this nothingness!"

Peeeeep! Peeeeep!

"Mum and me get along just fine."

"That's right, John, you tell her!" cackled Mum.

"Your Mum doesn't own you!"

"He's my son and you can't do nothin' about that, Jennifer!"

Mum was pulled out of his arms and dumped on the sand.

John was aghast: "You can't do that to my mother!"

"Why not? You should have buried her years ago! Come with me, John! What's wrong! Is it my hump?"

"Didn't they tell you what happened to me!" He tried to demonstrate the invisible cord but she was already dragging him away.

"It hurts! It's hurts!" he cried, clutching his stomach.

"Everything hurts! What's that got to do with anything?"

The invisible cord was towing Mum behind them. She stopped screeching and began thrusting her hands into the sand as if braking a sled.

Peeeeep! Peeeeep!

"Yee-haar!"

Mr. Lorum burst from the bushes like a fiddler crab (his beating arm was amazingly overdeveloped). "Jenny! Jenny my love! You know what Daddy wants, don't you, my lovely dumpkin!"

He clutched Mum and helped to anchor her.

"Pull, John! Pull!" gasped Jennifer.

"I'm no good at games!"

"You have to help! I can't do it for you!"

John pulled with all his strength, although his navel burned like fury.

"Come here and give Daddy a kiss and let him mount you!"

"Never give up!" gasped Jennifer, her breasts squirming against him. There was something like an explosion and suddenly John was further away from his mother than ever in his entire existence. How small she looked. Almost like an ordinary person.

***

Did John become a shipping magnate who collected vintage cars? Or did he look into a cannon to see why it hadn't fired? Did Jennifer become a best-selling novelist or was that someone else with the same name? Did John mount her and gallop away into the sunset, or did she pile rocks on the three corpses and set off towards the mountains? All we know for sure is that Mrs. Podger and Mr. Lorum sheltered in the lee of a gigantic boulder.

"He don't take after my side of the family!" she said, spreading out a frayed piece of cloth.

"A generation of serpents," he muttered.

"You ought to clean yourself up, Bill."

"So I shall, my dear, as soon as the rain comes."

She reached into her corsage for a teapot and two cracked cups. "A cup of tea?"

"I can always do with a nice cup of tea."

She dripped a few drops into his cup.

"I'm afraid that's all there is."

"Squeeze it!" he said, and they cackled at the old joke.

A snake writhed under a rock with Mum's wedding ring wedged inextricably in its jaws. The first raindrops splattered down. After the storm the desert would bloom with more flowers than there are stars in the Milky Way. But not for long.

OPEN SEASON

Traipsing through the woods, mute with boredom, one boot waterlogged, insects feasting on him, Martin vacillated between tears and rage. Mum had said that he and Dad needed to spend some quality time together but this was ridiculous.

"Ow!" he cried.

A branch had whipped him in the face.

"Don't follow so close then!"

Dad had planned this day to be a great experience but they'd been plodding for hours. The woods were meant to be a test of manhood, not an instrument of torture.

"Cheer up, Martin! The rain's stopped and our clothes is getting dry. God's in his Heaven and all's well with the world."

"My boot's squelching."

"Well then – take it off and squeeze your sock out!"

"There's nowhere to sit!"

"Don't be so feeble."

"Oscar Wilde said Nature was uncomfortable and he was right."

"Well, that's funny, 'cause he was queer as a coot."

Dad laughed at his own joke. As Martin sat on the ground to remove his boot his rifle tipped forwards making Dad leap sideways.

"How many times do I have to tell you never to point a gun at anybody!"

"I'm sorry!"

"No good being sorry if you'd blown my head off!"

Martin was squeezing water out of his sock.

"And stop sulking! This is what life's all about! This is nature! I suppose you'd rather be at one of them music lessons your mother pays for."

"Music doesn't blow animals to pieces."

Martin dropped his sock and bent to retrieve it. The rifle lowered towards Dad again.

"Augh!"

"Sorry!"

Dad bottled up his rage. Sometimes the boy seemed to have fallen from another planet. And now, dear God! – what was he doing now? Reading a magazine!

"Give me that!" he said. He read the title: *Dance Today*. He made a disgusted noise and stuffed it into his knapsack.

"Don't crease it! The Reverend Beecroft lent it to me."

"Well he'd be a funny sight leaping about in his cassock! You don't bring magazines when you come out for a day's hunting!"

"I wanted something to read."

"Don't you understand that nature is all one great book to them what can read it? Take that pile of droppings over there – that was made by a moose what's blind in his right eye."

"How do you know that?" said Martin, with a flicker of interest.

"Because over there you can see where he kept bashing into the trees on his right-hand side. And see those feathers? That's where a wood-pigeon blew itself to pieces – they eat the grain when it's wet and then it swells up inside them up till they explode."

There was a pop and a squawk in the bushes.

"There goes one of them now. And lookie here – what do you make of that?"

A gleam of white on a twig had caught his attention: he dabbed his finger into it and smelt it.

"Bird droppings?" said Martin.

"Theatrical make-up! And over there!" he said, pointing at the ground. "What does that tell you?"

"Looks like someone's been scuffing his feet."

"Very good, Martin. He was walking on the spot – that's a dead giveaway. And here – where the leaves are all rucked up. That's where he was moving crabwise, doing the 'wall'."

"Who was?"

"Use your head, can't you? The 'sideways walk'? Theatrical make-up?" For a boy who did well at school Martin could be slow on the up-take.

"A mime," said Dad, spelling it out.

Martin perked up. "Do you think we'll see one?"

"He's close, that's for sure."

They peered between the trunks of trees to more trees and yet more trees.

"You have to unravel the woods with your eyes, Martin. Never look for the whole mime. Keep scanning for a glimpse of white-face, or a patch of striped sweater."

Martin was interested in mimes but he didn't see why he had to shoot one.

"They can't help being mimes, can they, Dad?"

"It's a choice they make. No one's born doing the 'mask that gets stuck on your face', or 'the umbrella that you turn upside down and paddle away in'. No, they buy those stretchy trousers and the striped tops and they go to mime class, and from then on they walk not in the ways of the Lord!"

"But why do people hate them?"

Dad quoted the Bible: "It is a shame even to speak of those things which are done by them in secret."

"Ephesians, Chapter Six."

"Chapter Five," said his Dad, dismissively, and then: "Ssssh!"

They froze. Something was moving in the undergrowth. There was an explosion and a squawk.

"Wood-pigeon," said Dad, relaxing. Then he stared in horror. "What are you doing?"

Martin was pretending to walk a tightrope. Dad slapped him, harder than he intended. "There'll be no mimes in our family!"

"I was only pretending."

"That's how it starts!"

They reached a fallen tree with boughs that they could sit on.

"How about some food," said Dad, trying to be genial. "Let's see what your mother's packed for us. Good little homemaker your mother –" he passed Martin a sandwich – "once I'd broken her in."

They ate sitting side by side.

"Is that why you married her, Dad? 'Cause she was a good little home-maker?"

"No… noooo… We was… we was…" He hesitated before choosing the word: "… passionate." He remembered her flesh gleaming in the back of the car. He took a swig from a small flask of whisky. "One day a woman will light a fire under you and then you'll know."

"Better to marry than to burn, eh, Dad? Corinthians, Chapter Seven, Verse Eight."

He'd intended to please but his quotation had the opposite effect.

"God is not mocked – Ephesians, Chapter…"

Martin was indignant. "I wasn't mocking."

Dad took out a small radio, searched for a classical station and began beating time to Tchaikovsky's *Swan Lake*.

"I thought you hated classical music."

"So I do, but mimes like it. Jig about as if you're enjoying it."

"I am enjoying it."

"Sssh!"

Dad had seen something. "Pick up that rifle very slowly," he said. "Slip the safety off."

"It is off."

"What!"

"Sorry."

Dad gritted his teeth. "Never mind that now. Gently does it. Oh, and he's a beauty."

A mime was darting from one tree to another, trying not to be seen (which was pointless since most of his trees were mimed). He began to sway in time to the music. His foot rose from the ground and he began to dance.

Martin couldn't imagine shooting such an extraordinary creature.

"Can't you do it, Dad?" he whispered.

"This one's yours Martin. Aim for the chest."

"I can't…"

"Course you can. What do you think we came all the way out here for?"

"But…"

"Don't argue! Now wait! Wait till he's a bit closer!"

Dad's hands began to vibrate. He crossed them, fluttering them like wings.

"Dad!" whispered Martin, in amazement. "You're miming."

"Of course I'm miming! I'm doing the 'butterfly'. Wait for it…"

He mimed launching the butterfly into a zigzag flight. The mime pretended to catch it and peer in at it through closed fingers.

"Now!" roared Dad. "Let him have it, Martin! Shoot! Shoot!"

"I can't!"

"Shoot for Christ's sake!"

The mime stared aghast and began to run frantically on the spot, getting nowhere, but still cupping the mimed butterfly.

"Fire! Fire! Are you chicken?"

Martin never knew quite how it happened, but the rifle slammed back into his shoulder and the woods became alive with the screeching of rooks.

The mime fell to his knees, pressing his hands to his chest where a red patch had begun to spread. He opened his hands and released the imaginary butterfly into the air.

Martin was as shocked as his Dad was elated.

"Well done, Martin! Couldn't have done it better myself!"

Dad silenced the radio and returned it to his knapsack: "This is what it's all about, Martin – survival of the fittest. You know you've made your mark in this universe when you can blast the daylights out of something!"

"I feel sick."

"That's just the adrenaline."

They walked over to the body of the mime. He had struck a dramatic pose even in death. Dad prodded it with his foot. Martin was awestruck.

"I think I saw him performing in the park."

"Then he should have had the sense to stay there."

"He's beautiful."

"He'll look even better when his head's over the mantelpiece: 'That's a fine specimen,' they'll say, and I'll say, 'Yes! My son Martin took him down with one shot!'"

"You're not going to cut his head off!"

"Talk sense, Martin! We can't drag him back to the truck, not in this terrain."

He poured some whisky into the cap of the flask, and passed it to Martin. "A toast to you, Martin," he said. "And to our future hunting."

Martin 'threw the drink back', imitating Dad, and had a fit of coughing.

"Don't worry, son, you'll get used to it. Oh, damnation!"

The mime had leapt up and bounded away, giving Dad no time to aim his rifle.

Martin was elated. "So I didn't kill him!"

"You just winged him! They love dying artistically! Well, that's puts the kibosh on it! Can't leave a wounded mime out here in the forest. It's against the hunter's code. We'll have to go in after him."

"Into the thickets?"

"A man's got to do what a man's got to do. Don't worry, son, he won't get far!"

They set off in pursuit.

"Keep your eyes skinned, Martin. Catch a mime unawares and the odds are in your favour, but a wounded mime is a force to be reckoned with."

Someone was playing a piano. Martin recognized the Chopin étude where the chords roll up and down the keyboard. "There can't be a piano out here in the forest can there, Dad?"

Dad made a disgusted sound. "He's miming it! He must be in agony and yet he's playing tunes! They got no sense."

"But how can we hear the piano if he's miming it?"

"It's different out here, son. Remember Uncle Joe? Fell into a mimed hole and it was hours before we could dig him out."

The music stopped.

"Clap your hands!"

"What for Dad?"

"They can't resist an audience. Come on! Bravo! Bravo! Encore! Encore!"

They applauded and the music started again.

"Come on!"

"But why do we have to shoot them? Couldn't the Government just cut their grants?"

"It's kinder this way, son!"

***

They were pushing their way through young saplings.

"Are you scared, Dad?"

"Of course I'm scared. There's nothing wrong with fear if it stops you taking stupid risks."

There was something lying among the leaves – the mime's bloody T-shirt. Dad picked it up.

"See this, Martin! He's throwing away his clothes. They always do that when they nearing the end. There's a bond between hunter and hunted that's indescribable, you… Auuugghh!"

An invisible force had slammed Dad to the ground amid a twanging of wires and splitting of highly stressed wood.

"Dad, what happened! Are you hurt? Is it a heart attack?"

Dad seemed dazed. For a few moments he could hardly speak.

"Are you all right?"

"He drops a mimed piano on me and you ask if I'm all right? Get it off me!"

Martin made ineffectual gestures. "But how?"

"Mime getting it off me."

"Mime!"

"Yes! Yes! Mime for God's sake."

Martin pretended to be heaving a huge mass off of Dad who began to breathe easier.

"Jesus H. Christ…"

"You're swearing, Dad."

"Of course I'm swearing. He must have hauled it up to that branch, and thrown his T-shirt under it deliberate. Good thing he'd lost so much blood, or he could have mimed something heavier."

He tried to stand up but collapsed in agony.

"He's crippled me."

"I could carry you back to the truck."

"We'd never make it before sun-down. Look up there! The sunlight's already off the tree tops. Once it's night he'll have us like frogs in a blender. It's up to you now, Martin. You'll have to go in and finish him."

"By myself?"

"It's him or us, Martin."

He took a chain from around his neck that had a bullet as an ornament.

"Here – take my lucky bullet. I made my first kill with that bullet."

"You told me."

He fastened it around Martin's neck.

"There's a time in every boy's life when he has to accept adult responsibilities. If you get lost, follow the railway line back to the truck. Then radio for help."

"I'll be all right, Dad."

"I know you will son. Look for spots of blood, and bits of broken twig – scan the ground to see where he may have dragged himself. I love you, Martin."

"I love you too, Dad."

"Make me proud of you, son."

***

Bang! Bang! Bang! Bang! Martin was firing in total darkness, each explosion lighting the nearest trees for a split second. He was crouched at the base of a gigantic oak, terrified by snufflings and rustlings. Could mimes see in the dark? Was that why Dad had talked about being trapped like frogs in a blender?

He reloaded and sat back against the tree, not daring to move a muscle as he tried to identify every little sound He didn't realize that he'd fallen asleep until he saw that a full moon was shining through the branches. How many hours had passed? The mime must have bled to death by now.

He stood up, easing his cramped muscles. Where was the railway line that would lead him back to the truck? He knew that the moon rose in the east and chose his direction accordingly.

"Auuuuughh!"

Something tiny had run across his feet.

"Daaaaad!" he screamed, and listened. "Daaaaad! I can't find the way back! I can't find the railway line!"

The moon made the woods look alien. Even if he'd been here a hundred times before he'd never have recognized the place. He spun round in terror but saw nothing sinister. "I'm not scared of stupid mimes!" he shouted, and plodded on, whistling as if hadn't a care in the world – and saw the mime.

"Hay! You!"

The mime had appeared from behind an invisible door, but as soon as he saw Martin he slammed it and disappeared. Martin ran to where the door had been and stabbed the air with his finger. A doorbell rang. The door opened and the mime gaped as if seeing Martin for the first time. Martin pursued him upstairs, and along corridors, and down firemen's poles, and through trapdoors, and out of windows, and among the trees until…

"Got you!" he cried as the mime sprawled headlong. "Now you're for it!" But there was something strange about the way the mime was lying – on his back and gesturing with hands that seemed fastened at the wrists. Martin scuffed leaves away and realized that the mime was tied to the railway line. He crouched over him and tried to pull him loose. A steam-train could be heard chuffing up some steep gradient.

"I don't know what to do! I can't see what's holding you!"

No sooner had the train's headlight begun flashing through the trees than it was already upon them. The mime rolled well clear but the train passed so close to Martin that he could feel its heat. Skeletons and clowns grinned down at him from the carriage windows. The mime had tried to kill him. "You'll pay for that!" he said, walking forwards, rifle at the ready, but the mime was heaving an invisible lever into a new position. Steel gripped Martin's foot and the rifle went flying.

"Auugghhhh! Open the points. You've trapped my foot in the rails!"

A second train was picking up speed: Chuff-chuff! Chuff-chuff-chuff! Chuff-chuff-chuff-chuff!

"Set me loose!" he cried. "I tried to help you! Aughh!"

The mime alternated between horror and mimed laughter.

CHUFF-CHUFF! CHUFF-CHUFF! CHUFF-CHUFF!

The train had eyes and blew flame like a dragon. Suddenly Martin understood.

"None of this is reeeeeaaal!" he screamed and there was total silence: no train, no rails clamping on his foot. He picked up the rifle – no hesitation now.

"Oh, you're going to get it!"

The mime retreated through mimed door after mined door but this time Martin walked right through them.

"You should have stayed in the park! Dickhead!"

The mime knelt and pressed his palms together. Martin thrilled with rage and power.

"All right, pray if you have to, but make it quick!"

The mime gestured heavenward and sang an Italian death aria with such power and sensitivity that Martin was overwhelmed. How was it possible for anyone to express such passion, such feeling, such courage, such utter despair? How could he ever have thought of the mime as a target, as a trophy, as something to be trashed?

"I can't do it!" he said. "Dad's right! I'm chicken!"

Where was the music coming from? He looked up and saw an orchestra perched in the branches with the Reverend Beecroft conducting.

He came to himself and realized that he was huddled against the same huge oak as before, that he'd been dreaming that he was awake. A full moon lit the clearing, just as in the dream, but everything was silent – not even an owl hooted.

"Why was I ever born?" he whispered. "Why don't I suck on this rifle and blown my brains out!"

The metal had a chemical taste. A little pressure on the trigger was all that was needed. The Reverend Beecroft would say it was an accident so that they could bury him in hallowed ground. Mum would be upset but Dad might be pleased. Seconds passed, any one of which could have precipitated him into nothingness.

"I don't have the guts!" he whispered.

Then he realized that he was not alone. The mime was beside him, close enough to be touched, bare-chested with his wound black in the moonlight. Martin made eyecontact.

"I didn't mean to shoot you. I just wanted to make my father proud of me! I'm sorry! I'm sorry!"

The mime peeled the wound away. It was just a stage effect!

Martin's face was being stroked. Make-up was being smeared onto his skin. He was being given a white face by the mime. The strange eyes gleamed and the alien mouth curved into a strange smile, but then a light bounced towards them. It was Dad holding a flashlight.

"Dad! You're walking."

"Course I'm walking! A mimed piano can't hurt anyone. You was supposed to be giving him the *coup de grâce*. It was to be your test of manhood. Move away so I can get a clear shot!"

Martin shielded the mime.

"If you shoot him you shoot me."

"Get away from him. Or, by God…"

"What?"

Dad lowered the rifle and walked up to them. Martin could feel the mime trembling.

"Where's my lucky bullet!"

Dad tore it from Martin's neck and hurled it into the bushes.

"Not your lucky bullet!"

"And get that muck off your face. You're a disgrace to our family!" He made chicken noises to show his contempt. "He was trying to make you into one of them."

"What if I am one of them?"

The mime hid behind the tree.

"Don't talk so stupid. He made an evil choice!"

"Did you make a choice?"

"Why would I have to make a choice?"

"If you didn't make a choice then you know sod-all about it! You think I've haven't cried myself to sleep believing I was the only person in the whole world who was like me! That time when I nearly drowned, I was trying to kill myself. That cleaning fluid I found under the sink – I knew it wasn't orange juice."

Dad was aghast. "God help us!" he said, bewildered, angry, appalled, sickened, distraught. Was this the child that he'd taken to Disneyland? What would Jesus have done? Shot the mime and left him to rot out here in the forest? Probably. Anyone who let sinners burn in Hell for all eternity couldn't be one of those bleeding heart liberals.

Finally he said: "How –" he sniffed back a tear – "How long has it been…" He was too upset to finish the sentence.

Martin sounded subdued: "I used to watch Marcel Marceau on *Sesame Street* when you and Mum were up in the bedroom."

Dad made a helpless gesture: "I'll ask the Reverend Beecroft to talk to you. He'll set you straight."

"It was him that taught me the sideways-walk."

"I… he… He did! You make me want to throw up!"

"That's just the adrenaline."

"Remember the Bible, Martin – 'a man that is a mime after the first and second admonition, ye must reject, knowing that he is subverted, and sinneth, being condemned of himself." Titus, Three; Verse Ten.

"Verse Eight. But what about the Gospel of Bozo the clown? And the Epistle of St. Keaton to the Straightmen?"

"Never heard of them."

"That's because the priests burned all the books they disagreed with. Who knows what Our Lord was really like?"

Dad glowered at the mime who was peering at him from around the tree. "Well he wasn't one of *them*."

"Why not? He turned water into wine. He blasted the fig tree. He did that trick with the loaves and fishes. He must have been some kind of entertainer."

Dad searched desperately for words that would convince Martin of the pit he was falling into. "But mimes are…" Words failed him. He was in torment. "They're… they're… It's no way to live!" he shouted.

Martin shouted back: "There's mimes that work in banks and insurance companies. There's mimes that are lion-tamers and scuba divers. Even the Pope does magic tricks."

"Well, he's the anti-Christ."

"You're just repeating lies that people invented so they could control you!"

Dad felt exhausted. "I always thought you were a bit… I don't know… I always…" He sighed and took a swig from the flask.

"Whisky won't help."

Martin was opening an envelope. "Mum said I should show you this."

"What is it?"

"It's a letter from the Mime School. They've offered me a scholarship."

Dad switched on the flashlight and read it without comment.

"Mum thought it would be all right."

Dad felt betrayed. "How long has she…?" He forced himself to be calm.

"It would be easier if you could help me a bit – financially."

A wood-pigeon exploded, making them jump.

Dad laughed to cover his nervousness. How was one supposed to act in a world that wasn't flat any more? Where human beings evolved from apes? Where life was being created in laboratories? Was it really possible that Jesus had done the "wall", and "the box that gets smaller"?

Martin and the mime were holding hands. Martin was almost unrecognizable in his white make-up.

"What do you say, Dad?"

In spite of all the years of disappointment, Dad loved Martin.

"Well…" he said, forcing the words out. "It's your life, Martin."

"I love you, Dad."

"I love you, Martin."

But they didn't hug each other.

The mime reached out a hand and said: "I'm Adrian."

Dad clasped it out of sheer force of habit, and shook it roughly.

"Come on!" he said. "Let's get back to the truck."

Mum was asleep when they got home (they had dropped the mime off at an all-night convenience store). She stirred as Dad climbed into bed.

"You're so late – I was worried," she murmured.

"I'll tell you about it in the morning," he said, and stared into the darkness for a long time.

THE WHEELCHAIR

I used to joke that I'd fed a Princess to a crocodile and had been sent back to Earth to work off the bad "karma". Not that I'm religious, but reincarnation seems more satisfying than the "one trip only" Christian Universe.

The Princess would have been beautiful, with those vividly outlined Egyptian eyes, and in the full freshness of youth. I mention her because she was on my mind as the doctors probed me. It was not a pleasant session and I was soon wondering if I'd fed an entire Royal Family to that crocodile.

I limped into the corridor, still hurting from the tests, and saw a small child. It was kicking its legs as it sat on a bench. I gave it a friendly smile but it glowered at me (a bandage covered its mouth).

A nurse followed me into the elevator. "You're getting to be one of our regular visitors, Mr. Johnstone," she said, cheerfully.

A wheelchair clanged into the doors, jamming them. Had the child pushed it? The nurse shoved the chair away and I studied the tiny blonde hairs on her neck as we descended.

The world outside seemed newly created (as always after a medical ordeal). Cars glistened. Leaves seemed exquisitely detailed. Clouds, whiter than any white that had ever existed, reared skyward – no wonder that the ancients had housed the Gods up there.

I was so exhilarated that I walked rather too swiftly to my car and had to rest my head against the steering wheel. As I drove out of the car park an empty wheelchair was rolling gently across the tarmac.

***

I woke up next morning much improved. Then I saw the pills that I should have taken at bedtime. Their side effects were obviously debilitating, but I swallowed them anyway and waited for them to kick in.

It was soon time for my "constitutional" (I was allowed to take moderate exercise). I wrapped up warmly and stepped out of the front door to be confronted by a wheelchair. It was soaking wet, as if it had stood there all night. Had the hospital confused me with some non-ambulatory patient? There was no letter of explanation.

I remembered the wheelchair that had jammed the doors of the elevator, and the one that had rolled gently across the car park. I had the amusing thought that they might all be the same one. I smiled as I imagined it asking for directions, and then being unable to climb up the step to reach the bell. I left it under the front porch, clearly visible, and latched the gate; "Try following me now," I thought.

I crossed the beach, taking care to avoid the patches of mud, and plodded up the path that led around the headland and to the lighthouse. Every hundred yards or so I checked my pulse. As always it was running fast, frittering my life away. I'd read somewhere that all creatures are allotted the same number of heartbeats, and I thought of the fluttering of a sparrow's heart and the slow pulsing of the crocodile's.

"Far enough," I thought, stopping halfway. I sat on a bench to catch my breath and squinnied at the bright shield of mud that stretched to the horizon. A group of people were plodding across the bay. I hoped they knew what they were doing – unwary visitors can vanish into quicksand or be caught by the tide as it flows back with the speed of a galloping horse.

I stood up, ready to trudge home, and saw that the wheelchair was blocking the path. It was some thirty feet away, the leather still dark with moisture, the metal gleaming. I willed it into non-existence, but it stayed as real as the unkempt grass and the cries of the gulls. I stepped forwards and it withdrew an equal distance. Was someone having a game with me? Had it been rigged to operate by remote control? "Shoo! Shoo!" I cried, flapping my arms, and saw it retreat a little. I walked away a few steps and saw it skid to a halt as if to hide the fact that it was stalking me. I threw a handful of gravel and it moved closer.

An elderly couple was approaching from the direction of the lighthouse.

"Excuse me," I said.

The man seemed confused but the woman was like a sharpeyed little bird. She was holding his arm as if to steer him.

"Arrr?" he said. "Arrr?"

"I wonder if I might accompany you for a while," I said. "Someone's been following me."

"Following you?" She looked around at the grass and the bench and the absence of threatening people.

"Strength in numbers," I said. I felt sure that the wheelchair would behave itself if I were in the company of other people.

"You've not done anything wrong?"

"Me? Not at all."

"Is that your wheelchair?"

"Not mine," I said.

"Perhaps some teenagers pushed it up here. Young people cause no end of trouble."

"Young people, arrr…" said the old man. She dabbed at some saliva that had oozed out of the corner of his mouth and he became more articulate. "Do you know," he said, "that I once ran a marathon?"

"The gentleman don't need to know that, Gerald," she said, as if she was used to squelching him.

"Three's company," said the man.

"We're only going as far as the café."

"That'll be fine," I said.

"Slow down for the gentleman, Gerald. We're none of us as young as we used to be."

We were within six feet of the wheelchair when it jerked forwards, intent on ramming me. I lumbered panic-stricken towards some steps that led to a small cove. I was a couple of flights down before I looked back and saw it teetering on the extreme verge. "Can't get me now!" I thought.

And then – it's not easy to describe this – I seemed to be in my bed, but it was tossing about as if in a rough sea. This seemed in no way remarkable – my brain was too damaged to know that it was damaged.

I wanted desperately to stay asleep, but then I understood that strong arms were lifting me, that I had fallen down the steps and was being carried to the top of the cliff where my rescuers were intent on pressing me into the wheelchair. I tried to explain that it had been chasing me, but I doubt that I was saying anything intelligible. Ever since the accident I have experienced myself as speaking clearly and reasonably, but people react as if I'm shouting obscenities.

***

My visitors arrive less frequently now. Some of them must be relatives, but I can no longer identify faces or read their expressions. Nor can I understand their speech. I hear their voices but my brain extracts no meaning.

My attendants handle me as if I were a piece of furniture or a potted plant. On fine days they wheel me onto a patio where I stare at leaves and sky. There are no buildings visible so perhaps it's a roof garden. The clouds drift past as if every day was like every other. (Sometimes I think they are the same clouds.) My sense of time has betrayed me. Each minute will last an hour, or night will come when day has barely started. Cramps and sharp interior pains torment me but I'm like a baby that can't tell its mother that a pin is jabbing into it.

I am no longer wheeled onto the patio – not since my left arm was gnawed off from the elbow down. Perhaps they believe that some wild animal attacked me. If so, then the patio was probably at ground level.

Doctors huddle together at the foot of my bed. They keep glancing in my direction. Yesterday, when the nurses serviced me, they discovered that my right buttock had been ripped off, necessitating further operations. They have supplied me with a special cushion so that I can sit level. I try to explain that the wheelchair is eating me, but they just roll me further away from the other patients.

Time passes and so much of me has been devoured that my eyes are now eighteen inches above the seat and I have to be wedged in with pillows. I can only see things that are directly in front of me so I deduce that my eyeballs have ceased to swivel. The TV is partly outside my field of vision, yet that hardly matters since they have misplaced my glasses.

I chant poetry that I learned as a child, and take imaginary walks (today I soared over the path to the lighthouse as if I'd been reincarnated as a seagull). I try to imagine that I'm having sex with movie stars, or with old girlfriends, but the boredom is driving me insane. Time moves in great leaps. One moment I am back in ancient Egypt, dangling the Princess over the Lotus Pool, and the next moment I am lying on a gurney and a sheet is being pulled over my head.

Either my eyes have been eaten or I am in darkness. Soil thumps and scatters onto a wooden surface that must be a few inches from my face. The sounds muffle into silence. I can't recollect the moment of my death so perhaps it was a kinder transition than I had anticipated.

What sort of headstone will they erect? And will the wheelchair be waiting up there like the dog that languished beside its master's grave? (As you can tell I have not lost my sense of humour.)

I imagine golden boats rowed by slave girls who wear diaphanous costumes, and I try to visualize the Princess and the terrible white mouthed crocodile as it surges up at her. Why torment myself with such images? Because it's better to be punished for some ancient crime, than to be squeezed out by an indifferent universe.

MY WIFE'S MADNESS

"You don't understand!"

"I'd like to understand."

"I don't need a doctor. There's nothing wrong with me!"

"We're here to help you."

"Look! It's perfectly simple. It's alone and in terrible fear. Its entire life is one long agony. It's contacted me, so it's my responsibility. I'm the only thing that it knows. I promised that I would help it, and now it's waiting for me and I'm shut in here. I can't waste time talking to you."

"Please sit down."

"I'm telling you I have to get out of here, you stupid man."

"Nurse!"

***

"Has your wife had these attacks before?"

"It's been coming on for some time."

"When did they start?"

"She was fine, until… well… until we watched a programme on television. A… a science programme about 'distant viewing'. Not exactly science, although they were presenting it as science."

"Distant viewing?"

"More like light entertainment. These professors were trying to send messages telepathically. Someone would travel to a destination at random and stare at something, a clock tower perhaps, while someone back at the university would draw a picture, hoping to capture whatever was being stared at. They claimed some correlation, but two vertical lines don't make a clock tower. I think they were seeing what they wanted to see."

"And your wife was disturbed by this programme?"

"We didn't take it seriously. But she thought we should try it, just for fun – as a game. When I went for lunch the next day I was to stare at some object and she would try to draw whatever I was staring at…"

"Go on. Please don't mind me making notes."

"She drew a park bench. That evening she showed it to me, and – well, she was quite wrong but I wanted to tease her. So I said, 'That's right! I'd been staring at a park bench!' And she was amazed and delighted.

"Next day when I came home she showed me a sketch of a dog. I had forgotten that I was suppose to stare at something, so I said, 'Yes, I was looking at a dog.' This went on for several days. She took it so seriously that I could hardly tell her that it was a joke. So for a few days I made sure that she was always wrong. Then she said that she was tired of the game. That's when I noticed the change in her."

"She had changed. In what way?"

"She had always been so playful and lighthearted, but now she seemed so serious. She'd be silent. She didn't chat about things any more."

"She seemed depressed?"

"I sometimes thought that she had been weeping but she denied it. She'd smile and laugh but it seemed unreal – just a performance."

"And you attribute this to the TV programme? And the joke."

"The joke?"

"The teasing of her?"

"Not at the time."

"Yet the situation became intolerable?"

"She confided in me – eventually. She had imagined that some 'presence' had contacted her. She felt that by opening her mind to catch the images that I was supposed to be sending to her she had become vulnerable to this… this 'thing'. At first she was fascinated. She said that the 'entity' – whatever it was – was unbearably lonely, and in such pain."

"And what was it?"

"I don't think she knows. It was in a space that was too small for it to turn around. At first it hardly seemed to know anything. She said she was educating it. Giving it concepts. She really believed all this. I told her that I'd been teasing when I said she was receiving my thoughts, and she became furious. I'd never seen her so angry. She was like a different person."

"How had she changed?"

"She wasn't taking care of her appearance. She'd stare straight ahead without moving, sometimes for hours. When I arrived home she wouldn't acknowledge me. The house was in chaos. The laundry was … well she wasn't functioning. She seemed to be listening to this – this 'thing' all the time."

"And when she disappeared – how did you…?"

"I came home and her VW had gone. She hadn't driven it for days, so far as I knew. I found her diary lying in the driveway. It must have fallen out of her bag as she left."

"And this note?"

"That was on the table."

"'Dear Phillip…' Is this her usual handwriting?"

"No, she usually writes very clearly…"

"'Dear Phillip. I know where it is. I have to go to it. Don't worry about me. I'll phone you when I get there. God bless!' – is your wife a religious woman?"

"Not at all. How… how is she? Is it possible for me to see her?"

"She became rather violent. It's probably best for you to visit her in the morning. I reckon you need a good night's sleep after all you've been through."

"You're right about that, Doctor."

***

DAY EIGHT – I am writing this to try to understand what is happening to me. Phillip says that it is all in my imagination, but no experience has ever been more real. Its thoughts are not verbal. They are more immediate than words. I will try to translate, but there is no way to express the nuances. At first I almost believed it to be a soul in hell, so vividly did it communicate its torments, torments not of fire, but of cramp, and loneliness and helplessness. I've managed to communicate the idea of punishment to it, but it doesn't seem to have ever done anything wrong.

What sex is it? When I realized that it had no such concept I felt sure that it was not of this earth, that it was a prisoner on some other planet. Food is supplied to it from one end of its narrow cell, and its wastes are excreted at the other. It can peer into the area behind it with one eye, and glimpse some sort of mechanism that deals with its wastes.

If this creature is a hundred metres long, then its "containment" shrinks by twenty or so centimetres each feeding time, and will soon crush it.

DAY THIRTEEN – I have been very confused by the paradox that it is actually at the centre of a larger space. Today a new flood of images makes me understand that it is one of many beings, all of which are confined in rows, each in its oblong "cubicle".

DAY FOURTEEN – It once shared a space with other beings like itself. It had room to turn around in, and there was a hugeness that seems to represent "goodness" to it. Could this "hugeness" have been some sort of mother?

There is no darkness but nor is there a sun. The light comes from above, but not from a "roundness" – "roundness" was such a difficult idea for it to understand – but from what it describes as "longnesses". These "longnesses" are not so bright that they cannot be stared at.

DAY SIXTEEN – Communication has become easier. I am in contact with a remarkable intelligence that was almost devoid of knowledge until my mind gave it something to latch onto.

At first I welcomed each contact, no matter how brief. I would scan with my mind until I found it. I soon discovered that I needed to cast my mind in a particular direction. It began to reach me in the few minutes before I fell asleep. And then, soon, it was crashing into my mind as I was watching television or frying Phillip's pork-chops. I've pleaded with it to contact me only once each day, but it doesn't know what a day is. And it's frantic. What began as a faint murmur is now a non-stop scream. God knows I pity it, but I can't live like this. I have to be able to find some way to shut it out of my consciousness.

If I know the direction that it's in, and the direction never changes, that means that it's not on another planet, that it's here on earth!

DAY NINETEEN – I begin to believe that its intellect is superior to mine. It's bargaining with me. It offers to exercise restraint and to only communicate with me when my mind is receptive. My part of the bargain is that I will find it and either kill it or set it free. It has the concept of death although it has never seen anything die – not exactly of death but of a state where there is no consciousness (by which I deduce that it is a creature that can sleep).

DAY TWENTY – I bought a compass and drove east of the city, towards the badlands. I saw the direction that the creature lies in keep changing. I have drawn lines on a map that intersect several hours, journey to the south. The thing cannot understand my method – it has no concept of a world larger than the space that it's in – but it is filled with excitement. It longs to be killed or rescued by me.

It asks so many questions. Why does it suffer? Why is it tormented by urges that it cannot satisfy? What is its purpose in this universe? What do I mean by ideas like "running" and "jumping" or "walking about"? What is a leaf? What is a stone? What is water? What are the stars? It has the concept of punishment now, and it is sure that it has been condemned for some terrible crime. How else can it make sense of its existence? I've given it the idea of God, but it insists that God hates it. I cannot communicate the idea of love, since it knows no creature that it could love or be loved by. Except perhaps by myself.

I must rest. It has agreed to let my mind alone if I will travel to it in the morning. (Remember to take the knife!)

***

"How is she, Doctor?"

"Your wife spent a quiet night, but we suspect that she is still hearing the voices. She denies it – but that's only to be expected. You did the right thing, but of course she blames you. It's important that you keep assuring her that your intentions are good. Has she any interest in farming?"

"I don't think so."

"She was in a field when you found her."

"I followed the directions in her diary. She had booked a room in the only motel. It's such a small town, hardly more than the filling-station and a motel-restaurant. Flat – the land. Prairie to the horizon. I drove around hoping to find her. I saw her when she was far away – wandering aimlessly. She spoke quite rationally. It seemed that when she came near to the 'thing' the signal was so strong that it seemed to come from all around her. It was only when I tried to lead her away that she began fighting with me. It had begun to rain. I couldn't leave her. There were some long windowless buildings. I ran there for help. She followed me and began stabbing at the wooden walls with a knife. I found a couple of workers who helped to overpower her. She had seemed almost rational just moments before, but suddenly she was stabbing the walls and screaming: 'It needs me! It needs me!'"

"These long low huts?"

"For pigs. Genetically identical pigs – cloned so that the customers can all get a standard product. Rows and rows of pigs. The workers keep the machinery in order. I looked in while we waited for an ambulance – through a window of course. No one enters except in airtight suits. The buildings are kept sterile. Amazing technology."

"Well… let's take a look at her. We'll keep her under observation a few days. Once we find the right medication I trust that we can look forwards to a full recovery."

***

"Where were you?"

"I was on medication."

"The place you told me about, with grass, and skies, and wind that makes the trees rustle, and moving water. Can you take me there before the walls crush me?"

"The walls are not shrinking – it's you, you're growing bigger. And when you're big enough people will eat you. So you won't suffer much longer."

"No! No! That's not possible! My existence has to have more meaning than that! There's been a mistake! Help me! Help me!"

"Someone owns you. You're someone's property. No one can help you."

"You're fading! You're fading! Stay with me!"

"My medication is beginning to kick in."

"You're fading! Hello?… Hello?… Can anyone hear me? Is anyone out there? Hello?… Hello?…"

Plays

FROG WIFE
A play for children based on the folk-story "The Frog Princess"

This play was written for performance at The Loose Moose Theatre, Calgary, Alberta. We had no front-curtain so the set-changes were done on a darkened stage, or in view of the audience. We often distracted the audience from the scene changes by having Prince Ivan travel through the audience – the architecture of our theatre encouraged this.

Cast
1. **THE KING OF RUS**
2. **PRINCE PETER**
3. **PRINCE ALEXEI**
4. **PRINCE IVAN**
5. **SONIA** – highstatus and cold
6. **MARSHA** – giggly, extrovert
7. **ANYA** – a frog
8. **PHILLIPS/THE STRANGER**
   Phillips can be played by a stage manager, or can be replaced by an *electric* wheelchair. He always doubled with the role of "The Stranger", but the Princes or the King could have played that role.
9. **THE NARRATOR** The Narrator's voice can be recorded and/or shared out among the other players, but it's nicer when it's live.

A curtain hides the backstage area. It allows at least two entrances. A frame stands up-stage centre (it becomes a bed in Scene 4, and in the last scene it becomes a drawbridge).
Hanging from this frame are:
1. A bow and arrows.
2. Three cloaks.
3. Three crowns (they could be just a coil of those glittering Christmas decorative strings).
4. A hulahoop.
5. Three blindfolds.

There was a strip of red carpet up-stage, parallel to the curtain.

A Narrator comes on stage, using a microphone. (This Narrator can sometimes be on tape or various players can share the role.)

PROLOGUE

NARRATOR (*on-stage*) Welcome to the Loose Moose Theatre Company (*or to wherever the play is being presented*) where the story of the Frog Princess is about to begin. A very distinguished audience here tonight. I can see some of the forest creatures are still taking their seats.

Perhaps the ushers have spoken casually to some children, asking them their names and what animals they like to be. Perhaps this information had been passed secretly to the narrator who fits them into the commentary. For example:

(*Ad lib*) I can see Tom the Squirrel over there with his mother. And I can see Betty Nightingale and her sister Jean. There are five little foxes here who have birthdays this month. Oh, and I can see Charlene the Turtle and Kevin the Duck. And some birds, and some deer, and there's David the little Badger with his Father, Mr. Eric Badger...

Back to the script.

Oh and I think something's happening; the lights over the forest creatures are beginning to fade. And something's happening on the stage. I can see that the expensive tapestries are moving. I believe that the three Princes will be coming through to take their places for the ceremony. I can see Prince Peter the Brave – a round of applause for Prince Peter, please.

SCENE ONE

Peter enters and acknowledges the applause. He takes his "place".
  … followed by Prince Alexei the Thoughtful…
Enter Prince Alexei enters and acknowledges the applause.
  The Princes are well known to everyone of course, and are waving to their friends among the crowd.
Prince Ivan arrives late, hurried, rather nervous and apologetic.
  And here is Prince Ivan, the youngest of the three Princes, making his first public appearance. A little shy perhaps. Oh and here comes the King.
Royal music.
  I'm sorry but the King won't make his entry until the forest creatures have stood up to honour him. The King perhaps just a little annoyed at this delay.
The audience stand and the King enters in a wheelchair that is pushed by his servant Phillips.

KING Thank you. You may be seated! I am the King of Rus, and my kingdom stretches as far as the eye can see. Welcome to the ceremony of the Choosing of the Wives. Now that I'm becoming old, it's time that my three sons got married, so that I can have some grandchildren. (*To sons.*) Is that understood?

Phillips puts the hula-hoop centre-stage.

PETER Yes sir. But we don't know who we should marry.

ALEXEI That's right, Father.

KING The way the Royal Princes choose their brides has always been kept a secret from you. But this is the day when I can tell you that every Prince of Rus has always chosen his bride not by his brain, but by his arrow. Each of you will spin around five times, and will shoot your arrow away from the Palace. You will find your bride where the arrow falls. Step into the Circle of Truth, Prince Peter, and put on the blindfold.

Peter steps into the hulahoop and Phillips gives him the blindfold – fake the blindfold, i.e. let it allow him to see at least which direction he's facing. (*To children.*) Will you help us count the number of times that he turns around? Thank-you. (*to Peter*) Take this bow and this arrow, now turn around five times, and fire the arrow. Is everyone ready? Would the forest creatures help us count? Off we go now. One… Two… Three… Four… Five.

Everyone counts as Peter turns around five times and pretends to shoot his arrow above a side-section of the audience. Actually he hides it under his cloak until someone else spirits it secretly away (note 1). He removes his blindfold.

PETER Where did the arrow fall?

KING I don't know. Go and look for it.

Peter goes into the audience and asks who has his arrow. Some "give-and-take" with the children. "Have you got it?", "Are you hiding it there?", "Has anyone got my arrow?" etc. Finally high-status Sonia stands up from her seat and says:

SONIA Over here, Prince Peter. I have your arrow.

KING Bring her to me.

Peter picks Sonia up as they get to edge of the stage and carries her on as if carrying a bride over a threshold.

What is your name?

SONIA Sonia. I was in the garden and Prince Peter's arrow landed right beside me.

KING Very well, Sonia – step into the Circle of Truth. (*The hula hoop.*) Are you strong and healthy?

SONIA (*proudly*) Oh yes. I've never had a day's illness.

KING Close your eyes and stretch your arms out and touch your nose with one finger.

She does it.

That seems to be all right. We'd better take her measurements.

The Princes measure her and call out the measurements. They have a tape measure each. The King writes the measurements down (this should be "chaotic", with the Princes clustered around her and shouting out the measurements).*

Very well, you seem suitable. Now for the intelligence test. What comes before five?

SONIA (*slightly insulted by the question?*)   Four.

Princes applaud?

KING (*To children*) Is that right? (*They tell him – then he speaks to Peter.*) Prince Peter, you may join Sonia in the Circle of Truth. (*To Sonia.*) And what do you think of my son? Do you like him?

SONIA   Oh yes, Your Majesty.

They dress her in a cloak, put a loop of tinsel around head for a crown, etc. One advantage of having the King in a wheelchair was that he could come in front of the standing couples without masking them.

KING   Well, the arrow landed beside you, so you are to be his wife. Do you promise to be nice to him, and try to understand him, and not lose your temper?

SONIA   I do.

KING   And you Prince Peter, do you promise to be nice to Sonia, and to try to understand her, and not lose your temper?

PETER   I do.

KING   Well that's settled then.

Trumpets. Cheers, congratulations, etc.

And now, Prince Alexei the Thoughtful, step into the Circle of Truth and put on the blindfold.

Alexei steps into the hula hoop that lies on the floor, and Phillips helps him on with the blindfold.

(*To children.*) Will you help us count the number of times that he turns around? Good. (*To Alexei*) Take this bow and this arrow: now turn around five times, and then shoot the arrow. Is everyone ready? One… Two… Three… Four… Five!

---

*   One Sonia objected that this measuring was "sexist". Well of course it is, but as the story is about *not* judging by externals, it's important that we see people being judged by externals.

Everyone counts as Alexei turns around five times.

Fire the arrow!

Alexei fires his arrow above the opposite side-section of the audience.

ALEXEI   Where did the arrow fall?

KING   Go and look for it.

Alexei goes into the audience and asks who has got his arrow. Some "give-and-take" with the children. "Have you got it?", "Are you hiding it there?", "Did my arrow hit anybody?" etc. Finally Marsha stands up from her seat shrieking with hysterical excitement as if at a pop-concert, or as if she is a contestant at an American give-away show.

MARSHA   Over here, Prince Alexei. I have your arrow.

KING   Bring her to me.

Marsha picks Alexei up when they get to the edge of the stage and carries him on like carrying a bride over a threshold.

What is your name?

MARSHA (*still giggling and shrieking*)   Marsha. I was in the garden when Prince Alexei's arrow landed right beside me.

KING   Step into the Circle of Truth. Are you strong and healthy?

MARSHA   Oh yes. I'm strong as a horse.

KING   Well, close your eyes and stretch your arms out and touch your nose with one finger.

She does it.

That seems to be all right. We'd better take her measurements.

They measure her like they measured Sonia.

Very well, you seem suitable. Now the intelligence test. What comes before five?

MARSHA   Four.

KING (*to children*) Excellent. (*To Alexei.*) Prince Alexei, step into the Circle Of Truth. (*To Marsha.*) And what do you think of my son? Do you like him?

MARSHA   Oh yes, Your Majesty.

They dress her in a cloak, put a hoop of tinsel around head for a crown, etc.

KING   Well, the arrow landed beside you, so you are to be his wife. Do you promise to be nice to him, and try to understand him, and not lose your temper?

MARSHA (*gasping and shrieking*)   I do.

KING   And you Prince Alexei, do you promise to be nice to her, and to try to understand her, and not to lose your temper?

ALEXEI   I do.

KING   Well that's settled then.

Trumpets. Marsha faints and is helped up among cheers and congratulations, etc.

What a splendid day this is turning out to be. My goodness. And now, step into the Circle of Truth, my youngest and favourite son, Prince Ivan, and put on the blindfold.

Ivan steps into the hula-hoop and Phillips puts the blindfold on him.

(*To children.*) Will you help us count the number of times that he turns around? Good. (*To Ivan.*) Take this bow and this arrow, now turn around five times, and then fire the arrow.

IVAN (*enthusiastic – and temporarily raising the blindfold.*)   I saw my wife in a dream, Father, and she has golden hair, and a laugh like sleigh-bells, and a swan-white neck, and eyes as blue as heaven. So I'm going to fire my arrow as far as I possibly can!

KING (*firmly*)   Is everyone ready? One…

Everyone counts with him.

KING   …Two… Three… Four… Five!

Ivan is so enthusiastic that he does ten turns. Everyone on stage takes cover. Does Phillips throw his body across the King to protect him?

ALL   Fire the arrow! Fire the arrow!

The Prince pretends to fire the arrow over the centre of the audience.

PETER   So high!

ALEXEI   Look how far it's going.

KING   It's lost in the clouds.

SONIA   What a show-off!

MARSHA (*admiring*)   He has muscles though!

IVAN (*removes blindfold*)   Where did the arrow fall?

KING Go and look for it.

Ivan goes into the audience – i.e. climbs over the seats at the centre of the audience – and asks who has got his arrow. Some "give-and-take" with the children – "Have you got it?", "Are you hiding it there?", "Oh I hope you found my arrow" etc.

KING What's taking so long?

IVAN (*from rear of audience*) I'm sorry, Father, but I can't find my arrow.

KING Of course you can't find your arrow. It went much further away than that.

IVAN (*moving away*) But Father…

KING Don't "but" me. You had the same chance as your brothers. If your arrow went further you'll just have to keep walking until you find it, that's all.

IVAN But… but…

KING Farewell, Prince Ivan.

Ivan is moving out of the auditorium.

IVAN Farewell, Father. Goodbye, Prince Peter and Princess Sonia. Goodbye, Prince Alexei and Princess Marsha.

They wave goodbye to him.

(*From the distance.*) Goodbye, forest creatures.

Fade lights on the aristocrats waving.

SCENE TWO

We spread the stage with an old parachute – dyed blue-green. It looked swampy or watery. Then we set little islands of "marsh plants" on top of the silk as "solid bits" that could be stood on (note 2).

We closed the centre of the curtains to hide the 'frame' that held the arrows, cloaks, etc. The strip of red carpet was hidden by the parachute material.

We rolled the frog-princess surreptitiously into an edge of the material to hide her "in the water" as it were – the children didn't notice this.

This set change was covered by the commentary.

NARRATOR Prince Ivan went over hills and through forests, and he came to a great swamp, where his feet were always in danger of sinking into the mud, and they squelched each time he put his foot down. The whole day had gone past and he still hadn't found the arrow.

Lights up to show Ivan entering. Every time Ivan takes a step, or leaps from clump to clump, squelching sounds are made on the microphone.

IVAN How could my arrow have reached all the way to here?

FROG (*hidden*) Welcome to the swamp.

IVAN Augh! Who's there?

He pulls out his sword?

FROG (*hidden*) Welcome to the swamp.

IVAN Show yourself.

Frog emerges from under edge of parachute material. She is dressed in a green frog-suit that has a yellow front, and she wears green frogman's feet and a smooth green rubber bathing hat. She should be wide-eyed, and very pleased and enthusiastic and cheerful.

IVAN Oh it's just a frog.

FROG Welcome to the swamp.

IVAN How big is this swamp?

FROG It goes on forever.

IVAN (*To frog*) Forever! I shot an arrow and where it lands I will find my bride. (*To audience.*) But I'll never find the arrow here.

FROG (*pleased*) Yes you will.

IVAN What do frogs know!

FROG Frogs know everything.

IVAN Frogs just sit out here in the swamp and eat flies all day. Anyway, what sort of wife can I find here? Perhaps a eel-catcher's daughter.

FROG Not an eel-catcher's daughter.

IVAN Perhaps a fisherman's daughter.

FROG Not a fisherman's daughter.

IVAN Just because you're an expert on mud and flies you think you know everything.

FROG Frogs do know everything.

Ivan begins to walk off-stage into the darkness.

I know something that you don't know.

IVAN (*sceptical*) Really.

FROG Yes, Prince Ivan.

Ivan returns.

IVAN How do you know my name? And what do you know that I don't know?

FROG I know where your arrow is!

IVAN You do!

She shows him the arrow.

So I am in the right place! Was there a woman here with golden hair, and a laugh like sleigh-bells, and a swan-white neck, and eyes as blue as heaven? (*Calls out.*) Haallooo! Haaallloooooo! Halloooo!

FROG No one like that in this swamp.

IVAN There must have been someone.

FROG (*pleased*) Only me.

IVAN Only you.

FROG The arrow landed beside me.

IVAN Beside you?

FROG (*pats stage beside her*) Right beside me.

IVAN Well that's not my arrow.

FROG (*points to name*) It's got your name on it! (*Reads.*) Prince Ivan. (*Points to name.*) Ivan.

IVAN Well, all right. I'll go back to the Palace and shoot it again.

FROG That's not fair!

IVAN My arrow, please.

FROG You're not going to marry me? (*To children.*) He's supposed to marry me! Isn't that right? He's got to marry whoever the arrow lands beside. (*They'll say "yes".*)

IVAN What! What did you say!

FROG Ribbit!

IVAN Did you say marry me? A Prince can't marry a frog.
FROG Marry me!
IVAN That arrow was meant for somebody else!
FROG Marry me!
IVAN I can't.
FROG Please marry me.

Frog weeps.

IVAN (*sorry for her*) Look …
FROG Why won't you marry me?
IVAN No! This is all wrong.
FROG Tell me – is it my colour?
IVAN No, no, it's a very good colour – for a frog.
FROG Is it my feet? Are they too big?
IVAN No, they're very nice feet – for a frog.
FROG (*takes a few enthusiastic jumps*) I'm good at jumping.
IVAN With legs like that, who wouldn't be?
FROG (*swims on the parachute material*) And I'm a wonderful swimmer.
IVAN Yes, well It's been nice talking with you. But just give me the arrow and I'll be off.
FROG It's because I'm a frog, isn't it?
IVAN (*impatient*) Yes, of course it's because you're a frog.
FROG I knew it! You're prejudiced! I knew that was why you didn't like me.
IVAN (*polite*) I do like you. As a frog, you're perfect. (*Really losing his temper.*) But look at you! You've got no neck. And no hair. Your breath smells of flies.
FROG (*still good natured*) I could brush my teeth.
IVAN (*trying to make amends – he's a nice person really*) Look, how could you live in a palace, with chairs, and tables and beds and where everything is dry and warm?
FROG I could splash about in the moat.
IVAN (*anger*) There is no way that I, Prince Ivan, could marry a frog. So forget it! Forget it! Now give me the arrow.

FROG No!
IVAN (*pursuing her from clump to clump*) Give it to me!
FROG Never.
IVAN Please!
FROG (*makes frog noises*) Ribbit! Ribbit!
IVAN Give me the arrow. Stop it! Come here!
FROG Ribbit! Ribbit!

The frog hops around the stage. Ivan tries to catch her but he keeps sliding on the parachute material. Once they are off the parachute it's pulled off-stage (by a rope that extends behind the curtain). Add a huge slurping down-the-drain noise on the sound-track as it vanishes (an excellent effect). Ivan and the frog are already off-stage as the "swamp" finally disappears.

SCENE THREE

The exit of the parachute has exposed the strip of red carpet as before, and the curtains have parted to reveal the "frame". A paper moon has risen and white "Christmas lights" high above have been switched on to suggest stars. The princes and princesses are more bored than would seem possible – they are groaning and sighing with boredom. They assume the most bored postures that they can imagine.

KING (*after a while*) Any sign of Prince Ivan?
SONS No, Father.
KING The whole day gone by and now it's night, and still he hasn't come back. How beautiful the stars are. (*Looks at the dozens of tiny Christmas lights on the ceiling.*) Perhaps I should take more time to stop and enjoy how beautiful everything is.

A bell tolls midnight.

PETER It's striking midnight, Father. Can't we go to bed?
SONIA We've been standing around since breakfast.
MARSHA And it is our Marriage Night after all!
ALEXEI I'm stiff as a board.

PETER You can't be stiffer than I am.

KING Well… I suppose… (*Sees Ivan.*) Ivan!

Enter Ivan from rear of audience with the frog who is covered by a green cloth which allows only her flipper feet to show.

We were worried about you.

They liven up.

SONIA It's about time.

PETER Where've you been?

ALEXEI And who's that!

MARSHA Or what's that?

IVAN I had to go a long way, Father.

KING And is this the woman who will be your wife?

IVAN There's been a mistake, Father. I had to cover her up so I could bring her through the streets.

SONIA Is she so ugly!

KING Have you got the arrow?

IVAN She won't give it to me. She said she'd only give it to you.

MARSHA Look at her feet!

The veiled frog gives the arrow to the King.

KING (*takes arrow*) Thank you.

FROG Ribbit.

SONS (*looking at each other*) Ribbet?

KING What is your name, my dear?

FROG Anya, Sir.

IVAN Look, father…

KING A very pretty name. Won't you unveil yourself?

IVAN Yes. Then my father will understand, and send you back where you came from.

She unveils. The princes and princesses are amazed and amused.

SONS It's a frog! It's a frog!

FROG (*delighted*) I was in the swamp and Prince Ivan's arrow landed right beside me.

KING Right beside you! Well, er… I don't know what to say. You'd better step into the Circle of Truth!

IVAN Father!

KING Are you… are you strong and healthy?

FROG Oh yes. I've never been ill.

IVAN You don't expect me to marry her, Father!

KING Close your eyes and stretch your arms out and touch your nose with one finger.

She does it.

That seems to be all right. We'd better measure her.

Peter, Alexei, Sonia and Marsha measure her as before. They laugh and giggle at the frog's measurements. Ivan is appalled.

KING Well, she seems fit enough.

IVAN Of course she's fit. She's fit as a frog. Please, Father…

KING Now don't worry yourself, Prince Ivan. She'll never pass the intelligence test. Well, Anya. Can you count up to ten?

FROG Oh yes, Your Majesty.

In this next section Prince Ivan gets increasingly desperate, and his brothers gloat over his impending fate.

KING What comes before five?

FROG One, and two, and three, and four, but four is the number immediately before five… One and two are three, two and three are five, three and four are seven, four and five are nine…

KING (*startled*) Yes, yes, quite! (*Decides to give tough questions.*) Er… er… Add together all the numbers from one to a hundred.

FROG Five thousand and fifty.

KING What is the square root of minus one?

FROG Minus one is an imaginary number that has no real existence.

KING What was Rumpelstiltskin's name?

FROG Rumpelstiltskin!

SONS (*applauding*) Correct.

KING Why did the Wolf have big teeth?

FROG All the better to eat Red Riding Hood.

IVAN Do something, Father!

KING What… er… What am I thinking at this very moment?

They crowd round, thinking that this question will demolish her.

FROG (*dramatic pause*) You're thinking that I… am a frog.

KING Augh!

SONS Is that right?

KING Yes, of course it is! (*Getting desperate.*) What number is bigger than the biggest number ever?

FROG The biggest ever number ever plus one!

IVAN I don't believe this!

KING (*inspired*) How long is a piece of string?

FROG Twice the distance from the middle to the end.

KING (*"driven into a corner", frantic*) What's the difference between a man in a uniform and a man not in a uniform.

FROG The uniform!

The King is appalled.

KING I give up!

FROG Frogs know everything.

KING (*exhausted. wheels himself to the side?*) This is no ordinary frog.

IVAN What can I do, Father?

KING (*to Ivan*) Step into the Circle of Truth!

IVAN No, Father, please!

KING (*firmly*) Step into the Circle of Truth!

IVAN (*stands in circle*) Oh!

KING What do you think of Prince Ivan? Do you like him?

IVAN But Father…

FROG (*adoring Ivan*) Yes, Your Majesty. I like him.

Tries to give Ivan a hug.

IVAN (*moving away*) Get off! Let me go. Slimy thing.

FROG (*following him*) I'm not slimy. Feel me.

She jumps on his back and he carries her round the stage piggy-back until he shakes her off. Uproar.

IVAN Father, you have to stop this.

The princes and princesses collapse in hysterics. They imitate the frog, etc.

KING Silence! Do you think it's funny that your brother – Prince Ivan – has to marry a frog?

PETER Ribbit!

He hides behind Sonia. Alexei is pretending to catch flies out of the air? Phillips wheels the King towards the audience.

 KING (*ignoring them*) And you forest creatures. I want everyone with a straight face. No smiling! I want every one of you looking as serious as possible. Getting married is a very important decision!
 SONIA What will the children be like?
 MARSHA They'll be tadpoles!
 IVAN You see, Father – everyone will laugh at me.
 KING But if your arrow decided that you should marry a frog…
 IVAN No!
 KING … then you have to marry a frog!
 SONS (*aping frog*) Ribbit! Ribbit!
 KING Silence back there! (*To frog.*) Princess Anya …
 SONS (*sniggering*) Princess!
 KING (*insisting*) Princess Anya may be a frog but there's no need to be rude to her. (*To Ivan.*) Get back in the circle. (*To princes.*) Put Prince Ivan back in the Circle Of Truth.

Prince Ivan is carried back into the circle protesting. Meanwhile the frog is dressed in robes and tinsel by the princesses.

 Do you, Anya the Frog, promise to be nice to Prince Ivan and try to understand him, and not lose your temper?
 FROG (*full of love*) I do.
 KING And will you, Prince Ivan, promise to be nice to this frog, and to try to understand her?
 IVAN How could anyone understand a frog?
 KING Well you'll just have to learn!
 IVAN I won't marry a frog. (*Talks to children.*) Would you marry a frog? Would you? Would you like your mummy to be a frog? (*etc.*)
Pleads on with knees with his father?
 KING We all have to do things we'd rather not do, Ivan, and if you have to marry a frog then you have to marry a frog, and that's all there is to it! Now, for the last time, will you promise to be nice to this frog, and to try to understand her, and not lose your temper with her?

Ivan with folded arms? He is obstinate.

PETER (*coming close to him*) Don't you wish this had never happened?

IVAN I do!

KING Good! So that's settled then.

IVAN What! Nooooo!

Has tantrum. The frog is shaking hands with the other princes and princesses.

I want a wife with golden hair, and a laugh like sleigh-bells, and a swan-white neck, and eyes as blue as heaven. Auuggghh! (*etc.*)

The frog hugs and kisses Ivan. The other princes and their princesses are helpless with laughter.

SCENE FOUR

During the scene-change the frame tips forwards to become a bed.

NARRATOR (*during blackout*) So Princess Anya, who was a frog, lived in the Palace with Prince Ivan, who was a human being, and they tried to be nice to each other, and to understand each other, and not to lose their tempers. And the frog taught Prince Ivan to help people and be nice to them, and not to think of himself all the time. And Ivan began to like the strange wife that he had found in the swamp.

The frog is lying in the bed. Prince Ivan sits someway to the side on a wooden chair and stares front.

FROG (*pause*) A whole month has gone by since we were married.

IVAN (*blankly*) Thirty-one days.

FROG Can't we go outside sometimes?

IVAN Why go out? We just ring the bell and the servants bring whatever we ask for.

Pause.

FROG I'd like to see the houses, and all the people. I'm bored.

IVAN You're bored! What do you think I am?

FROG (*out of the bed, instantly*) How about a game of leap-frog?

IVAN I'm sick of playing leap-frog.
FROG I could teach you my frog dance.
IVAN Frog dance?
FROG The amazing frog dance never seen before by human beings.
IVAN (*interested*) Well, all right.

She prepares to teach him the frog dance.

FROG Let's have all the forest creatures do it as well. Everyone stand up. Make sure that your mummies and daddies stand up too. And they'd better hold your popcorn for you.
IVAN Stand up! Everyone stand up.

They get audience to stand.

FROG It's called the Froggie-Woggie.

They get the audience to do a version of the hokey-cokey.

You put your left flipper in,
You put your left flipper out,
You put your left flipper in
And you shake it all about,
You do the Froggie-Woggie
And you turn around,
That's what it's all about!

Repeat this a couple more times, doing the right leg, and then the nose.

IVAN That was fun!
FROG (*eagerly*) Time for bed!

The frog gets into bed. Ivan tucks her in (like a parent). Gives her a fatherly kiss.

FROG I like the way you tuck me into bed every night. You're very nice to me, Ivan.
IVAN Well – it's not your fault.
FROG Are you coming to bed too?
IVAN I'll stay up and read this letter from my father. Good night.
FROG Good night!

Frog goes to sleep and Ivan wonders what is in the letter from the King. He takes his time opening it. He reads it and is horrified. He screws it up and throws it down. He tears his hair.

Oh no! Oh no!

Tries to strangle himself? Beats his head on the floor? The frog has woken up. She looks at him, at first curious, and then afraid.

FROG   Ivan?

Ivan continues.

Ivan? What are you doing?

IVAN   I'm going to end it all! I can't go on living like this. I'm going to jump out of the window!

A struggle. They end up with him on the bed and her squatting over him and holding him down.

IVAN   Ow! Augh! Let me up!

FROG   I'm not going to let you do bad things to yourself.

IVAN   But I'm so unhappy.

He gets up and walks around the stage expressing despair but the frog hasn't let go. It's as if he doesn't notice that the frog is still clinging to the front of him. He circles the bed and then drops her on it.

FROG   (*releasing him*)   What's wrong, Ivan?

IVAN   Everyone thinks I'm a fool for marrying you. I mean look at you!

They sit side by side at the foot of the bed.

Every time I walk out of a room I hear them making up jokes about us. What's white on the outside, green on the inside, and jumps about?

FROG   A frog sandwich.

IVAN   You knew!

FROG   Frogs know everything.

Pause.

You want me to go back to the swamp? I will, you know.

Pause.

You want me to go back to the swamp?

Pause.

I will.

Pause.

The swamp's not such a bad place. For frogs. But I'll miss you, Ivan.

No reply. She starts to walk away, totally rejected – she's going back to the swamp. Perhaps she takes a sad look back.

    IVAN (*inner torment*) No, don't. I didn't mean to hurt your feelings. Here, dry your eyes.

    FROG It's crocodiles that cry – not frogs.

Brings her back to the bed and sits on the end of it beside her.

    IVAN I'd say you were about the best frog in the whole world. You're fun to be with. And I'd be lonely without you. But now this letter from my father has spoilt everything.

Gives her the letter.

    He wants a competition to see which of his sons has the best wife. Each Princess has to sew him a shirt by breakfast tomorrow. That's easy for Princess Sonia and Princess Marsha, but how can a frog sew a shirt?

The frog folds up the letter purposefully. Ivan is trying not to weep but is very upset. She rocks and soothes him. She puts his head in her lap.

    FROG You let me worry about that. It always seems darkest before the dawn.

She sings a lullaby.

    Splish, Splash, in the water,
    Who can find the Frog King's daughter?
    Flip and Flop with great big feet.
    Always lots of flies to eat.
    When in trouble jump for blue,
    That is what a Frog must do!
    When you're feeling very sad,
    A Frog has ways to make you glad!

Ivan is asleep in her arms.

    (*to audience*) Poor Prince Ivan, what trouble I've brought him! I know that he likes me really. It's not his fault that life is sometimes difficult. But life's not so easy for frogs either.

Fade the lights. Stand the bed up on end and close the curtains to conceal it.

SCENE FIVE

The princes and their princesses are lined up on the carpet. Each princess holds a shirt (folded in such a way that we can't judge it).

PETER Well I'm sure Princess Sonia's shirt will be better than that Frog's!

ALEXEI Of course, if it was a swimming competition…

Ivan is embarrassed. Anya comforts him.

PETER It'll certainly be one of our wives who gets the medal.

Enter the King in his wheelchair (pushed by Phillips).

This is the day of the Competition. Prince Peter – are you ready to present your wife's shirt?

PETER (*proudly*) Here it is, Father.

The King opens box with shirt. Sonia comes forward, sure that she will be the winner.

KING It's… it's terrible!

PETER Terrible, Father?

KING I can get my head through the button holes. This shirt is a disgrace!

Gives it back. Sonia is terribly upset.

ALEXEI (*confidently*) Would you like to see my wife's shirt then, Father?

KING Thank you. I'm sure that Princess Marsha will have taken a little more trouble.

ALEXEI Here it is, Father.

Marsha squealing and giggling with excitement. The King opens the box.

KING I wouldn't have believed it.

MARSHA (*thrilled*) Thank you, Sir.

KING I wouldn't have believed that you've made a shirt that's even worse than the one made by Princess Sonia! What did you use for a needle – a harpoon?

Marsha is terribly upset. The King is about to leave.

PETER (*resentful*) What about Princess Anya's shirt then, Father?

ALEXEI (*angry*) You did ask for a shirt from each one of us, Father.

PETER And if hers is even worse, one of us will still be the winner.
KING Very well.
IVAN Here it is, Father.

The King opens the box. We used one of our decorated children's show T-shirts which were on sale in the foyer.

KING What's this! No one ever gave me such a magnificent shirt. What a talented wife you have, Prince Ivan. Princess Anya is the winner, and she certainly deserves this medal.

The King hangs a medal around the frog's neck.

PETER It's not fair, Father.
ALEXEI This frog just happens to be very good at sewing.
PETER We want another competition.
KING Another competition!

(*Kids are always interested in competitions.*)

(*Thinks.*) Very well, let me think! All right! I want each of the Princesses to bake me a loaf of bread for my breakfast tomorrow. Prince Ivan and Princess Anya – you can walk with me in the palace gardens. I'd like to hear about life in the swamp.

IVAN She could show you her Froggie-Woggie, Father!

They exit. The princes and princesses are furious.

ALEXEI He must be married to a witch.
PETER You're right. She must be a witch. We'll have to spy on her.
SONIA Yes. We'll watch her.
MARSHA And we'll see everything she does.

They exit as the lights fade.

SCENE SIX

A fire to one side of the stage. The frog squatting on the floor, rolling "dough" on a board with a rolling pin (if the sightlines are bad give her a table to make the bread on).
The fire is four of five feet across – actually it was the "well" that we had

built for a production of "The Frog Prince". *The flames are red and yellow paper streamers tied to an electric fan's finger-guard. The fan is facing upwards and makes the paper streamers flutter. We put a light in the well and the paper "flames" made the light flicker – a excellent effect (many of the children thought the "flames" were real).*

    NARRATOR (*at end of scene change*)   Princess Anya was in her kitchen and rolling out the dough to make bread when she heard something suspicious.

    FROG (*to children*)   I thought I heard something. Will you tell me if you see someone?

Peter and Alexei and the princesses peep through the curtains. The children yell but they hide again and the frog doesn't see them.

    FROG   Are you sure? I thought I heard something but I didn't see anyone. (*Ad lib.*)

Play this game for a while. Then the frog comes close to the audience and confides in them.

    Can you whisper very quietly? I thought I saw Prince Peter and Prince Alexei, and the two Princesses. Is that right?

Children whisper "yes".

    FROG (*whispers*)   I'll play a trick on them. I'll take some of the dough and throw it into the fire and that will spoil it, and then they'll think that's how I make bread.

She throws the dough into the fire and then says this verse (close to and towards the gap in the curtains?). Princess Sonia is writing it down.

    Put the dough into the fire,

    Till the crust is black as night,

    But the bread that's in the centre,

    Will be soft and taste just right.

The frog runs into the audience and hides. The princes and princesses enter and look into the flames.

    PETER   So that's the secret!

    MARSHA   Now our bread will be as good as hers!

    ALEXEI   What was the spell?

    SONIA (*reading*)   Put the dough into the fire.

ALEXEI   Till the crust is black as night!
SONIA   … black as night…
PETER   But the bread that's in the centre…
ALL   Will be soft and taste just right.

Delighted with themselves they rush off. The frog comes out of the audience. Enter Ivan.

Oh Ivan, I've done a wicked thing.

IVAN   What happened?
FROG   I can't tell you.
IVAN (*to children*)   What happened?

They tell him.

FROG   I saw them spying on me, and I played a trick on them. I put some dough right into the fire. And now they've rushed off to bake their loaves of bread in the same way, and they'll be all burned black and taste horrible. I've been a bad frog!

The frog puts head on Ivan's chest.

IVAN (*thinks*)   Well… serve them right for spying on you. And for being nasty to you just because you're a frog. You can't help the way you were born.

Lights fading.

FROG   Yes, but it's mean to play tricks on people.

SCENE SEVEN

The frog and Ivan stand to one side, Ivan is holding something on a tray covered by a cloth.
There is a dispute off-stage. The curtains move. The King is off-stage roaring with anger.

KING (*off-stage*)   It's the worst loaf I've ever seen!
SONIA (*off-stage*)   But I put it in the fire!
KING (*off-stage*)   In the fire! Bread is supposed to go in the oven! I'm not eating this. I'll throw it away!

A black heavy loaf hurtles through the curtains opposite to Ivan and the frog. It thumps noisily onto the stage. Sonia enters and picks it up. Peter enters.

    PETER I've never seen Father so angry!
    SONIA I just did what the frog did!
    PETER (*picking up loaf*) It's just charcoal! No one can eat this!
    SONIA It was your fault as well.

They quarrel. They hit each other? The King is heard roaring with anger again. They listen.

    SONIA He must be looking at the bread Marsha baked.
    KING (*off-stage*) This bread is just as bad as Princess Sonia's! You don't put bread in the fire! Bread is supposed to be baked in the oven! I'm not eating this. I'll throw this one away as well.

A second-hard and blackened loaf comes through the curtains and bangs onto the stage.

    MARSHA (*off-stage*) No!

Marsha stamps on followed by Alexei.

    He didn't like it, and after all the trouble we went to!
    ALEXEI It's that frog's fault!

Phillips wheels the King onto the stage.

    KING I've never heard of such a thing!
    SONIA The frog put her loaf in the fire.
    MARSHA We saw her!
    PETER What about Princess Anya's loaf anyway, Father?
    ALEXEI Yes, let's see the frog's loaf, Father.
    SONIA Yes, I bet her loaf is burned twice as much as ours.
    MARSHA Why should we get all the blame?
    KING Ivan!

Ivan brings loaf over covered by cloth.

    IVAN Here you are, Father.

King removes cloth to reveal a marvellous loaf that has a city made of icing on the top of it.

    KING What's this?
    IVAN Anya put a city made of icing sugar on the top, Father.

KING Looks aren't everything. Let me taste it. (*He breaks off a piece.*) Why, this is better than cake. Princess Anya gets another medal.

He hangs a second medal around the frog's neck.

I'm so pleased with this wonderful loaf of bread, that I shall give a party this evening. And the guest of honour will be Princess Anya herself.

The other princes and princesses are outraged.

PETER It's not fair, Father.

ALEXEI This frog just happens to be very good at baking bread.

SONIA It's just luck!

MARSHA (*mutters*) Or witchcraft!

PETER We want another chance.

ALEXEI That's right, Father!

KING Let me see. All right, we'll have a competition at the party to see – to see who… To see which couple are the best dancers! And we'll let the forest creatures decide who the winner shall be. I'll tell the servants to start making the preparations.

Phillips wheels him off.

PETER Well, I'm certain we can dance better than any frog!

SONIA I shall wear my new dress.

MARSHA I shall have my dancing instructor give me an extra lesson.

ALEXEI Yes, we'd better practise.

PETER (*turning back to Ivan*) Think how the people will laugh when they see you dancing with your frog!

Ivan is angry.

ALEXEI If I were you, I wouldn't bother to come.

SONIA Mind you don't step on her feet!

MARSHA People will think you're really stupid you know.

They leave. Ivan stares out at the audience. The frog approaches him. She makes faces, or funny ears with her hands or whatever, trying to cheer him up.

FROG Why so sad, my love?

IVAN You're the best frog in all the world! But everyone will laugh if they see us dancing together.

FROG Let me worry about that. Go to the banquet alone, and when you hear trumpets and a noise like thunder, just say – "That's the wheels of Anya's carriage!"

IVAN "That's the wheels of Anya's carriage."

FROG Perhaps the forest creatures can say it with you so that you can remember. (*Turns to audience.*) Are you ready? Say: "That's the wheels of Anya's carriage."

Get children to repeat it.

IVAN How will that help?

FROG Trust me.

IVAN (*to children*) Should I trust her?

The audience say "yes"

SCENE EIGHT

Lower in chandeliers? You can make them out of tin cans that you cut to shape. And/or use Christmas lights, etc. We put a couple of low pillars at each end of the red carpet with trays of drink etc. on them.

Peter has a large "Number 1" hung round his neck. Alexei has a large "Number 2" hung round his neck. Sonia and Marsha wear party dresses? The king is impatient.

KING Has anyone seen Prince Ivan, and Princess Anya? We can't start the dance competition without them.

SONIA I hope he's not going to keep us waiting.

MARSHA Like when he shot his arrow.

KING Perhaps they've sneaked in the back door so that the peasants won't laugh at them. I'll see if I can find them. Wheel me out Phillips!

Exit King.

SONIA I expect he's bathing in the moat with his frog!

The prince and princesses are laughing hysterically.

MARSHA Or she's teaching him to make fly soup.

Enter Ivan.
>IVAN I'm sorry I'm late.
>ALEXEI Here's your number.

They put a "Number 3" on him.
>PETER Where's your frog? (*To others.*) I expect she's still putting her lipstick on!
>ALEXEI With a paint-roller.
>SONIA (*spiteful*) Are they serving frog-legs tonight?
>MARSHA (*giggling*) I hear they're turning one of the washrooms into an aquarium.

Enter King.
>KING Ah Ivan, but where is your frog? (*Genuinely sorry for the lapse.*) I mean, where's your wife?
>IVAN She's coming later in her carriage.
>SONIA A frog in a carriage!
>MARSHA A frog can't ride in a carriage!

Trumpets. Thunder and lightning.
>KING Thunder? I hope it won't rain and spoil the party.
>IVAN That's not thunder. That... (*He prompts the audience.*) That's the wheels of my wife coming in her carriage. That's Anya coming in her carriage.

They repeat it with him.
>AUDIENCE That's Anya coming in her carriage.
>KING Come now Prince Ivan, no one's carriage makes a noise like thunder. And what about all this lightning!
>IVAN That's the sparks from the iron wheels.

The others are laughing but a new burst of thunder scares them. The curtains billow, and the actors shake about, clasping the pillars as if for support and shaking them too.
>ALL (*staring to the rear of the audience*) Look! Look! Whoever saw such a carriage. It's enormous! (*etc.*)

The frog enters through the audience. She is now a woman who is wearing a wonderful white dress and lots of glittering jewels.
>ANYA I'm sorry to be so late, Your Majesty.

SONIA She knows the King.

ANYA Good evening, Prince Alexei, Good evening, Princess Marsha, and to you, Prince Peter, and to you, Princess Sonia.

MARSHA She knows us!

ANYA Good evening, forest creatures. Don't you know me, Ivan? Oh well, women are always changing their appearance.

IVAN Are you… Could it be possible that you are…

ANYA My name is Anya!

IVAN You can't be Anya the frog!

ALL It's the frog! It's the frog!

Anya startles the princes and princesses by rushing at them.

ANYA (*in frog's voice*) Welcome to the swamp! Ribbit! Ribbit!

IVAN You *are* my frog!

ANYA Yes. I climbed out of my frog skin but I must put it on again before midnight.

IVAN Is it true? Are you really my frog?

KING So the arrow made the right choice! But we can't wait any longer. We have to begin the dance competition. Music!

A mirror-ball starts rotating – it throws circling spots of light onto the stage and onto the audience. Cut the stage lights and use a follow-spot to illuminate the dancers.

NARRATOR (*ad lib this commentary*) And here we are at the Royal Dancing competition. Couple Number One, Prince Peter and Princess Sonia, a beautifully matched couple, oh but Princess Sonia is dipping him – they'll lose points for that.

Peter and Sonia seriously screw up, maybe she falls over?

KING Thank you. Next couple, please.

Peter and Sonia move to the side or rear, sure that they've won the prize. Marsha and Alexei start to dance.

NARRATOR (*ad lib*) Prince Alexei and Princess Marsha having some disagreement – I think she's complaining that he stepped on her feet … (*etc.*)

Maybe Alexei falls over.

KING Thank you. Next couple, please.

ALEXEI Give us a chance, Father.

MARSHA We can do it!

KING (*firmly*) Next couple, please.

Ivan and Anya step are picked up by the follow-spot. The waltz music changes mid-dance into something lively and jazzy. They do an astounding dance with cartwheels, acrobatics, whatever.

NARRATOR Couple Number Three, Prince Ivan and Princess Anya are taking everyone's eye here. (*Ad lib.*) It's Prince Ivan and Princess Anya, and they're doing an amazing new dance. I've never seen anything like it. The audience is applauding. Even the King is applauding. There can't be much doubt who is the winner of this competition. Bravo! Bravo! The King is congratulating them…

SONS ETC. It's not fair! It's not fair, Father!

KING And now we will let the forest creatures decide the winners.

Peter and Sonia come forwards, still confident of winning. (Ad lib dialogue). If Alexei and Marsha boo then probably the audience will boo as well.

NARRATOR Couple Number One, Prince Peter and Princess Marsha.

PETER (*to audience*) Cheer! Clap, can't you!

SONIA We were the best!

They go to side or to the rear, quarrelling.

PETER It was your fault.

SONIA Oh no it wasn't.

NARRATOR And now couple Number Two – Prince Alexei and Princess Marsha.

Marsha and Alexei come centre-stage – confident of winning. They bow to audience. (Ad lib dialogue.)

And now couple Number Three, Princess Anya and Prince Ivan.

Lots of applause.

KING (*giving Anya another medal*) And Princess Anya earns another medal, and is the best of all the wives!

Phillips holds up applause board.

Everything goes into slow motion (or freezes) and the lights dim. Ivan comes forward into the reduced circle of the follow-spot.

    IVAN (*to audience*)   So my wife doesn't have to be a frog! I wonder what she did with her frog skin? If I can find her skin and burn it she'll never be able to turn back into a frog ever again.

SCENE NINE

    NARRATOR   Ivan slipped away from the party and went back to the Royal Palace. He ran up the circular staircase, and along the corridors, and opened door after door, searching everywhere for the Frog skin.

Ivan mimes all this (meanwhile the "fire" has been wheeled on-stage again).

    At last he went into the kitchen and took the bellows and made the fire burn brighter.

Add more light.

    Then he noticed a trapdoor that had been opened very recently.

We used a trapdoor in the stage and hung the frog skin (a duplicate) from the underside of it, but a trunk will do. If you use a trunk say: "Then he noticed an old trunk that he hadn't seen before."

    He opened it and there was the skin of Anya, the frog. How strange and heavy it felt as he lifted it. But there was no time to lose. Already his wife might have noticed that he had left the dance, and be hurrying after him.

    IVAN (*to children*)   If I burn it she'll never turn back into a frog again. What shall I do with it?

They answer him.

    Why don't I put it into the fire?

They answer him.

    Then she'll be mine forever.

They answer him.

    What would you do?

They answer him.

I don't care! I'll burn it so that she stays with me forever. Goodbye, frog skin.

He throws the skin into the flames. Thunder. Lightning. Strobe light. A puff of smoke goes up from the fire (use powder for the smoke?).

I've done it. I've done it! I'm sure I did the right thing. (*Startled.*) Someone's coming!

Ivan shrinks back. Anya enters.

ANYA Ivan? Ivan?

She doesn't see him. She hurries to the trapdoor (or trunk). She is appalled to find the frog skin missing. She sees Ivan.

ANYA Ivan! What have you done with my green frog skin! Where is it?

IVAN I've solved the problem.

ANYA What have you done with it?

IVAN We won't be laughed at any more, not ever.

She asks the audience?

IVAN Yes! I burned it!

ANYA You burned it!

IVAN So now you can't be a frog ever again.

She screams and rushes to the fire. He pulls her back.

It's too late. It's gone! Now we can live together like human beings.

She weeps, utterly distraught.

What's wrong? Isn't being human better than being a frog?

ANYA You've spoiled everything.

IVAN How? What have I done?

ANYA My father was a magician and he was so angry when I refused to obey him that he turned me into a frog for three whole years, and threw me into the swamp. But in three more days the time would have been up. And I would have been yours forever!

IVAN Three days!

ANYA If I don't put on my frog skin before midnight I have to go back to him.

IVAN But it's all burned to ashes!

Midnight strikes.
> ANYA I must go!
> IVAN Will I never find you again?
> ANYA Even a frog can't tell you that.
> IVAN I'll get everyone in the kingdom to search for you.
> ANYA No! You must search for me alone or you'll never find me!
> IVAN I love you! I'll never let you go!

He tries to hold her, but her robe falls on the floor and she slips effortlessly away.
He stood upstage of her as she vanishes, leaving him with her cloak in his arms. (He held the wired top of her cloak while she crawled between his legs and into a tunnel that was inserted secretly through the curtains – without the tunnel her white dress would have made her exit visible. The tunnel was made of cardboard and triangular in cross section – see note 3.).

> Anya! Don't leave me! How can I ever be happy again? Anya! Anya! Will I really never find you unless I search for you alone?

Fade out.

SCENE TEN

Ivan mimes a journey.
> NARRATOR Prince Ivan left his palace, and wandered for years through the whole kingdom.

While Ivan goes through the audience, a tombstone is placed on the stage (by the Stranger).

> In the summer he sweated under the hot sun, and in the winter he froze in snowdrifts. He climbed great mountains and crossed terrible deserts.
> IVAN *(calling)* Anya! Annnyaaaa! Annyaa! Has anyone seen her? *(Ad lib.)*
> NARRATOR Some people say that one day he came to a tombstone standing all by itself in the forest.

Ivan on stage again.

IVAN What's this? (*He reads the inscription.*)
"Splish, Splash, in the water,
Who can find the Frog King's daughter?"

NARRATOR And then he read these words: "This is the grave of the Frog Princess who died because Prince Ivan burned her skin".

Ivan weeps beside the grave.

And some people say that he stayed there until he turned into a statue made of the hardest stone. But other people say that Prince Ivan met a stranger.

Enter a Stranger (played by Phillips?).

STRANGER Hello! Why are you looking so miserable?

IVAN Because I'm Prince Ivan.

STRANGER Prince Ivan! Oh, you mean the fool who married a frog.

IVAN Yes.

STRANGER The idiot who couldn't wait another three days.

IVAN That's enough!

STRANGER The one they make up all the jokes about.

IVAN My frog taught me to ignore unkind remarks.

STRANGER The cheat who ran back from the party and burned his wife's skin!

IVAN My wife taught me to admit my faults.

STRANGER Better a clever frog than a stupid Prince.

IVAN Leave me alone!

STRANGER (*pulls out sword*) And did your frog teach you to be a coward!

An exciting sword-fight – in our production Ivan's sword was set behind the tombstone. No one mentioned that he hadn't had one until then.

Ivan wins.

Are you going to kill me?

IVAN No! The frog taught me that I should be merciful. So go your way.

Ivan turns away.

STRANGER Then you're a fool for not killing me!

The Stranger attacks him again but Ivan is ready.

IVAN My frog taught me to expect treachery!

He defeats the Stranger again.

STRANGER Go ahead! Finish me off.

IVAN No! My frog taught me that every creature is as precious as me. But this time I'll keep your sword. Go on your way.

Ivan turns away and the Stranger leaps on him and they wrestle. Ivan wins.

My frog taught me that bullies have to be taught a lesson. So apologize!

STRANGER You may be a Prince, but you're still a fool.

IVAN Prove it?

STRANGER Only a fool believes something just because it's carved in stone.

IVAN But this is Princess Anya's grave.

STRANGER This stone was put here by her father to trick you if you ever reached this far on your journey.

IVAN Anya is alive!

STRANGER She's in a castle guarded by a huge giant.

IVAN Who are you?

STRANGER (*leaving*) I'm the man with the streamers – take them. (*Gives him streamers.*) Throw them and they will lead you to her. She is locked in a tower, and a terrible giant stands guard ready to tear you to pieces.

IVAN I'll fight him!

The Stranger is leaving the auditorium.

STRANGER Good luck!

IVAN Which way do I go?

STRANGER Follow the streamers.

He leaves.

IVAN (*to the children*) Should I throw the streamers?

The children say "yes".

Ivan throws a streamer into the audience, and follows wherever it lands.

He asks everyone who catches a streamer if they have seen Anya. He mimes to the commentary again, becoming gradually very old in body and voice.

    NARRATOR So Prince Ivan followed the streamers, and they led him through a part of the forest that was full of wolves! Can we hear the wolves please?

The audience make wolf noises.

    And then he came to a valley that was full of hissing snakes.

The audience make snake noises.

    And then he climbed a mountain where bears growled and waved their claws at him. Can the bears wave their claws?

The audience growl and wave their claws.

    The journey was so terrible that Prince Ivan became old, and weak, far too weak to fight a giant, but then one day he came into a clearing, at the centre of which stood a tower surrounded by a moat.

During this streamer-throwing adventure we opened the curtains to disclose a raised drawbridge (it was the frame that became a bed). We arranged the parachute material in front of it as a moat. We also placed the remains of a giant in a heap on stage – gigantic skull, ribs, bones of a couch-size hand, etc. Plus a broken key. (Ivan has a stick?)

    NARRATOR (*Ivan is back on stage.*) And there were the bones of the Giant who had been waiting so long for Prince Ivan that he had died and had fallen to pieces. And beside the body was a key that the Magician had broken so that Ivan would never be able to get into the tower.

Ivan examines the Giant, making sure it's dead. Then he turns to the castle.

    IVAN (*calling out*)   Hello! Hello! Is anyone there?

Anya speaks from behind the drawbridge (using a megaphone?)

    ANYA Who speaks?

    IVAN Prince Ivan.

    ANYA What is more precious than gold?

Ivan asks the forest creatures and tries out answers. If they say stupid or mean things like "silver" or "being strong" nothing happens, but if they suggest something wise for him to say he repeats it and there is thunder and lightning. He consults the audience each time.

IVAN (*for example*) Happiness.

Thunder and lightning.

ANYA And what is better than power?

IVAN (*for example*) Kindness.

Thunder and lightning.

ANYA What is better than being young?

IVAN Being wise.

Thunder and lightning. Eerie or powerful music. The drawbridge lowers. Anya stands on the drawbridge. Ivan turns away and crouches with his back to her.

ANYA Ivan.

IVAN Is it you?

ANYA Why won't you look at me?

IVAN Because my eyes are dim from the glare of the snow. Because my skin is withered by the desert sun. Because my bones ache and I've become so old and ugly.

She glides over to him.

ANYA Once I was ugly. But you learned to love me.

She puts her arm around him and leads him across the drawbridge as he slowly becomes young again. Fade lights as the mirror-ball fills the theatre with swirling light.

NARRATOR And Princess Anya, who was a frog for two years and three hundred and sixty-two days, took Prince Ivan into the Castle and made him young again, and they lived happily ever after.

If you have the money and the resources, fill the stage magically with flowers.

Blackout. Curtain call. Actors bow.

NOTES

1. Firing the Arrows

As you pretend to release the arrow you bend it back and conceal it along the back of the arm that 'fired' it. The others, Princes, etc., come forwards to watch the flight of the arrow and one of them sneaks the arrow away from you instantly, so that even if the audience noticed the 'sleight of hand' they still won't know where the arrow actually went. (Paint the arrows black.)

2. The Swamp

We placed 'tufts' of 'marsh plant' on the parachute at random. The Prince only stood on the tufts and strode or leapt from one to the other, but the frog could move anywhere.

3. Vanishing Princess Anya

Princess Anya wore a red cloak with wired shoulders. Prince Ivan held the cloak and she went between his legs into a black triangular tunnel made of cardboard which had been thrust in through the curtains, and which was withdrawn as soon as she made her exit. This made for an effective 'vanish'. Ivan was left holding the cloak the top of which was wired. This 'vanish' was possible because almost all the stage light came from the fire, and from a follow-spot that lit only the top halves of their bodies. The tunnel was necessary because she was wearing a white gown (for the ball-room scene) and many of the spectators would have seen the white shape moving through the darkness.

THE LAST BIRD

The first productions of this play were in 1971 and 72 (in Denmark). It's usually been played in a proscenium theatre, but I wrote it for the State Theatre School in Copenhagen where we built a T-shaped stage and sat the audience at either side of the "upright" of the "T". This allowed each half of the audience to see how the other half was reacting. Fortunately they reacted as I wanted them to, rather than looking bored.

My productions of this play have always been on a black stage with black, or with very dark, drapes (velvet if possible to absorb light). We never curtained the stage off from the audience. Scene changes were made in the light from a rotating mirror-ball that was hung above the stage – an excellent method because the scene-shifters can see rather well, but the audience can't quite grasp what's happening. More elaborate productions are possible, but the blackouts must not hold up the play (although the use of excerpts from the Bach's B-Minor Mass make it unnecessary to rush the scene-changes). Dead leaves should be strewn along the edges of the stage. Replace them each performance and dampen them to keep down any dust.

A half-curtain closed off the horizontal top of the "T", and a full curtain closed off the base of the "T" (see notes). A head of Jesus drawn in black paint on a papered hoop was placed above the centre of the half-curtain. A small trampoline was level with the stage at the "base" of the "T" (this trampoline was fun but not essential). Bare branches that had been suspended on ropes and then tied back (ready to be swung forwards) were visible in the gloom above the half-curtain.
The play needs at least seven actors (plus an Assistant S.M. who "walks on" as an "Executioner"). The use of Masks makes the doubling very easy and satisfactory – see the chapter on Masks in my book *Impro*.
I had intended to write each scene in a different style but the first performance took place three weeks after I began writing, so I was a bit rushed. Traces of this "many styles" approach are still evident in the

play. *Struggle against the emotion. Don't wallow in grief or you will kill the comedy.*

Two quotes that were a source for this play
The Sunday Times, November 1969
On the night of September 23, 1966, a squad of nine Marines were assigned to ambush duty near the hamlet of Xuan Ngoc in the province of Quang Ngai. There had been very little VC activity in the area for months and it should, logically, have been a routine, actionless night. The squad, however, decided to do a little freelance VC suspect hunting in the neighbouring hamlet.

In all they hit ten huts. The general pattern was a severe beating on the husband, roughing up of the wife and terrorizing of the children. In one hut they sat five children on a bunk and surrounded them with a pyre of firewood which they threatened to ignite. In another they prepared a 16-year-old girl for a gang rape. She was loosed, however, when the Corpsman, after examining her loins by flashlight, diagnosed venereal disease. As there was a complete linguistic barrier it was impossible for the villagers to pass on information about the VC, even supposing they had any. The climax of the operation came at the tenth hut. The Corpsman, employing his flashlight again, found the young mother there free from infection. Five of the squad raped her in succession.

The husband, under guard outside the hut, set up such a din that the Marines became rattled. They proceeded to gun down the entire family: husband, sister, wife and two children.

Coming back with their lieutenant next morning the squad attempted to make the carnage look like an engagement with the VC in which civilians "accidentally" got killed. While constructing this scenario they discovered that one of the children, a five-year-old girl, was still alive. One of the marines beat her head in with the butt of his M14. Their cover story was ultimately blown by the recovery of the mother who had been left for dead.

Source: facts filed in Washington in the office of Judge Advocate General. First pieced together in narrative form by Normand Poirier in August 1969 issue of *Esquire* magazine.

The Sunday Times, November 1969

On the evening of 17 November 1966 a five-man US reconnaissance patrol set off on an assignment in the Central Highlands. They stopped briefly at the hamlet of Cat Tuong, in the district of Phu My, and kidnapped a young Vietnamese peasant girl. The original intention was to keep her as a collective concubine for the five-day stint and kill her before returning to base. Four of the GIs raped her on the first day out.

The girl showed signs of illness after this treatment and the squad leader feared that her cough might attract the attention of the VC. This necessitated a change of plan. The girl was disposed of – stabbed to death – after only 24 hours, acquaintance with the patrol.

Source: Court files. Pieced together narrative form by Daniel Lang in a recently published book, *Casualties of War*.

This happens in the play

Scene 1. His Wife helps Headstone to dress as an Executioner.
Scene 2. Three Cripples cripple a fake Cripple.
Scene 3. A Monster claims that she has come to destroy a monster.
Scene 4. A Waif and her Grandfather set out to rescue the last bird.
Scene 5. The Doctor diagnoses Headstone's wounds as the "stigmata".
Scene 6. Granddad and the Waif take Death to the Cathedral.
Scene 7. Death challenges Jesus to a duel.
Scene 8. The Last Bird – an Angel – is rescued from interrogation.
Scene 9. Granddad is shot.
Scene 10. The Executioner tortures his Wife (forgetting that he is at home).
Scene 11. The Monster has an affliction that the Doctor cannot cure.
Scene 12. The Novice Monk cannot protect the Angel.
Scene 13. Death wins a re-match with Jesus.

Scene 14. Jesus heals the Cripple who was broken in Scene 2.
Scene 15. The Waif befriends a worm.
Scene 16. The Family that shelters the Waif is destroyed.
Scene 17. Headstone explains himself to Jesus.
Scene 18. Headstone dies.
Scene 19. Some Executioners meet Jesus and the Waif in Heaven.

1. DAWN

A tremendous chorus from the Bach B-minor Mass welled up as the lights faded.
During the "blackout" Headstone entered and moved centre stage. (No mirror-ball was used for this change.) A wooden chair with clothes draped over it stood near him.
Headstone stood naked except for his black socks (and black underpants if the actor didn't want to be naked). He was in a pool of light that streamed sharply down, shadowing his muscles. We had time to study him. No wounds were visible. (Slowly add more light?)
Begin "matter-of-factly". ("Bore" the audience a little?)
    WIFE *(from off-stage)* Harold!
Headstone made no response. The wife entered with a cup of coffee. Was she afraid that he'd hit her? Was she trying to hide her fear?
    Your coffee is getting cold.
    HEADSTONE *(inarticulate grunt)* Orgf.
She held it for him so he could drink it.
    WIFE Did you go back to sleep? You know how it upsets you when you're late for work.
    HEADSTONE There's still time.
She began dressing him.
    WIFE Did you sleep all right?

HEADSTONE   The pain kept waking me. Those pills are useless. That doctor is useless.

WIFE   You're too old to be out in all weathers. You should have accepted that promotion.

HEADSTONE   Where's the belt?

WIFE (*she fetches it*)   The baby was playing with it.

HEADSTONE   It's not a plaything. She might scratch it.

WIFE   I washed your helmet. I wish you'd put it in to soak. It's so difficult to get the blood out once it's dried. (*Sees lint.*) You've got bits of lint. (*Did she go over him with a lint roller? Or did she mime picking bits of lint off of him? – We didn't see any lint.*) The way this stuff picks up the dust! You'd think they'd use some other material.

HEADSTONE   The colour's traditional.

WIFE   Some other fabric.

HEADSTONE (*unreadable – ominous*)   Some other fabric.

Was there a pause as she continued to dress him?

WIFE   Harold. You know you come home all shaky. Let me phone in and say you're not well.

HEADSTONE   No, no! Some of them may crack this morning.

WIFE   When you joined up they went on about opportunities for foreign travel, they didn't say you'd be …

He had gradually become more frightening. She tried to slide his black gloves onto him gently.

HEADSTONE   Auugghhh!

WIFE (*flinches*)   I'm sorry…

HEADSTONE (*raging inwardly*)   My hands are burning like fire! That doctor said this was psychological! How can this be psychological!

WIFE   He said you need a holiday.

HEADSTONE (*laughs trying to be reasonable*)   I need something.

She had put a black leather "executioner's" helmet onto his head. It exposed only his mouth and chin – the eyes were barely visible. It had a tape dangling at each side of the mouth (see illustration in appendix). He was now a terrifying executioner. He showed both sets of teeth and mouth-breathed audibly.

(*Heavier and coarser voice.*)   Give me a hug.
They hugged gently – but it hurt a wound high up on his side.
   (*Gasps with pain.*)   Ahghh!
   WIFE (*tries to draw away*)   I'm sorry.
   HEADSTONE (*holds on to her*)   It's all right.
   WIFE   We haven't made love for ages.
He released her. She gave him his lunch-box. He was about to leave.
   Your sandwiches. I put in the ointment for your sores. Oh, and bring home a pint of milk.
   HEADSTONE   I'll remember.
   WIFE   Make it a quart. Go careful.
   HEADSTONE (*running to the exit*)   Gerrroonniimmoooo!
He jumped onto the small trampoline, and vanished through the curtains on an upward trajectory like a super-hero. Note (1).
Fade in one of the great choruses from the Bach Mass in B-minor.

2. CRIPPLES

Three happy Bruegel-like Cripples were laughing. Was the second Cripple on crutches? Was the third Cripple in a wheelchair? Or was he kneeling on a little trolley like "Porgy" in Porgy and Bess? *They wore those plastic spectacle frames that have noses and mustaches attached. Paint the noses to remove the gloss. Note (2). Were they in a good mood? Were they drinking? Were they sitting around a "cloth fire"? Note (3) Perhaps not.*
   FIRST CRIPPLE   That was such a party.
   SECOND CRIPPLE   We got one of those kids from the amusement arcade…
   THIRD CRIPPLE   Stuck his legs though the railings, tied his feet to a truck…
Laughter. A fake Cripple using a crutch tried to limp past.
   FIRST CRIPPLE (*loudly*)   Excuse me, Sir.
   FAKE CRIPPLE (*politely*)   I'm sorry?

FIRST CRIPPLE Just a quick word…

FAKE CRIPPLE I'm late for my bus.

FIRST CRIPPLE (*soothingly?*) There'll be another along in ten minutes. No need to distress yourself. (*To the others.*) Watch out! This one'll probably run like a hare!

FAKE CRIPPLE (*indignant*) How can I run with this leg?

FIRST CRIPPLE The thing is, Sir! We have it, on good authority – that sometimes you limp on one leg and sometimes on the other.

FAKE CRIPPLE It's a lie!

SECOND CRIPPLE And sometimes your spine's all twisted, and sometimes it isn't.

FAKE CRIPPLE You're confusing me with someone else!

FIRST CRIPPLE (*brutally*) Are you a cripple!

FAKE CRIPPLE (*outraged*) Of course I'm a cripple! I had ten men at my breaking.

FIRST CRIPPLE Where were you broken then?

FAKE CRIPPLE In Church!

SECOND CRIPPLE What Church?

FAKE CRIPPLE (*gesturing towards it?*) All Saints.

THIRD CRIPPLE Look at him! He's getting more crippled every second. He's trying to convince us. Hold him!

The fake Cripple tried to escape but they seized him. (Did the third Cripple keep muttering, "Yes, that's right! We believe in you! There! There! Yes, that's right! We believe in you…" while stroking him and brushing him and pretending to sooth him?)

FAKE CRIPPLE Let me go! Get your hands off!

The fake Cripple is struggling to get papers from some inner pocket.

I've got certificates!

FIRST Anyone can have certificates!

They snatched the papers from him (if they were printed on light-weight paper and if there was a "cloth fire" we threw them in the "flames" and let them flutter up as he tried to grab them.)

FAKE CRIPPLE Augh! You've no right to stop me!

FIRST CRIPPLE No right! Doesn't every citizen have to be crippled as his parents were crippled? Doesn't each generation have to be broken so as not to outstrip the last! (*To Cripple.*) You coward! You were scared of the breaking! You thought the real cripples wouldn't know the difference!

FAKE CRIPPLE (*struggling towards audience*) I'll go away! I'll run into the audience! Don't break me!

SECOND Smash his face in!

THIRD CRIPPLE Rip his guts out!

FIRST CRIPPLE He's no cripple!

FAKE CRIPPLE (*as they drag him back on-stage?*) Help me! Help me! Auuuggghhhh!

ALL THREE (*chanting*) Smash and wrench and rip and tear!
Break the bones beyond repair!
Make the agony unceasing,
In the cause of proper policing.

As they broke him we heard loud snapping sounds.

THIRD CRIPPLE He'd been better off having it done in Church!

Cripples One, Two and Three exited happily, laughing and singing.

ALL THREE (*song*) Every man is faaaated.
To be educaaaated!
You must be,
Same as me!
That's why we're creaaaated!

Their victim tried to stand but couldn't. He began to crawl away (perhaps down the "upright" of the "T" if more time was needed for costume changes. B-minor Mass.

3. MONSTER

Two Executioners entered at the side of the half-curtain. They were stretching a red or orange sheet between them to conceal whatever was crouching behind it as they edged crabwise to the centre of the half-curtain. They showed both sets of teeth, or just the lower teeth, and breathed audibly (as should all Executioners).

A woman who had entered behind the sheet became visible as the sheet was wrapped around her to become part of her costume. She stood astride a man who lay face upwards on a low bench – his body was up-stage of the curtain and his feet were towards the audience so that all we saw of him were his legs. The woman's legs were hidden in pillow-cases. We seemed to see a seated female giant who had bare hairy male legs. These "legs" had been slid through the curtains together with the bench when the sheet reached the centre. Note (4). This "double figure" should be physically unstable, sometimes needing to be saved from toppling to one side or another, she should be played with exuberance. Double figures don't work unless they're extrovert.

A Bishop entered and stood beside this "double figure". More Executioners arrived as soon as they'd completed their costume-change. They were armed with "airship" balloons that had been painted black. Note (5). They threatened people in the audience, grimacing and growling (don't do this unless you pretend to be terrified of the audience).

> **DOUBLE FIGURE** Headstone! Help me adjust my dress! (*Hissing at the Executioners who are adjusting her costume.*) Careful now! (*Then:*) Stop the music! I said "stop the music!" (*The music stops.*) Can everybody see my legs? (*Ad lib if more time is needed.*)
>
> **JAKE** (*accusing spectators in brutal way*)   Are you thinkin'! Are you using your intellect! (*It's not clear whether they should or shouldn't be.*)
>
> **DOUBLE FIGURE**   Let each common voice be stilled!
>
> **HEADSTONE** (*to a spectator*)   Sit up straight. Get into the "Yes, Sir" attitude!
>
> **SLUD** (*to audience. He was "Number two" to Headstone.*)   Quiet down!
>
> **DOUBLE FIGURE**   Is everyone assembled? Is everyone looking at me?
>
> **EXECUTIONER** (*unexpectedly*)   Silence in the Theatre!

The Bishop in regalia had taken his place to one side of the Double Figure. His staff was a cross – not a crook.

Should we make an example of someone?

BISHOP (*fearing a disembowelling?*)   Perhaps not at this juncture, Madam.

DOUBLE FIGURE (*points into the audience*)   That person rather irks me!

HEADSTONE   Jake!

JAKE (*heavily – to the audience member*)   Do you have a programme? No one gets in here without a programme!

Jake seized the audience member's programme and tore it up. The Executioners guffawed (tear up a "palmed" programme rather than depriving an audience member). Note (6).

EXECUTIONERS   Har! Har! Har! Har! Har! Har! Har! Har!

HEADSTONE   Silence!

DOUBLE FIGURE (*facing the spectators*)   Seal the entrance!

HEADSTONE   Let the doors be closed.

EXECUTIONERS   Let the doors be closed!

Did we hear huge steel doors being slammed all around the auditorium?

HEADSTONE   Anyone who makes a sound
Shall be stamped into the ground.

DOUBLE FIGURE (*begin elegantly*)   My Lords, Princes of the Church, Executioners. Bureaucrats, peasants, insignificant but well-intentioned riff-raff!

The Executioners stared down anyone who seemed likely to respond.

Why, you may ask, have we burst into your little world with our machines, with our military advisers, and with all our marvellous apparatus of war? We come to admire your ancient culture, your museums and traditional ways of life, to visit your noble mountains, to picnic on the banks of your great rivers, to stroll through your secluded valleys, and to refresh our spirits in your fabulous orchards. (*Change gear?*) I, who am childless (due to an unfortunate proclivity to eat my children), seek peace and fulfilment here – but we also come to ally ourselves with you. And to warn!

EXECUTIONERS (*loudly – en masse*)   To warn!

A canvas was unrolled (like a roller blind?) that showed a huge monster that was ripping people to pieces while stamping their houses into rubble.

We have eyes in space that survey each inch of this world. These eyes have detected a beast that will ravage your lands and destroy your children. No family will be untouched by his flame. If this creature is allowed to spawn, all this loveliness – will burn to ashes!

EXECUTIONERS (*en masse*)   Ashes!

DOUBLE FIGURE   Only we, with our machines and military might, have the power to destroy this beast. I am an enchantress of unimaginable power! (*Indicates Executioners.*) These, my executioners, have achieved all that man has ever dreamt. They have stood in the depths of the deepest ocean. They have flown their flag on the airless moon! They can rip out a man's heart and set it beating in the breast of another! They hold sleep in a bottle… (*An Executioner waves a small bottle.*) … and life in a syringe. (*An Executioner brandishes a syringe.*) Here is a pill that kills despair… (*She brandishes a bottle of pills.*)

EXECUTIONERS (*en masse*)   Despair!

She swallowed a pill.

EXECUTIONER (*showing vial*)   Here is a poison so profound,
A trillionth part shall you confound!

EXECUTIONER (*showing vial*)   Here is a plague that breaks your back.
One breath of this your bones will crack.

EXECUTIONER   We have a burning glass in space,
That can incinerate this place!

EXECUTIONER   If our enemy should hide,
At the round earth's furthest side…

HEADSTONE   … Within his flesh his bones we'll burn
So that he shall our lesson learn!

EXECUTIONERS (*en masse*)   We shall be cruel to be kind,
As those that love the beast shall find!

DOUBLE FIGURE (*reassuringly?*)   Thus, with our power, our massive apparatus, military and of thought, we shall destroy this monster. A quick, neat operation, then to depart – like surgeons who remove the cancer and heal the flesh. We are the creators and annihilators of worlds. Those who are less than us – are less than men! (*Savagely?*) Isn't that so, Bishop!

BISHOP (*was he attending?*)   A golden tongue speaks always truth.

Part of the Double Figure's costume became the sheeet again. It was held open to conceal her exit through the centre of the half-curtain (together with the "legs"). The Executioners drew attention by brandishing applause-boards. Note (7).

The Bishop followed the Double Figure off-stage as the sheet was being folded – did he take it with him? (This next section allowed him time to change into Granddad.)

EXECUTIONERS   Applaud! Applaud! Clap, damn you!

EXECUTIONERS   Applaud! Applaud!

SLUD   There will now be a short musical interlude, sponsored as by the Executioners as part of their 'hearts and minds' programme.

Did the Executioners play Beethoven's "Ode to Joy"? Or was it a Sousa march? They used trumpets, tin drums, accordions, flutes, kazoos, tubas, or whatever else they could manage. They enjoyed their music. They hummed, and tapped their feet, and danced lugubriously. They shouted: "No laughing!" "No laughing!" and beat cheeky people in the audience with their long, black-painted balloons. (Only beat people if they laugh while holding eye-contact – and always pretend to be terrified of them.)

Granddad entered, carrying a parcel. He was a half-mask.

JAGGER   And where do you think you're going?

GRANDDAD (*trouble speaking*)   H… H… H…

JAKE   Speak up, Grandpa!

GRANDDAD   H… H… H…

CAUNTER (*mocking the stutter*)   H… H… H…

GRANDDAD   H… Home!

EXECUTIONERS   H… H… Home!

JAGGER   What's in the parcel?

GRANDDAD   A… p… p… p… present!

JAGGER   Open it!

JAKE Open it!

GRANDDAD It's for my G… G… Granddaughter. For her b… b… birthday.

*Laughing and seemingly good-natured, they ripped a teddy bear from the parcel (*choose one with arms that stick out sideways*). They threw it to each other over Granddad's head while he tried to catch it. They shoved or kicked him off-stage amiably and threw the teddy bear after him.*

JAGGER We don't trust you gooks with parcels!

EXECUTIONERS Fuck off G… G… Granddad.

GOUGER And send us that little G… G … Granddaughter! We'd like to f… f… f… fuck her little a… a… a… arse!

EXECUTIONERS (en masse) Anything that is not compulsory is forbidden!

They were laughing as the B-minor Mass faded in.

4. THE LAST BIRD

*Granddad relaxed in his old armchair. He had removed his overcoat. He wore trousers and shirt and waistcoat (*and slippers?*). He wore a half-mask. The Waif was on the floor near him, playing with the teddy bear. She wore a pale blue dress made of a light silky material. She usually wore a flattish hat. She was slight, seemingly prepubescent. She wore a half-mask.*

WAIF (*idly*) Granddad…?

GRANDDAD Yes dear?

WAIF What did you do before you were a night watchman?

GRANDDAD (*remembering with pleasure*) I used to look after the birds in the park. I put nesting boxes for them up in the trees. I built platforms out in the lake for the swans to nest on. People used to be surprised at how many birds there were.

WAIF What was a bird, Granddad?

GRANDDAD (*appalled*) You don't know what a bird was! Have I have lived so long!

WAIF (*pleased that she has galvanized Granddad*) Tell me!

GRANDDAD They were flying things.

WAIF With people in them?

GRANDDAD Oh no, they were alive! And they made noises like this. (*Makes various bird noises.*) You would have liked the birds. At dusk the starlings used to pour into the trees like God emptying his tea leaves.

WAIF Starlings. Were they from the stars?

GRANDDAD No, no... they were corporeal things. There were wrens, sparrows, kingfishers, robins, blue-tits, coal-tits, thrushes, swifts, swallows, the stork, the heron, the passenger pigeon, the great auk, the coot, the moor-hen, the humming bird, the stormy petrel, the fish-eagle, the crow, the chaffinch – there were owls, ostriches, penguins, chickens, turkeys, geese, pullets, partridges, ducks...

WAIF (*excited*) But what were they like, Granddad!

GRANDDAD (*confused?*) Haven't I told you? (*Realizing.*) Ah well, their mouths and noses were all one thing – like this (*Making a "beak" with his hands.*) – and their eyes were on the sides of their heads, and their legs were scaly, and they had feathers – soft as your cheek or stiff to beat the wind with.

WAIF Were their faces always pointed?

GRANDDAD They were all shapes.

WAIF (*excited*) I've seen one!

GRANDDAD No, no, an aeroplane.

WAIF A big white flappy thing!

GRANDDAD (*alerted by the word "flapped"*) Flapped? It flapped? How did it move?

WAIF Like this! (*She does a imitation of an elegant frail bird.*)

GRANDDAD You saw it on television.

WAIF No. It dropped something. Wait! I've got it here somewhere. (*She shows him a white feather.*)

GRANDDAD (*overcome. Ecstatic.*) A feather! A feather! A real feather from a living swan! A swan! A swan! A real feather from a living swan! (*Urgently.*) Where did you see it!

WAIF   In the wilderness.
GRANDDAD   Perhaps it's hurt! Perhaps its wing is broken! A swannnn! A swannnn! A real feather from a living swan! (*Ad lib.*) We must help it. Get your coat on.

He put his own coat and scarf on, and helped the Waif with her coat and scarf (*clothing was usually handed through the curtain by black-covered hands and arms*).

(*New thought.*) There weren't two of them?
WAIF   It was alone.
GRANDDAD   Pity! Pity! (*New thought!*) Bread! They used to eat the bread! (*He speaks with great passion.*) A swan! A swan. A white swan. That I should live to see it! A swan. A real feather from a living swan. A swan! A swan! (*Ad lib.*)

They exited through the audience where Granddad shook hands with people and showed them the feather and cried out the news about the swan estatically.
B-minor Mass.

5. AT THE DOCTOR'S

This scene was played in the area in front of the half-curtain.
The Doctor had a chair on wheels so that he could move without standing up (if he felt the impulse). There was a small table with instruments on it (glue or tie these instruments to the table?). There was a plain wooden chair for Headstone (was it the chair that the clothes were on in Scene 1?). The scene change was effected while Granddad was still shaking hands with audience members and enthusing about the Last Bird.
Headstone had wounds in this scene (none had been visible in Scene 1). This scene began very matter-of-factly.

DOCTOR   And what seems to be the trouble?
HEADSTONE   Sores, Doctor. I wear these gloves to protect them.
DOCTOR   Let's have a look, then.

HEADSTONE If you could just help me slide them off.
Doctor pulled the gloves off. Headstone cried out in pain.
DOCTOR (*reproving*) There, there, a big fellow like you. Humm…!
The Doctor was baffled. Did he get a magnifying glass?
Is this the result of some accident?
Headstone shook his head.
You haven't been scratching them?
HEADSTONE I try not to rub them even.
DOCTOR They seem quite deep.
HEADSTONE (*holds his hands up*) You can see daylight through them. Would this be an infection?
DOCTOR Infection?
HEADSTONE Infection!
DOCTOR Well, it's not syphilis if that's what you mean!
HEADSTONE I saw another doctor. (*Handing him a tube.*) He prescribed this ointment. (*Reluctantly.*) They're on my feet as well.
Headstone groaned as the Doctor removed the boots.
DOCTOR Must be painful.
HEADSTONE It's worst at night when I try to sleep.
DOCTOR Humm… (*Ponders.*) Are these sores anywhere else?
HEADSTONE (*reluctantly*) Well, er… here, Doctor.
DOCTOR Let's see.
Headstone lifts his tunic to show a bloody wound below his ribs (there were no wounds visible in Scene 1).
DOCTOR Thank you. Hummm. (*Ponders for a while.*) Married?
HEADSTONE Seven years. Got a family. Baby girl. Best thing that ever happened to me.
DOCTOR No, er… (*How to put it?*) … marital difficulties?
HEADSTONE (*reluctant*) The sores do make… intimacy… a bit awkward.
DOCTOR (*pauses before taking the plunge*) You know that skin conditions are influenced by states of the mind – Warts for example…
HEADSTONE (*no patience with this*) I'm not an imaginative man, Doctor!

DOCTOR I suppose not. (*Awkwardly.*) What exactly do these sores suggest to you? (*Headstone won't answer.*) In your professional opinion?

HEADSTONE (*reluctantly*) They look like nail-holes.

DOCTOR (*ploughing on*) There are cases of… (*He wonders how to phrase this.*) … practising Christians who have the wounds of Christ …

HEADSTONE (*getting angry*) Wounds of Christ?

DOCTOR The stigmata.

HEADSTONE (*enraged?*) With my profession! Don't I know that a nail will tear out of a man's palm? (*He shows the Doctor a place above the wrist.*) But drive a nail through here and the sinews have to rot first!

Impasse. The Doctor tried a new tack.

DOCTOR Problems at work?

HEADSTONE Oh no. I enjoy being outdoors. Wouldn't want to be cooped up in an office.

DOCTOR What exactly does your work entail?

HEADSTONE (*matter-of-factly*) Usual pacification programme. Flushing gooks out of the forest. Gassing them in the tunnels. Spraying them with fire.

The Doctor made sympathetic noises. Headstone brooded? Sighed? Muttered? Retreated into some terrible "inner space"?

It's the interrogations that get you down, Doctor. There's a certain type of screaming that goes on inside your head for hours. (*Wrenches at head?*) I can hear it now. I'll always hear it.

DOCTOR (*ponders?*) Can't you delegate the work to subordinates?

HEADSTONE (*gasping with pain?*) No! No! They throw them into convulsions. They let them drown in vomit. You know how easy it is to kill a man, Doctor. They don't understand you got to play a man like you play a fish. (*He gradually becomes more frightening, more violent.*) To keep a client alive and yet make him talk before the next shift can get the credit, that's what's so exhausting, Doctor. (*He's becoming insanely violent.*) Some of them are so stubborn you feel like smashing your own head against the wall! It's as if they're torturing *me* ! Auuggghhh! Auuggghhh! (*He slams the Doctor against the wall?*

He overturns the table? Whatever violence he does hurts his own hands.) It's as if they holding out out of sheer blind malice! (*Climax?*) I'm not a Christian! I'm not a spiritual man! So why do I have His Wounds! (*Subsiding? Burned out? Staring at his hands – then roaring in pain and despair.*) Auuggghhh! Auuggghhh!

The Doctor was desperate to calm him.

    DOCTOR (*"stepping on eggs" as he struggles to be professional*) You need a psychologist who can resolve the unconscious conflicts so that you can function without undue stress and anxiety.

    HEADSTONE (*broodingly*)   Perhaps you're right. (*Sighs?*) A man should enjoy his work. (*Brightens up?*) Isn't that the truth, Doctor?

We faded out on this tableau as the B-minor Mass faded in.

6. DEATH

The lighting came from ground level (we masked the ground-level lamps so that they didn't dazzle the audience). Please don't use dry-ice – it's too distracting.

Music continued quietly throughout this scene. (One production used the "Death" section from the B-minor Mass, but I prefer the Ligeti piece that was used as "space" music in the film 2001.)

    GRANDDAD (*as if in a trance*) Granddad did not recognize anything he had known as a child. Arms and legs stuck out of the soil. The ground rose up like an angry sea. Thousands of craters overlapped into the distance. "Is this where you saw it?" said Granddad.

    WAIF   Oh, Granddad – someone's here!

    GRANDDAD   She said.

A traditional Death had entered – in silhouette against the light. (Frank Totino as Death wore "dry-waller" stilts and even wore them during the fight in Scene 6. He wore a skull mask that sat on his head like a helmet. He saw through a scrim in the "neck" of the mask.)

"Perhaps he's seen the Last Bird", thought Granddad. "We're looking for the swan… Have you seen the swan?" he said.

DEATH Don't you recognize me?

GRANDDAD Said the shadowy figure. "My eyes aren't what they were."

WAIF Said Granddad.

DEATH Come closer!

WAIF Said Death!

GRANDDAD Weren't we at school together?

DEATH When the bombs discomforted the children?

WAIF Said Death.

DEATH Come closer.

Waif tried to pull Granddad back, but Granddad was polite.

GRANDDAD "Was it in the mountains?" said Granddad?

DEATH "When the shells scattered the horsemen?" said Death.

GRANDDAD Granddad began to remember the shadowy figure. "You were in the next bed at the hospital!"

WAIF (*frantic, delaying the inevitable*) We were looking for a bird!

DEATH (*taken aback*) A bird? (*Surveying the audience in grim amusement.*) They might as well ask for a flower!

A flower appeared in his hand. He crushed it and a fine dust fell from his fist (use a dried flower).

DEATH pointed a finger at the old man. "Come with me!" he said.

WAIF Don't take my Granddad!

GRANDDAD (*collapsing, dying*) She said.

DEATH Answer me a riddle, said Death, and you can keep him for another hour. (*In a different manner.*) Where is Jesus?

WAIF Er… er… er…

DEATH (*to audience, sure that the Waif doesn't know*) The answer used to be: "In every glass of wine, in every piece of bread."

WAIF (*frantic*) In the Church!

GRANDDAD (*quite dead*) She said.

DEATH (*amazed*) "In the Church!" said Death. (*Peremptorily.*) "Take me there!"

GRANDDAD (*staggering to his feet, aghast*) Oh no! No! Aughgh! No! Don't! You'll break me! You're too heavy! Ugh! Ugh! God help me! I can't! I can't! (*Ad lib.*)
Death climbed onto Granddad's shoulders.
WAIF (*she follows them*) Death climbed onto the old man's shoulders, and the three of them set out towards the Cathedral, the old man gasping and panting, and the girl crying out that Death was too heavy and would crush her Grandfather.
Death's robes hid Granddad's body and made Death (those "Deaths" that didn't wear stilts) seem much taller. The Waif gave inarticulate cries as she followed them off.
The mass in B-minor drowned out the Ligeti.

7. THE CATHEDRAL

Jesus stood on a low box that was against the centre of the half-curtain. He wore a linen loincloth. His arms were in a crucifixion position. (Give his hands something to clutch or the position soon becomes painful.)
The box was large enough for small items to be placed in front of his feet and to provide a surface for Death to sit on later in the scene.
Brother Klausius dusted the pedestal and then Jesus with a feather duster – yellow for visibility. He wore sandals and a monk's habit, plus a plastic bald-head-and-spectacles (see notes). He was short and slight.
Klausius had just been accepted as a novice monk and was still very enthusiastic. He began the scene with a permanent smile achieved by drying the space behind his upper lip and then pushing it to reveal his top teeth. (The lip descended during the scene.)
Bartholomeus entered at the trampoline end – stepping on the little trampoline so that he bobbed – was it a ritual obligation? He was dressed like Klausius with identical bald-head-and-spectacles and with his top-lip dried and pushed up. He was plumper than Klausius.

BART (*unctuous*)   Good day, Brother Klausius.

KLAUSIUS (*respectfully*)   Good day, Brother Bartholomeus.

BART   Settling in, are we?

KLAUSIUS   Yes, indeed, Brother Bartholomeus. It's so peaceful here, away from the cares of the world.

BART   Ah, but you should have seen it in the old days, before the stained glass was put into storage.

KLAUSIUS   One of the Executioners was here earlier. He wanted some holy water for his hands.

BART   How heartening.

KLAUSIUS   Terrible times, Brother Bartholomeus.

BART   Terrible times, Brother Klausius. (*Heartily.*) But God is on the side of the big battalions. (*Realizing how late it is.*) Brother Klausius! The Bishop will be here! We must begin the ceremony!

They performed a ritual. In one production this involved holding those springy shoe-straighteners. They were black, with white crosses painted on them, and they were clacked together at key moments in the ritual. Potato crisps were blessed and "wine" sanctified. The ritual took them to and fro between the audience and Jesus.

At a moment when Bartholomeus was looking away from Jesus, Jesus smiled good naturedly at Klausius, who was startled.

(*Not seeing this.*) Brother Klausius! Is something wrong?

KLAUSIUS (*unable to believe his eyes*)   Er… ah… no …

BART   Proceed with the ritual! Have you forgotten everything that I showed you?

KLAUSIUS   I'm sorry, Brother Bartholomeus. A momentary faintness.

The ritual continued until Klausius saw Jesus moving again.

KLAUSIUS   Augh! Ulp! Hoooo! (*Ad lib.*)

BART (*enraged*)   Brother Klausius!

KLAUSIUS   It moved!

BART   What moved?

KLAUSIUS   The crucifix!

BART   A trick of the light! Many of us have seen it!

KLAUSIUS (*amazed*) You have!

Jesus moved (or made a face?).

Augh! Look! Look!

BART (*still not seeing Jesus*) Brother Klausius! There is no room for hysterics in the church!

KLAUSIUS (*seeing Jesus move again*) There! There!

BART (*grabs Klausius*) Take hold of yourself! Now then! (*Turns Klausius's head forcibly away from Jesus.*) Look carefully! (*Turns Klausius's face back towards Christ.*) See how you are mistaken!

Jesus was now a motionless crucifix again.

KLAUSIUS It was making fun of me.

BART (*furious*) Christ does not make fun! Leave this Church, or continue the service.

Klausius kneels. Bartholomeus lays a crisp on Klausius's tongue and sees Jesus moving.

Augh!

KLAUSIUS (*elated*) There! You saw it too! (*He prays.*)

BART (*crossing himself?*) I saw nothing!

KLAUSIUS You did!

BART (*horrified*) If the Bishop should see this!

KLAUSIUS Hallelujah! Hallelujah! (*Continue ad lib*)

BART (*panic*) He's… He's drinking the wine!

Jesus sipped the "wine" and ate a crisp and then froze in his crucifix position again as the Bishop entered. The Bishop was wearing his robes and carrying his cross and with an identical bald head. Note (8). The Bishop also had his top-lip dried inside and pushed up.

BISHOP (*enraged*) What is the meaning of this hooliganism? Brother Bartholomeus! Brother Klausius! Have you taken leave of your senses!

Jesus had frozen into the crucifix position. The Bishop became aware of the audience and changed tack.

I… I do apologize, ladies and gentlemen, for this unseemly conduct.

Jesus was clowning whenever the Bishop looked away. Bartholomeus tried to stop the Bishop from seeing this.

BART Brother Klausius has succumbed to a fit of religious ecstasy.

KLAUSIUS (*trying to enthuse audience*)   A miracle! A miracle!

BISHOP   How distasteful.

KLAUSIUS   My Lord! The crucifix, it moved!

BISHOP (*to audience? to God?*)   Another Galileo! (*To Klausius.*) Brother Klausius, you are new here! If the crucifix were to move you would not be the first to see it!

BART   I'm sorry he's so overwrought, Bishop. He's done nothing but pray since he came here.

BISHOP   Continue the service!

The Bishop joined the ritual. Jesus fooled about good-naturedly, knocking the Bishop's mitre off, pushing him, etc. The Bishop blamed the monks but finally saw what was happening.

What! Why… Who… who is responsible for this devilry?

BART   Brother Klausius saw it first!

KLAUSIUS   A miracle! A miracle! (*Ad lib.*)

BISHOP (*re: Klausius*)   Stop him praying!

BART   Silence!

KLAUSIUS (*kneeling*)   A miracle!

BART   Hold your tongue!

Bartholomeus slapped Klausius. (*Mime it with Klausius making the sound of the slap?*)

KLAUSIUS   I turn the other cheek.

BART   Very well! (*Slaps him again.*)

Klausius strode about the stage singing "Onward, Christian soldiers" and encouraged the audience to join him (*sometimes they did*). *Note* (9).

BISHOP   This must not be allowed to go beyond the walls of this church. We must… we must… (*Baffled as to what to do.*) We must… We must… (*Looks around him?*) Ah yes!

BART   Your Holiness?

BISHOP   Fetch the hammer! And the nails! (*Urgently.*) Hammer hammer hammer hammer hammer! Quickly now! (*To Jesus.*) And you! You…! Get back up there where you belong! Go on! Making faces! Drinking the wine! You're not wanted here! (*To audience?*) What a catastrophe!

They nailed Jesus back using foam rubber mallets – miming the nails (the hammering sound was made from behind the curtain). Jesus became a crucifix again – accepting this passively.

    KLAUSIUS (*to audience*)   Stop them! Stop them! Help! Help! What are you doing! Stop! Stop! Help! Help!

Klausius ran off to get help but reeled back in horror as he met Death who was on the way in. (Any character who came within a six-foot radius of Death screamed and fell over and kept screaming until he could scrabble away, or until Death moved away.)

    DEATH   Where is Jesus!

They panicked.

    Where is Jesus! Nowhere on Earth can I find him! Is he in the Church that bears his name!

Bartholomeus and the Bishop were too terrified to speak.

    KLAUSIUS (*pointing at Jesus*)   There! On the cross!

Death saw Jesus who was now a statue again.

    DEATH (*triumphant*)   Have I found you at last, my old enemy? All these years locked in a dusty Cathedral!

Death knocked hollowly three times on Jesus's chest. Make the sounds live from off-stage using a microphone? (When we did this scene at a pop-festival near Tübingen Death knocked on Jesus with the microphone that he was holding.)

    This is wood! (*Wheels round.*) Where is Jesus!

    BISHOP (*terrified*)   You… you have no business here!

    DEATH   No? You think that old heart is going to tick away forever!

Bishop clutched his chest.

    (*Demanding an answer from the Bishop.*) Where is Jesus!

    BART (*to divert death from Bishop*)   He had an accident!

    DEATH (*sarcastic? elated?*)   You call that an accident! (*Gestures to Bart's head.*) Why don't I tweak that aneurysm in your brain?

    KLAUSIUS (*running in to distract Death from Bart*)   Get out of God's house! (*He rushes away, screaming in terror.*)

    DEATH (*sitting on the edge of the box that Jesus is standing on, genially*) Can't I be baptized?

ALL Baptized?
DEATH (*making himself comfortable*) Yes! Perhaps I'll take over the organization. Start a few religious wars. (*Terrifyingly.*) Baptize me!
BISHOP (*to Bartholomeus*) Well?
BART (*to Klausius*) Get the holy water!
KLAUSIUS Me!
BART You're reinstated.

Klausius got the holy water and passed it to Bartholomeus who passed it to the Bishop who passed it back to Bartholemeus who passed it back to Klausius. Meanwhile…

BISHOP Er… do you… er… Do you accept the articles of the Christian Church?
DEATH I've killed millions of unbelievers! I think the body is disgusting! Won't that do?

Death stood up, still unbaptized, but growing tired of this game. He prepared to reap the audience.

Enough of this play-acting! Since Jesus is nowhere to be found – why don't I save time by reaping the whole damned lot of you! Augh!

Jesus had put his hands over Death's eyes. Death knew that no mortal would have had the temerity. From now until the end of the fight, Bart and the Bishop screamed whenever they were close to Jesus, just as they did with Death. They are terrified as Death asks questions.

(*Expectantly.*) Who is this?
JESUS (*country accent*) Guess?
DEATH (*it must be someone really interesting*) Er… Buddha?
JESUS No.
DEATH Allah? (*Certain.*) Thor!
JESUS No.
DEATH Um… Krishna?
JESUS No.
DEATH (*triumphant*) Jesus!
JESUS And is that your final answer? (*Or some other cliché from whatever TV quiz or game show is popular at the moment.*)
DEATH We meet again! Let us fight for dominion over this world!

Jesus snapped his fingers and a crimson-coloured silken gown was thrown on-stage from over the half-curtain. He put it on. Packets of potato crisps descended or were thrown in from over the half-curtain. We labelled the bags "Crisps, pass them on".

JESUS   I'm a pacifist!

DEATH   (*astounded*)   You! A pacifist!

JESUS   Turn the other cheek. Do unto others... you know! (*He hands packets of crisps to the audience saying...*) Make sure everyone gets one.

BART   An imposter!

BISHOP   (*outraged*)   Show him the door!

Jesus looked at Bart and the Bishop and they quailed and retreated.

JESUS   Misrepresenting me! Getting me in here just so you could use my name on the notepaper!

DEATH   (*growls impatiently*)   Grrrr! If you won't fight, name a substitute!

JESUS   (*looks around the stage and the audience and the universe – who will he choose*) Um... er... er... er... Him!

ALL   Brother Klausius!

KLAUSIUS   Me!

BISHOP   Ludicrous!

BART   He only started yesterday!

JESUS   Do you volunteer?

BART   (*aghast*)   No!

BISHOP   (*aghast*)   Not I!

JESUS   Then Brother Klausius it is!

Klausius fainted.

Let me touch him!

Klausius, touched by Jesus, jumped up invigorated. Death was practising karate kicks etc. well away from them (near the trampoline).

I'll just have a few words with my second! (*Takes Klausius aside.*) Come out of your corner fighting.

KLAUSIUS   Yes, Lord.

JESUS   Don't let him get you in any clinches! He's a terrible in-fighter.

KLAUSIUS   I'll be careful, Lord.

JESUS (*furtively*)   And take this, you may need it!

KLAUSIUS (*stowing it away*)   A revolver, Lord?

JESUS   Remember, squeeze the trigger: don't jerk it.

DEATH   Well?

JESUS (*giving Klausius the Bishop's cross*)   Seconds out!

1. *Klausius and Death rushed at each other, clashed scythe and cross together (like kendo), and then both rushed away screaming and roaring with terror.*

2. *Death did some kung fu leaps to over-awe Klausius. The scythe and the cross clashed a few times until Klausius found himself straddling the blade which stuck out behind him like a tail. He tried to push it down with the cross while Death jerked him up and down. He managed to roll off of the scythe and lay helpless as Death raised the sythe to stab the blade downwards to impale Klausius.*

JESUS   Break! Break!

3. *Death was furious (sure that Jesus was cheating to aid Klausius). Jesus began to count Klausius out like a boxer while Death pranced about, eager for the kill. Klausius stood up at the count of "nine".*

4. *Klausius swiped downwards at Death and missed. Death stepped on the cross, making it slam to the stage. Death seized it and thrust it horizontally to audience members sitting in the front row who let it lie across their laps.*

DEATH   Hold this!

5. *Klausius ran off-stage, bouncing off of the trampoline like Headstone in Scene 1) and 'flew' out through the full curtain's centre entrance. Death bounced out after him as Klausius re-entered below him. Klausius, raised his arms and took the scythe from Death in mid-flight – Death was holding it horizontally so that it wouldn't have gone through the slit of the curtain anyway. Note (10).*

6. *Death poked his head out of the curtain and was horrified to discover Klausius in possession of the scythe. Bart and the Bishop were cheering Klausius in wild excitement but Klausius was too over-awed to use it. Death advanced on Klausius, holding out his hands for the scythe, willing Klausius to surrender it. Klausius lost his nerve as Death closed in on*

him. *There were shouts and groans from the monks as he tossed the scythe horizontally to Death who caught it and was determined to kill Klausius instantly for such hubris.*

7. *I had Klausius dive into the "moat" that surrounded the "T-stage", with Death trying to reap him each time his head bobbed up, and with Bart and the Bishop screaming each time. (However you achieve this climax, Klausius must seem doomed until the last possible second.) Then Klausius squirted Death with the water-pistol and Death forgot about him, horrified that his scythe blade might rust.*

    DEATH What's this!

    JESUS Holy water!

    DEATH (*berserk*) You squirt me with water-pistols!

He started to dry his scythe – his precious implement.

Jesus took the pistol from Klausius and squirted some water from the pistol into his own mouth.

    JESUS (*to Bishop*) Have you been thinning out the holy water?

    BART We spray it over the bombs and ammunition.

    BISHOP A Bomb, properly blessed, has 2.6 more chance of hitting its target.

    JESUS (*arm round Klausius?*) Well, you couldn't cure a leper with *this*!

    DEATH I do not accept your substitute! (*He hit Jesus in face with a glove.*) I challenge you, Jesus of Nazareth, personally. I will not take part in this circus! (*Stalking out.*)

B-minor Mass.

8. THE WHITE BIRD

Had the branches that were visible behind the half-curtain been untied so that they swung forwards and projected over it? Probably not but if they were they had no apples or leaves (see Scene 15.). Were the Executioners chanting as the Bach faded out:

This is your cock!
This is your gun!
This is to kill
This is for fun!

Did they shout in exhilaration? (Were shadows of running men seen?)
    EXECUTIONERS (*off-stage. Overlapping?*) Look! Look up! The sky! The sky! The bird falling! The white bird! The bird in the sky! (*Ad lib.*) The white bird! The white bird falling! (*They start cheering.*) In the trees! The bushes! The trees! The white bird! The white bird falling! Don't kill it! Capture it! It's valuable! The white bird! The white bird falling! That way! Over here! The white bird! The white bird!
(Use as much of this as you need – it's to give time for costume changes.)
A barefoot female Angel wearing a "paper mask" limped on and knelt centre-stage, facing front. Note (11). We added more light so that when it spread its wings the dark stage would blaze with radiance. Her arms were through shoulder-loops and she was clutching hand-holds in the stiff wire frame of the wings (so that she could flap vigorously). The wings were covered, as was the rest of her costume, with overlapping tongues of white fabric that suggested plumage. (If more time was needed for costume changes she watched a helicopter fly over – "whop-whop-whop".)
She could see very little, except perhaps through invisible pin-holes around the eyes of the paper mask. Most "Angels" performed completely "blind". After all, they only had to enter and then crouch or kneel facing front. From then on they were in the hands of the Executioners.
The shouts grew louder. (Were bodies heard crashing through bushes?) Executioners entered from all sides – not necessarily at the same time. They were torn between exaltation and terror as they approached the Angel.
    EXECUTIONERS Don't get too close! Careful now! Break your leg with one flap of that wing! (*They grabbed it and struggled with it.*) Hold it! Don't let it escape! (*Ad lib.*)
Did they pretend to be holding the Angel down while secretly helping to lift it? Certainly they eventually forced it to kneel and began caressing it, thrusting against it, moaning and gasping (but not copulating with it).

So smooth! Oh God! Feel that! Christ! What an arse! Oh fuck it smells good! Shit! Oh fuck! Oh shit! Fuck! Shit! (*ad lib.*)

Enter Headstone.

> **HEADSTONE** (*enraged*)   Slud! Jagger!
>
> **SLUD**   Sah!
>
> **HEADSTONE**   I'll have those men on jankers! Line them up!
>
> **SLUD** (*dragging them off of the Angel*)   Back! Back! Get back! Get off it! (*Ad lib.*) Get these men in line!
>
> **JAGGER**   Positions! Positions!
>
> **HEADSTONE** (*to Jake who was holding the Angel down*)   Not you! You keep hold of it! Don't let it flap into the air!

The men lined up except for Jake who held the Angel.

> **SLUD**   By the right! Number!
>
> **EXECUTIONER**   Aye!
>
> **EXECUTIONER**   Aye! Aye!
>
> **EXECUTIONER**   Aye! Aye! Aye!
>
> **EXECUTIONER**   Aye Vee!

Etc., depending on how many they are (they're using Roman numerals).

> **HEADSTONE**   Slud?
>
> **SLUD** (*at attention? saluting?*)   We've captured a bird, Sir!
>
> **HEADSTONE** (*sarcastic*)   A bird! You call this a bird?
>
> **EXECUTIONERS** (*various*)   Could have fooled me! Its got feathers! Wot is it, then? (*Ad lib.*)
>
> **HEADSTONE** (*spelling it out as he seethes with rage*) This… is… an… Angel!
>
> **EXECUTIONERS** (*marvelling. Looking at each other.*)   An Angel!
>
> **HEADSTONE**   Can't you smell the odour of sanctity!
>
> **JAKE** (*smelling the scent of the Angel on his own body?*)   Oh yeah!
>
> **CAUNTER**   So that's what it is!
>
> **EXECUTIONERS** (*muttering*)   Yeah! Of course! (*Ad lib.*)
>
> **SLUD**   Silence!

The Executioners stared aghast. Was Headstone about to punish them? They were longing to rub up against the Angel, or against each other, or against audience members, but they didn't dare to.

HEADSTONE   This is Heaven's creature! This is a... living... breathing... creature of *God!* And all you can think to do with it... all that occurs to your warped little minds... is to *fuck* it?

The Executioners looked up, expecting to see God hurling a thunderbolt.

(*Smiling?*) Well done, men!

They laughed and relaxed – happy that Headstone was only teasing them.

JAGGER (*proud*)   One of the practice boulders struck it when we was testin' out the new catapult, Sir.

SLUD (*to quelch Jagger?*)   It was coming in low to dodge the radar.

Headstone pressed his hands into the Angel, hoping it would heal him.

HEADSTONE (*whispers?*)   Why won't you heal me?

CAUNTER (*muttering*)   What's he tryin' to do – tickle it?

SLUD   No talkin' in the ranks! (*Turns on Gouger in rage.*) Are you smiling, Gouger?

GOUGER   No, Sir! It's my grimace.

SLUD   God help you if I see you smile.

HEADSTONE   Does it speak?

CAUNTER   Got a funny-shaped tongue, Sir – more like a bird.

HEADSTONE   See if it sings!

They tried to hurt the Angel but with no effect.

Twist its balls can't you!

CAUNTER (*fumbling under Angel's costume*)   Smooth as a Barbie doll!

HEADSTONE   What's that tied to its ankle?

An Executioner ripped off a card that was tied with ribbon to the Angel's ankle and gave it to Slud.

SLUD (*tearing the envelope to see what's inside*)   It's a birthday card.

He gave the card to Headstone.

HEADSTONE (*contempt*)   "... Many happy returns on your ..."

The Angel struggled – wanting to protect the birthday card. Headstone crushed the card and threw it down.

Hold it still! (*He shouted at the Angel's face as if she were deaf.*) Now then! What's your real message? Speak up! How can we get into Heaven! Is it true the streets are paved with gold? How many battalions does God have? How can we catch St. Peter unawares? Do you understand?

EXECUTIONER   What about the water torture, Sir?

EXECUTIONER   The Swiss roll!

EXECUTIONER   The Turkish delight!

EXECUTIONER   The Swedish polka!

EXECUTIONER   The Australian outback!

The Executioners reacted according to their preference for or dislike of these tortures. Now they looked at Headstone expectantly.

HEADSTONE   Fetch the saw!

The Executioners marvelled at Headstone's audacity.

JAGGER (*affirming the order*)   Move it!

An Executioner went for the saw. Headstone took Slud aside.

HEADSTONE (*admiringly*)   Look at those wings! With wings like those we could fly right up past the sun and be up under the Vestal Virgins' skirts before you could say "knife". (*He says "wings like these" not "those" if the wings are close to him.*)

The Executioner arrived back with a large painted plywood saw – a "clown" saw. Headstone turned back to the Angel.

Do you know what this is? You see how sharp this is? Don't you like flying! Answer me if you know what's good for you! How do we get into Heaven? What is the secret of eternal life! Speak or by God I'll … (*Makes the decision – panting as if needing rest?*) Right then! She's made her choice! (*Gestures to one of the Angel's wings*) Get on with it!

The Executioners were overwhelmed by the terror and daring of the deed. They looked in fear at the sky. Jake mumbles?

(*To Jake.*) Something wrong, Executioner?

JAKE   What will God do?

EXECUTIONERS (*mumbling, en masse*)   Yeah! What will God do!

HEADSTONE   What he always does! (*Threateningly.*) And what might that be?

EXECUTIONERS (*confused – their sentences overlapping*)   We don't know, Sir. We don't remember! (*Ad lib.*)

GOUGER   No one told us!

EXECUTIONER   We haven't been trained!

HEADSTONE   When we shoved those prisoners in the helicopter to give them a flying lesson – what did God do?

EXECUTIONERS   We don't know! What did he do? Search me! (*Ad lib.*)

HEADSTONE   When we threw that surprise party for the Nuns? What did God do?

EXECUTIONERS (*in mental agony*)   We don't know! We don't remember! It's slipped our mind! (*Ad lib.*)

HEADSTONE   When we burned down the orphanage? What did God do?

EXECUTIONER   We don't know! It was an accident! (*Ad lib.*)

SLUD   You'll have to tell us, Sir!

HEADSTONE (*rhetorical*)   What did God do? He did what he always does! (*Make them wait?*) He did fuck all!

EXECUTIONERS (*baffled: then laughing and gloating?*)   That's right! He did fuck all! (*Roaring with laughter.*) He did fuck all!

They scampered about laughing and pointing at the sky.

Strike me! Strike me dead! Strike me first! Strike me! Me! No, me! Me! (*Ad lib.*)

Rude gestures were made towards heaven. But then a loud clap of thunder terrified them (did it flatten some of them?).

HEADSTONE (*after a pause*)   Anyone hear the weather forecast?

JAGGER?   Thunder.

HEADSTONE (*expectant*)   So?

The Executioners looked at each other.

You want B-Company to say we're a bunch of old women? Are you men? Or a pack of schoolgirls?

EXECUTIONERS (*beating their chests*)   We are men! We are men!

GOUGER (*an "aside" to an audience member?*)   B-Company will shit themselves when they hear about this!

Suddenly they were glorying in their power, laughing, having intense pleasure. The Angel faced the audience – as always. Both wings were held wide as they sawed off one wing (did they vocalize the rasping noise?).

The wing was severed. Pieces of red silk were untucked to represent the wounds.

HEADSTONE   Done!

SLUD   Are you prayin', Caunter?

CAUNTER   No Sir, cursing!

HEADSTONE   (*to Angel, triumphant*)   Now do you see how it is here on earth? So how do we get into Heaven? What siege-machines can penetrate those walls? How do we force God to forgive our sins? Answer!

JAGGER   Perhaps it's dumb.

HEADSTONE   (*in rage*)   I'll give it dumb! Saw off… the other wing!

The Executioners hesitated.

For Christ's sake! Give me that! (*He grabs the saw – his hands hurt terribly.*) Augh! Hold her down! Keep her still for me! Stop her struggling, arsehole! Auuugghh! Spread out her wing for me! (*Cries in terrible agony.*) Auuughh! (*Saws.*) Oh fuck! Fuck! Fuck! (*etc.*)

They pressed the Angel down (facing front). I don't think she was struggling. Did they make a rasping noise at each stroke?

EXECUTIONERS   (*in chorus. Solemnly?*)
Let God Almighty hide his face,
And never look upon this place!
Generations yet to come,
By our courage, be struck dumb!

Did they groan erotically – longing to push their faces into the wings and to rub against the Angel?

SLUD   Careful with those wings. Don't besmirch them!

HEADSTONE   Bring them here! Perhaps they'll work on me! If not, I'll give them to the wife to hang over the mantelpiece (*The Executioners laugh. They start putting the wings onto Headstone's arms. Note (12).*) Aaaauuggh! Go careful! I burned my hands rescuing a child from a burning orphanage! (*Deflected rage?*) Put that Angel to everlasting interrogation! And if it won't talk, get it to draw a map!

The Executioner slung the Angel over his shoulders and carried her off. Headstone wore the wings.

HEADSTONE   Perhaps I'll fly up to Heaven and spy out the fortifications! Stand back! (*Bounces on the trampoline.*) Higher! Higher! Higher! Higher! (*Ad lib.*)

EXECS   Higher! Higher! Higher! Higher! (*Ad lib.*)

HEADSTONE   How am I doing?

GOUGER?   Might need practise, Sir.

HEADSTONE (*rage*)   Don't tell me what I need, Executioner! How far am I off the ground?

The Bishop and Klausius entered, plus an Executioner who was carrying the Angel. The Angel was dumped on the stage.

BISHOP (*loudly*)   Headstone! (*Berserk?*) Headstone!

HEADSTONE (*mutters*)   Oh shit!

GOUGER (*mumbles*)   What the fuck does he want?

BISHOP (*trying to be calm*)   What… is the meaning… of this outrage!

HEADSTONE   That Angel was in a free-fire zone.

BISHOP (*enraged? Boggling? Scornful?*)   Free-fire zone! (*Looking around?*) How could any reasonable, sane, no matter how … (*Gives up the attempt to express his outrage.*) Arrrugh!

HEADSTONE   Anything that moves in a free-fire zone is ours to mutilate and kill, Geneva Convention, Article three seven four!

BISHOP   This is a Celestial Being! Angels and other Celestial Beings are under the jurisdiction of the Church, Article Seven, Nine, Six! (*He goes to Headstone to speak personally.*) This Angel was on the way to the Cathedral as an advertisement and fund-raiser.

HEADSTONE   It was delivering a birthday card!

Perhaps an Executioner handed the Bishop the crushed card but he rejected it.

BISHOP   This is our Angel, Headstone! (*Announcing.*) I claim this Angel in the name of the Mother Church!

HEADSTONE   Tough!

Impasse. The Executioners waited for the order to kill the Bishop.

BISHOP (*threateningly*)   Do you want to be excommunicated? Do you want to burn in Hell till the Day of Judgement?

The Executioners groaned in a deep rumbling.

Do you wish us to preach against the atrocities? (*Starting to repeat the sentence.*) Do you want us to …

HEADSTONE (*impotently*) Take your Angel.

The Executioners seethed but Headstone quelled them.

BISHOP (*sarcastic*) Thank you! Thank you so very very much.

HEADSTONE Much good may it do you.

A Monk goes to the Angel. (Add more monks if you have them.)

BISHOP And the wings!

HEADSTONE (*appalled*) Not the wings!

EXECS (*outraged – overlapping?*) No, Sir. It's not right! It's our Angel! We found it! Finder's Keepers…(*Ad lib.*)

BISHOP (*inexorably*) The wings.

HEADSTONE (*desperate?*) Those wings could revolutionize modern warfare!

BISHOP The wings!

HEADSTONE (*crying out in rage and pain*) Arrughh!

BISHOP (*aware that they might tear him to pieces*) Your decision, Headstone? (*He waits for them to give in?*) Very well! (*He raises his cross to God and starts to start to excommunicate them.*) In nomine Christi…

HEADSTONE (*impotently*) Take your wings.

A monk takes the wings. The Executioners seethe.

BISHOP (*smug?*) Thank you. (*Vicious.*) I shall remember this, Headstone! Now then – line your men up in proper order!

SLUD Move it. Hup-two-three-four. Hup-two-three-four! From the right, Number!

The Executioners begin to shout their numbers in Latin as before.

EXECS Aye… Aye aye… Aye aye aye…

HEADSTONE (*interrupting*) All right, that's enough!

BISHOP And now – a short prayer of reconciliation and thanksgiving.

The Executioners bowed their heads reluctantly.

(*Walking up and down the line as if inspecting them.*) We thank ye oh Lord, for sending us this thine Angel, as proof of the spiritual nature of this universe. And we crave your indulgence for these men who have so desecrated thy incomparable gift! Amen.

MONK(S) Amen.

EXECUTIONERS (*grudgingly*) Amen.

BISHOP Your men can carry it to the Cathedral. Have them sing Hymn 666!

JAKE You heard!

EXECUTIONERS (*singing mournfully*) God sits on his throne above,
Blessing all things with his love.
Those who do not praise his name,
Roast in the eternal flame.

Exit in procession, led by the Bishop. Headstone is alone.

HEADSTONE (*finally*) To soar into the sky as if I were a God! (*Pause?*) Shit! Shit!

The branches are hauled back into the shadows. The B-minor Mass.

9. GRANDDAD DIES

There were distant sounds of war – explosions. Machine-gun fire. The Grandfather entered, followed by the Waif.

WAIF Granddad! Granddad! Don't go so fast now!

GRANDDAD (*gasping*) Oh, oh my, oh dear, oh dear. Better rest I suppose. Perhaps he means me to run my old heart out.

WAIF (*looking back*) I can't see him. He's not following us.

GRANDDAD (*looking around*) What a mess they've made! So hard to build things – so easy to trample it all down. (*Looks at audience?*) Who'll bury all these people? (*Looks around.*) Nowhere to hide! We might as well have stayed in that cathedral!

Death leaned over the half-curtain (like a glove puppet?), swung his scythe towards Granddad, and killed him quickly and neatly.

WAIF No, no. I told you where Jesus was! (*Desperate.*) Please!

DEATH I'll give you five minutes to say goodbye!

Death vanished. The Waif and Granddad didn't know what to say.

WAIF (*finally*) Oh Granddad, does it hurt?

GRANDDAD (*in pain but trying not to show it*) I've known worse.

Pause while the Waif wonders what she should do to help.

WAIF (*feeling awkward*) Goodbye then, Granddad.

GRANDDAD Goodbye.

WAIF Oh!

She hugged him.

GRANDDAD There's some money buried to the left of the fireplace. It's all yours now, the house, everything.

WAIF (*hands covering her face?*) Yes. Yes.

GRANDDAD Hide if you hear the soldiers coming.

WAIF (*looks up, wiping her eyes?*) They give me chewing gum.

GRANDDAD No, no, you keep away from them. They do bad things.

WAIF Don't cry, Granddad!

GRANDDAD If I only could have seen the white bird! The bird! The white bird!

WAIF Shall I climb up and see if I can see it?

GRANDDAD Don't leave me.

WAIF Only for a moment. (*Lying.*) I can see it, Granddad! Yes, there it is!

GRANDDAD Is its wing broken? Can it fly?

WAIF It's flying high up.

GRANDDAD Is it coming nearer?

WAIF Yes, can't you hear it? (*She makes bird sounds.*)

GRANDDAD That's not a swan – it's one of the little birds.

WAIF There are little birds, thousands of little birds.

GRANDDAD They've come back! Feed them the bread! Feed them the bread!

She threw fragments of soft bread to the audience (only do this in an intimate theatre and make sure it's fresh). Granddad prodded himself and realized that he was still alive.

WAIF Oh Granddad, are you still alive?

    GRANDDAD Yes. It must be more than five minutes! (*Sudden hope.*) Take my hand!

She helped him up. Did she mime brushing "bits" off of him?

    He's forgotten me! He's forgotten! Well, why not? I'm not so important.

Two Executioners entered. They had bicycle-horns instead of guns.

    JAGGER You there! What are you doing in the free-fire zone?

    GRANDDAD (*stuttering*) We… we were… w… w… we were… f… f… feed… feed…

    JAGGER Speak up, old man!

    GOUGER Look out!

Granddad had reached for inside his coat. Gouger "honked" him dead with a bicycle horn. Granddad died. The Waif shrieked and ran off-stage.

    JAGGER Idiot!

    GOUGER Only a couple of gooks.

    JAGGER Shoot *after* interrogation! Christ, why won't you ever learn?

    GOUGER He was reaching for his gun.

Jagger felt inside Granddad's coat and found a card.

    JAGGER (*scornful*) A gun! (*Reads.*) "My name is Henry Lazarus. I have an impediment in my speech that makes it difficult to speak when I am nervous."

    GOUGER Honest mistake.

Two manic journalist/photographers (Media) entered and photographed Granddad and the Executioners. Did the Executioners pose for them? Or did they beat them away with black-painted balloons? Or both?

    JAGGER Let's find that girl!

They ran out.

The photographers photographed Granddad. Make sure the camera flashes don't dazzle the audience.

    MEDIA 1. See that beggar this morning? His skin was a crust of napalm.

    MEDIA 2. What did you give him?

    MEDIA 1. A fortieth of a second at F-twenty two.

Mass in B-minor.

10. HOME

Did a "baby" sit on a sofa? Could it be operated through a slit in the back of the sofa? If so, don't move the baby for a while – wait until the violence starts.
A skipping rope lay on the floor.
The wife was sweeping the floor. The head of the broom kept falling off, infuriating her. She didn't fix it back on properly – she just jammed the stick into the hole of the broom head with an ineffective piece of newspaper.
Headstone entered.

WIFE Had a hard day?

HEADSTONE (*sitting on sofa*) Terrible. We captured an Angel. (*Relates to baby?*) Who's Daddy's little girl?

WIFE An Angel?

HEADSTONE (*he pushes his helmet up onto his forehead to expose his face*) That Bishop took it away from us. (*To baby – if there is one.*) Coochy coochy coo. (*To audience? Or wife?*) I'd like to burn that Cathedral with him in it.

WIFE A real Angel?

HEADSTONE One of the boulders from the practice catapult caught it.

WIFE That's unusual, isn't it?

HEADSTONE Unusual? (*To audience? To himself?*) I tell her we caught an Angel and she asks if it's unusual!

WIFE Did you remember the milk?

HEADSTONE What milk?

WIFE I asked you to bring some milk home.

HEADSTONE You didn't tell me about any milk.

WIFE (*To audience?*) I did.

HEADSTONE She did not.

WIFE What are we going to have in our tea now?

HEADSTONE Isn't there tinned milk?

WIFE Of course there's tinned milk. It doesn't taste the same.

HEADSTONE (*roars*) For Christ's sake! Tinned milk, cows milk! (*To audience?*) She blames me for everything! (*To wife.*) You think I slog my guts out to come home to this?

WIFE It's not much to ask. I hardly ever ask you to do anything. You're useless round the house.

HEADSTONE You know I can't hold things properly! (*To audience?*) It's like a flame in my hands and feet and my side all the time! (*To wife.*) What do you expect me to do?

WIFE (*to audience.*) I expect you remember the milk when I ask you.

HEADSTONE Shut up about the fucking milk! So you asked me you didn't ask me! I'm sick of your yap! (*To audience.*) She did this to me! She makes this pain in me!

WIFE Harold... don't.

Did the baby start crying and continue crying until the end of the scene (if a baby was in this scene)?

HEADSTONE (*he pulls the helmet over his face*) I'll learn you!

WIFE What are you doing...! Don't!

HEADSTONE (*he's screaming with pain as he attacks her*) Bitch! Fucking bitch!

He tied her wrists with the skipping rope. Then he pushed her knees through the loop made by her arms, and inserted the broom between her knees and elbows. She cried: "Harold! Harold!" "Stop it, Harold" (*Ad lib.*)

I'll show! You! I'll...

WIFE Harry, the baby! Ahhhhh!

HEADSTONE (*sniffing her body?*) You stink of the Beast. Show you how we treat you scum! You don't speak out of turn ever!

WIFE You're hurting me.

He exits and returns with pliers (or did he take them from his pocket?).

The rope's cutting me!

HEADSTONE More than rope will cut!

WIFE What! No, Harold! No!

HEADSTONE (*is he going to rip her teeth out?*) Now call me out for not fetching the milk!

WIFE (*terror – trying to inch forwards*) Harold! It's Thelma! It's me, Thelma! You're not at the office! Harold, you're not at the office! You're home! You're home! You're not on patrol!

He came to his senses. He removed the broomstick from behind her knees.

HEADSTONE (*sitting on sofa? going to face a wall? weeping?*) Forgive me! Forgive me!

She crawled away from him. The B-minor Mass faded in and drowned out the gasps and moans and the crying baby.

INTERVAL

11. VAGINA DENTURA

The auditorium lights cross-faded with the music (as in Scene 1) but this time there was no blackout. The Executioners shuffled on as in scene 3, holding the sheet so that the Double Figure could enter.

DOUBLE FIGURE Headstone, help me adjust my robes. (*Ad lib as necessary while adjusting the costume.*) Tell me now! The monster! – has it spawned?

HEADSTONE No, Ma'am. But its footprints have been found in the Palace Gardens.

DOUBLE FIGURE (*angst?*) In my gardens! (*Rage?*) Have we not cauterized this land with fire?

HEADSTONE Until the smoke blacked out the sky.

DOUBLE FIGURE Have we not seeded every path with death?

HEADSTONE Until more peasants have one leg than two.

DOUBLE FIGURE (*fury?*) They must be feeding it.

HEADSTONE Let's bulldoze all the soil into the sea!

DOUBLE FIGURE Remember the election, Headstone! We'd lose votes!

(*Broods?*) But is there no end to our suffering?

Do they not know we bleed for them with gold?

Each hour's expense would build ten nursery schools!
Each bomb costs more than would an orphanage!
Each plane denies us one more hospital!
(*Demanding an answer.*) Why don't they love us? Headstone! Answer me!

HEADSTONE (*reluctantly*) Madam – they say the beast is us.

DOUBLE FIGURE (*screams on one long breath? Then, coldly.*) Headstone, I shall remember this.

An Executioner thrusts the Doctor, and then his bag, on stage.

EXECUTIONER (*oafishly*) We've found the doctor, Ma'am!

DOCTOR (*enraged*) You drag me out of an operating theatre…(*sees Double Figure.*)

An Executioner pushed a small low tea-trolley onto the stage.

DOUBLE FIGURE (*politely*) So gratifying that you were able to join us, Doctor. (*Making conversation.*) A touch of autumn in the air.

DOCTOR (*recovering – finally*) Yes, the… er… the herbicides.

DOUBLE FIGURE It's autumn all year round I'm afraid. Such a poetic season. Tea?

The Doctor was handed a cup of tea (*by the Executioner*).

DOCTOR You've read my report on the women who give birth to monsters? Is that why you sent for me?

DOUBLE FIGURE Ah… No.

DOCTOR Was it about the lack of hospital beds?

DOUBLE FIGURE No.

DOCTOR The use of glass in the cluster bombs so that the shrapnel doesn't show up on the X-ray plates?

DOUBLE FIGURE (*rage*) Contain yourself! (*Icy self-control.*) One would have thought you were beyond romantic notions as to the nature of war! (*Sweetly.*) More tea? No? (*To Headstone imperiously.*) Leave us! (*To the Doctor, discreetly?*) I have an ailment of a personal nature. This letter will explain.

Headstone – and any other Executioners – exited with the tea things.

DOCTOR (*reading the letter*) You want a gynaecological examination?

DOUBLE FIGURE Certainly.

DOCTOR But this note is from a dentist!

DOUBLE FIGURE Yes! There's a tooth in it! Tooth, teeth – it's so humiliating. I have to gnaw on broomsticks!

DOCTOR A rare affliction, Ma'am.

DOUBLE FIGURE It's so embarrassing.

DOCTOR Er... very well, Madam. (*Gives a notebook and pencil to an audience member, ad libbing if necessary. Note (13).*). I wonder if you would be so kind as to take notes for me? Thank you. (*To Double Figure.*) Er... open wide...

The legs splayed outwards. The Doctor crouched between them, masking what he was doing as he groped. (No visual obscenity.)

DOCTOR Upper two, occlusal... (*To audience member.*) Are you getting this down? (*Spells it out.*) O.C.C.L.U.S.A.L. Right molar... Augh!

DOUBLE FIGURE What is it, Doctor?

DOCTOR (*Shows spatula. To "note-taker"?*) It's bitten the end off my spatula! If you could just relax, Ma'am ... (*Explores again.*) Hum... There does seem...

DOUBLE FIGURE Have you found something?

DOCTOR (*brandishes a button held with serving tongs*) It's a button!

DOUBLE FIGURE It bites them off the upholstery, Doctor. Once it had all the foam rubber out of a cinema seat.

DOCTOR (*to the "note-taker"*) Make a note of that. (*Probes again.*) Breathe, Madam... Breathe... Try to relax... (*Soothingly.*) There we goooo... (*Probes – then screams.*) Arruugh! (*His hand is bleeding.*) It bit me!

DOUBLE FIGURE Is it serious, Doctor?

The Doctor crawled – dragged himself – slowly away down the stem of the "T".

DOCTOR (*gasping*) My own fault. Should have realized... Augh! Just need a few stitches...

DOUBLE FIGURE (*anger*) I mean my own condition! (*Increasingly frantic.*) I'm beautiful! I'm intelligent! My wealth increases faster than anyone can count! My powers are infinite. And yet I have this thing in me that won't be satisfied! The Palace is full of my discarded lovers. Screaming young men bleed to death in every corner! Can't you hear them, Doctor? Why should I care about women who give birth to monsters when I do such terrible things to my own poor boys? (*Start to fade lights on her but perhaps keep them on the Doctor as he crawls in agony to exit over the trampoline.*) Why should I care about women who give birth to monsters when I do such terrible things to my own poor boys? (*Repeat if necessary. Perhaps scream it until the sound is swamped out by the Bach?*)

The Executioners helped her to leave (as in Scene 3). Maybe she was shouting over the top of the sheet. I've never tried adding the sounds of discarded lovers moaning towards the end of this speech, but I think Xenakis composed a piece that had a chorus screaming – perhaps one could use that? Something I've never tried is to have her fall in half at the end of this speech and scream until the Executioners reassembled her as the lights fade. If I direct this play again I might see if this works.

The B-minor Mass began to fade in towards the end of the speech.

12. ANGEL

The wings were hung on the half-curtain to either side of the centre opening. A "chart" entitled "Map of the Angel" had been unrolled (perhaps identical in size to the "beast" chart in Scene 3?). It showed the outline of the Angel, perhaps made by drawing around its outline.

Jake (and another Executioner?) stood guard in front of the half-curtain. Jake was gruff, large and often ponderous. He enjoyed life. He was a "rough diamond", a simple, seemingly good-natured fellow. He spoke in an uncultured country accent.

Many of his lines could be directed at the audience – "You're Brother Klausius" could become "He's Brother Klausius." "Christ knew you had the guts" could become "Christ knew he had the guts!" And so on.

Klausius approached him. Start this scene low-key.

    KLAUSIUS Please, Sir, this part of the Cathedral's closed –
No visitors allowed till ten o'clock.
I'll be in trouble if they find you here…

    JAKE (*from the side of his mouth.*) You'll be in trouble if you don't fuck off!

Klausius was perplexed. He decided to try again.

    KLAUSIUS Forgive me, Sir – the Bishop ordered it…

    JAKE (*toying with him*) Who's goin' to make me then? A runt like you? Don't make me laugh!

    KLAUSIUS (*apologetically.*) Well, yesterday I went two rounds with Death.

    JAKE (*enthused*) I've heard of you! You're Brother Klausius!
Well done, my lad! I have to shake your hand!
By all accounts you beat him fair and square!
Well done! Well done!

He shook hands with Klausius admiringly.

(*Genial.*) How long you been a monk?

    KLAUSIUS Since yesterday.

    JAKE You'll be promoted then!

Klausius shook his head.

Of course you will!

    KLAUSIUS (*apologetically.*) I'm just a novice here.
They think Christ should have chosen one of them.

    JAKE (*amused*) Those jealous bastards would've shat themselves!
He knew you had the guts! (*Confidentially.*) So why'm I here?
My job's to see the Doctor's not disturbed.
(*Indicates the half-curtain.*) He's back there wiv' her now!

    KLAUSIUS (*overjoyed*) Then God be praised!
I thought she'd bleed to death without her wings.

    JAKE (*ponderously.*) Do you not know an Angel cannot die,
Being a thing created outside time?
(*Aside.*) He's wasted here! (*To Klausius.*) You should enlist wiv' us!
We're rock-stars when we wear this uniform!

And in a war
The rules of civilized behaviour
Don't mean Jack Shit!
(*Refers to audience.*) Well, even they know that!
(*Clinching the argument.*) And when you're pensioned off
You'd have enough to buy yourself a pub!

KLAUSIUS   I hate the world!

JAKE (*taken aback. Pauses?*)   Ah well, you've suffered then.

Klausius retreated into himself while Jake pondered.

(*Confiding.*) See where I slit my wrist!
It hurt too much to do the other one.
I lay there in the dark and would have died
Had not my friend stepped in the blood! But now
I've learned that pain and pleasure co-exist
That nothing cancels out! And all that's here
Is here to be enjoyed!
Like dancing to accordions! And songs
That tear your heart out! And the comradeship
Around the fires at night. (*Thinks a moment?*) Might you be gay?

KLAUSIUS   Oh no.

JAKE   I am. (*Pleased with himself.*) Well on and off I am.
(*He pulls forward the top of his trousers.*)
See that? A bullet went in there!
By Christ that hurt!
Gave me two arse-holes till they stitched me up!
But guess what I want for my epitaph?
(*Waits to see if Klausius will respond?*)
Not "Rest In Peace"… (*Triumphant?*) … but "Thanks for Everything!"

Did they brood?

KLAUSIUS (*finally?*)   I'm not like you.

JAKE (*philosophically.*)   Well, different upbringin'!

The Doctor looked through the gap in the half-curtain (or over the half-curtain?)

DOCTOR (*to Jake*)   I need your help again. (*To Klausius.*) Respect our privacy.

JAKE (*gruff but friendly*)   You best stay out!

Jake and Doctor go behind the half-curtain. Did we hear drilling and tearing sounds? Was Klausius tempted to look?

WAIF (*just off-stage*)   Jesus! Jesus!

She ran on-stage, distraught.

KLAUSIUS   What's happened, child? Has someone been unkind?

WAIF   Can Jesus bring my Granddad back to life?

KLAUSIUS   He could if he were here!

WAIF   So where's he gone?

KLAUSIUS   To see the world.

WAIF (*devastated?*)   So now I'm all alone!

Klausius comforted her. Did he dry her tears?

KLAUSIUS   Just like myself.

WAIF   Can you look after me?

KLAUSIUS   I'm just a monk! (*Inspiration.*) Come back at ten o'clock. (*Kisses her forehead?*) We'll ask the Angel for a miracle.

Jake and/or the Doctor pulled the curtain aside to reveal the Angel. It was strapped to a tilted and wheeled platform (its feet toward the audience). The torso of the Angel was fake – the centre of the actor's body being below the surface of the platform. Note (14).

WAIF (*awestruck*)   The Last Bird! Look!

KLAUSIUS (*shakes head and whispers to her*)   A bird's an earthly thing. This is an Angel sent from paradise.

WAIF   They're *hurt*ing it!

The Angel was wheeled forwards (unless opening the half-curtain was sufficient).

JAKE (*indicating the Doctor*)   The Doctor needs more light!

WAIF (*whispers to Klausius*)   They're hurting it!

KLAUSIUS (*whispers to her?*)   Oh no, they're experts here.

WAIF (*pulling at Klausius?*)   They're hurting it.

Was Jake (and/or the Doctor) tightening the Angel's straps?

JAKE (*quietly*)   The girl don't need to see this – take her out.

Fade in horror music?
> WAIF They're hurting it!
> KLAUSIUS (*perturbed*) What's happening here!
> JAKE The Bishop ordered it!

He held a cable and looked for somewhere to plug it in. Klausius followed him.
> KLAUSIUS (*outraged*) A wounded Angel needing care and love! God's messenger!
> DOCTOR Go tell the Bishop then!

Jake plugged the cable into a power-point that was some way away from the Angel. It powered a chainsaw (minus the chain) that the Doctor had taken from his bag. The Doctor tested it. When the chainsaw was used we wavered the lights as if the system was being overloaded.
> KLAUSIUS (*re: chainsaw*) You stay away from her!

Did Klausius wrestle with the Doctor for the chainsaw?
> DOCTOR (*to Jake*) Remove this fool.
> KLAUSIUS He can't do that!
> JAKE 'Oo sez he can't?

Jake grabbed Klausius and put a hand over his mouth or held him in a headlock.

The Doctor started the chainsaw and was about to slice open the Angel (was he now wearing surgical gloves and mask?).
> WAIF They're hurting it!

She ran out screaming "Jesus! Jesus!"
> DOCTOR (*to Headstone*) You're paid to see that no one interferes!

Klausius broke loose from Jake's grasp.
> KLAUSIUS (*to audience*) Help! Help!

He ran offstage. An Executioner pursued him (if there was one on-stage).
> (*Off-stage.*) Demons in the Church! Demons in the church! My Lord! My Lord! (*Ad lib.*)

The Doctor recovered his composure.
> DOCTOR (*to audience – reassuringly*) What seems like pain is only reflexes.

JAKE (*aside*) But just in case – he's cut 'er vocal cords. (*To a woman in the front row?*) Best close your eyes, my dear. Last Angel that we had was full of pus!

The Doctor "sawed" the Angel's fake (and velcroed) torso from throat to groin. A line of red silk pushed out to represent blood. The Angel accepted this passively (rather passively?). If there were extra Executioners on stage during this scene I'd crowd them around to partially obscure the view while they made interested sounds.

Were hooks on elastic cords (bungee cords) used to hold open the slit and reveal internal organs made of stuffed cloth or plastic?

(*Chatting to pass the time?*)

I studied Science to know the Mind of God.

But then I could not pray.

JAKE Why might that be?

DOCTOR (*chuckles*) I was afraid that he might notice me.

JAKE Look out!

Klausius swung back in, Tarzan-like, and grabbed the chainsaw. (Or he ran in and grabbed it, or crept in concealed behind a sheet, as in Scene 3 – insert a rod so that the sheet can stretch wide even when only one person is holding it?) Or he could leap in over the half-curtain, holding its rail for support, or he could push the half-curtain down and step in over it if it was suspended from a long "bungee cord".

Jake chased Klausius who switched on the chainsaw and became the pursuer. Did it pull him about until he got it under control?

Bartholomeus entered.

BART (*appalled*) Dear God in Heav'n!

They stopped, they were all gasping for breath. (Hold this tableau?)

Klausius switched off the chainsaw (or did someone unplug the cable? Either way he still kept hold of it, guarding the Angel).

KLAUSIUS Look what he's done to her!

BART Put that thing down! (*Apologizing to Doctor.*) He's just a novice here!

KLAUSIUS He's got to stitch her up!

BART Are you quite mad!

KLAUSIUS (*still with the chainsaw?*) You keep away!

BART Do you not know why God created us?

To punish Angels! And we're good at it!

JAKE (*ponderously – trying to help*) Compared to Hell Earth is a Paradise!

Therefore we say that God is merciful!

KLAUSIUS (*aghast*) Then Jesus is not God!

Jake grabbed Klausius. Was there a slight rumble of thunder?

JAKE (*ominous*) 'Oo is he then?

KLAUSIUS The enemy of God!

Was there thunder and lightning?

JAKE You watch your mouth.

He gave Klausius a savage beating (with an "airship" balloon that had been painted black?).

BART The Bishop must be told!

KLAUSIUS (*collapsing*) Christ suffered more!

Bartholomeus ran off-stage shouting "My lord! My lord!" Klausius lay unconscious.

JAKE (*aside – with regret*) I liked this little Monk, (*sniffs?*) but once I start,

I've no more choice than has a bayonet!

DOCTOR Oh let's get on.

They yanked out the Angel's internal organs. The Doctor pressed them against the chart and drew around them? (Or printed them with their own blood?)

The Bishop entered through the audience, accompanied by Bart. He seemed in an excellent mood. Was he shaking hands with audience members like a politician?

BISHOP Good morning, Admir'l, good to see you here.

And you, Lord Mayor, fond greetings to your wife.

Congratulations, Judge, keep sending them to jail!

(*To Bart, quietly.*) Where is this monk?

JAKE (*quietly*) He's over here, my lord.

Bart showed the unconscious Klausius.

BISHOP (*quietly*)   A heretic! What shall we do with him?
BART (*quietly?*)   Burn him alive? It's good publicity!
And keeps the rest in line.
BISHOP (*shakes head*)   We have to be God's Sheep – until the pendulum
Swings back!
(*To Jake – re: Klausius.*) Remove his robes and throw him in the street!
(*To Bart.*) Then add his name to those who'll burn in Hell!
(*To audience?*) Salvation lies through us!
(*To an Arab or Jewish audience member?*) And only us!
JAKE (*hesitates*)   My lord! He's very young.
BISHOP   They are the worst!
(*To audience?*) The gift of knuckling under comes with age.
JAKE (*distraught*)   My lord, he was the champion of Christ!
BISHOP (*furious at being resisted?*)   A cardboard Christ!
BART (*threateningly*)   A false disciple too?
JAKE (*caving in. kowtowing?*)   My lords – I was deceived.
BISHOP (*after a pause?*)   Well then? Obey!

The Executioner and Jake removed Klausius's habit. Klausius's "loincloth" was like Jesus's. Did he groan, or try to sing a feeble "Onward, Christian soldiers" as they carried him off-stage?

The Bishop approached the Doctor.

BISHOP (*urbanely? Quietly?*)   Well, Doctor, what conclusion have you reached?
(*Re: the Angel, hopefully.*) Is this the proof the Red Sea turned to wine,
And sheep in Bethlehem sang madrigals?

Had the Doctor removed his medical mask and gloves?

DOCTOR   Just one more species to be catalogued.

The Doctor and Jake pushed the Angel back behind the half-curtain which they then closed.

BISHOP (*still hopeful*)   It was the same when Jesus walked the earth
Yet as he floated up into the Heav'ns
His flesh transformed to less offensive stuff.

(*To audience, briskly.*) But now my news! Last night, at 3 a.m.,
Almighty God exposed his rear to me,
Just as he did to Moses long ago
On Sinai: "Strap on those wings!" he said,
"And fly to Heav'n to help the Saints compose
Ten *new* commandments for this Modern Age!"

Applause signs are held up by the Monk?
(*To Doctor, challengingly.*) If that's a dream all revelation's false!

DOCTOR Perhaps.

Did he now exit behind the half-curtain?
Bart was unhooking the wings from the curtains.

WAIF (*off-stage – closer*)   Let me go! (*Ad lib?*) Stop it! (*As she enters.*) Jesus! Jesus!

Jake and Bart dragged in the struggling Waif.

BISHOP Who is this child!

JAKE She made herself a bed between the pews.

BART (*dishevelled? Panting*)   She ate the wafers, and she drank the wine.

JAKE She pinned this drawin' up!

BISHOP Well, give it here!

WAIF (*not drunk*)   I drew my Granddad! Some men murdered him!

BISHOP (*matter-of-factly*)   Tell me their names! We'll break them on the wheel!

WAIF (*not drunk*)   The Executioners!

Consternation. The Bishop is appalled.

BISHOP Not murdered, child!
(*To audience?*) For those who take up arms against the beast
(No matter what misfortunes may ensue)
Are never murderers! (*To Waif.*) Say rather "slain"
Or "handled robustly".

WAIF He's still dead though!

Did the Bishop give the drawing to Bart who screwed it up? Were the wings being put onto the Bishop about here?

BISHOP (*irritated*) She can't stay here! The orphanage burned down! (*To Waif.*) Wait over there!
(*Flapping his wings a little.*) We'll let you light a candle later on (*Quietly to Bart.*) And then get rid of her!

Two or more photo-journalists (Media) rushed in. They vied for the Bishop's attention. They took photos – taking care not to dazzle the audience. They could wear similar hats, raincoats, and "men" masks.

MEDIA (*wanting to take a photo*) Please look this way, my lord!

MEDIA (*another photographer*) Please spread the wings, my lord!

MEDIA Will God help us destroy the beast, my lord?

BISHOP This is a war impossible to lose.

MEDIA Will there be universal censorship?

BISHOP The Church must save men from their baser selves. (*To the audience.*) What use is knowledge if men won't be good?

MEDIA My lord! When Christ was born the earth was flat, But now which way is up?

BISHOP (*points up*) That way is up
Because God tells us so!

He flapped up about a foot and then landed again. Cameras flashed. (In the first production we hoisted him straight up with a block and tackle.)

BART (*to Media*) No further questions – take your place outside.

BISHOP I'll circle low for the photographers
Then soar aloft to give God my advice!
So – chocks away!*

MEDIA My lord! My lord! This way, my lord! Give us a smile, my lord!

There was ecstatic music from the Bach B-minor Mass as the Bishop flew off-stage with Media shouting "My lord!" "My lord!" . Note (15).

MEDIA (*leaving*) My lord! Was Jesus gay?

BART (*leaving*) The Bible has the facts!

MEDIA (*leaving*) You saw the arse of God – hairy or smooth?

BART (*leaving*) That's classified.

---

* Chocks were wedges placed under the wheels: see Battle of Britain Spitfire movies.

Cheers came from off-stage (and the Hallelujah chorus?). The Waif was alone on-stage. Did she carefully unwrap the screwed-up drawing?
Jesus entered quietly and put his hands over her eyes.

    JESUS Guess who!

    WAIF (*instantly*) Jesus! (*She pulled the curtain open to show the Angel.*) Oh Jesus! Look!

    JESUS Yes. God teaches them to fly by throwing them over the edge of Heaven. This one didn't open its wings in time.

    WAIF Can you bring Granddad back to life?

Jesus suddenly had a camera.

    JESUS (*taking her picture*) Smile please.

    WAIF I'll put you in my prayers!

Jesus tucks the camera away.

    JESUS And will that help?

    WAIF Of course! If I believe in you!

    JESUS (*laughs*) I don't have long.

    WAIF I'll take you there! Come on!

The lights faded out and the Bach faded in as they were leaving.

13. RE-MATCH

Muted sounds of war were heard. We turned individual lights up and down at the start of the scene to suggest flares. Granddad lay dead. Other corpses lay face down – the skull masks that they wore were hidden.
Jesus and the Waif entered.

    WAIF Walk in my footsteps.

    JESUS What for?

    WAIF Because of the mines.

    JESUS Is it all like this?

The Waif sees Granddad.

    WAIF Oh Granddad!

If Granddad was slow changing costume (from the Bishop) we added an explosion and he threw himself on-stage – as if hurled there. But I've allowed more time in this version. Note (16).

    JESUS (*reluctant*) Make sure no one sees, or they'll all want it. Rise up, Granddad.

    WAIF He's not moving.

    JESUS I'm a bit rusty. Granddad! Rise up! Hear me!

Granddad stirred.

    JESUS Done it.

    WAIF (*happy*) Ohhhh!

    GRANDDAD I had such a dream…

    WAIF Jesus brought you back to life.

    GRANDDAD Oh! Thank you, thank you! We have to get home before the soldiers find us. (*To Jesus*) Would you like to come in for a cup of tea?

    WAIF The men bulldozed our house!

    GRANDDAD But winter's coming.

Granddad was appalled. Death entered – enjoying himself. (In this scene he usually entered in some unexpected way.) Note (17).

    DEATH Death isn't just going to sleep, old man. It's rocks, sticks, stones, trees, loved ones – gone forever.

    JESUS Now look here!

Death exited after killing Granddad (scything Granddad?).

    WAIF Do something. Poor Granddad!

    JESUS Rise up, Granddad! Rise up!

    WAIF (*pulling open one of Granddad's eyelids?*) He's still in there.

    GRANDDAD (*reviving. Staring around.*) Augh! That was t-t-terrible!

Death re-entered and killed Granddad again.

    WAIF Look out!

    JESUS (*to Death*) That's enough now!

Death swept out.

    (*Mops brow?*) Come back into the flesh! Granddad! Rise up!

    GRANDDAD Augh! Oh… augh!

WAIF (*hugging Granddad*) Oh Granddad, let's go far away from here.

GRANDDAD W-where am I?

Death entered.

JESUS (*to Death*) I won't have this man killed and resurrected like a yoyo!

DEATH Try squirting me with Holy Water then!

Death snapped his fingers – Granddad died again.

JESUS (*he blows into Granddad's thumb*) That should do it!

GRANDDAD (*reviving*) Augh!

Granddad died – Death had stayed on to "snap" him dead again.

JESUS Why don't you give up!

DEATH I never give up!

JESUS (*furious?*) I am the resurrection and the life!

DEATH (*leaving*) That was then! This is now!

Death exited.

JESUS Rise up, Granddad! (*To audience.*) If everyone could try to add to my spiritual energy instead of looking in your programmes to see who's playing me, we might get somewhere. Rise up, Granddad! All together now! Rise up, Granddad!

WAIF He's not moving.

JESUS (*To audience*) Are you concentrating? All together then! One… two… three… Rise up, Granddad! (*Ad libs as he encourages the audience to join in.*) Rise up, Granddad!

GRANDDAD (*confused*) Augh! I was… Augh… No… Augh… Please…

WAIF Granddad! It's me! (*Showing him the teddy bear.*) Look! It's Teddy!

GRANDDAD You're the little girl that I r… rescued from the b… burning orphanage.

WAIF (*pleased that he recognized her*) Yes! Yes!

Death entered.

We don't want you here! You are cruel!

She threw the teddy bear at him. He stabbed it to the stage with a knife.

    DEATH I am kind!

He "snapped" Granddad to death and sat at ease on the edge of the T-shaped stage.

    WAIF Oh Granddad!

    JESUS Hold this!

He gave the Waif a plasma bottle to hold.

    DEATH (*shows a bullet to audience member*)   This bullet! This bullet made a mother die of grief!

Jesus honked a bicycle horn, or blew a toy trumpet (not near Granddad's ear).

    GRANDDAD (*groaning*)   Augh! I though it was last trump!

    WAIF (*whispers*)   You're hurting him.

    DEATH (*shows another bullet*)   You see this one? This bullet turned the father into stone.

    GRANDDAD Augh! No! No!

Death snapped his fingers to kill Granddad.

    JESUS (*to Waif*)   Just hold that plasma bottle high.

    DEATH (*showing bullet*)   This little darling ate a family's wealth.

Jesus thumped Granddad's chest.

    WAIF (*whispers*)   You're hurting him!

    JESUS (*panting?*)   Just trying to get his heart started.

    DEATH (*shows a bullet*)   And this one put a sister on the streets.

    GRANDDAD (*trying to crawl away*)   Leave me alone! I've had enough! I'm t… t… too tired! Let me be!

Death 'snapped' Granddad dead, and homed in on someone in the audience — perhaps someone who's name he already knew.

    DEATH Stephan isn't it? Yes, Stephan. I thought…(*muttering as he searches through a small notebook.*)

    WAIF (*to Jesus*)   Stop it! Stop it!

    JESUS What's wrong?

    WAIF I don't want him back!

    JESUS You don't want him back!

    DEATH (*finding Stephan's name in the notebook*)   Ah yes, Stephan! I have an appointment with you in Samarkand! Better book your flight!

JESUS (*sudden inspiration*) What was he interested in?

WAIF Birds.

Jesus snapped his finders and we heard a magnificent "dawn chorus". Death watched sardonically.

JESUS Rise up, Granddad.

WAIF It hurts him too much!

Granddad revived.

GRANDDAD Let me go!

WAIF Listen, Granddad! Is it birds?

GRANDDAD Oh yes! They always sang when the dawn came. M-m-messy things they were.

A bird lowered from above landed on Jesus's hand (it was a herring gull made of folded newsprint in the first production). Note (18).

WAIF Look, Granddad.

GRANDDAD I'm blind!

JESUS Let me touch him! (*He touches Granddad's eyes.*)

GRANDDAD No, no. I've seen enough.

WAIF There's a message tied to its leg! (*A strip of paper – not a birthday card*)

JESUS (*reading*) "Many happy returns on your birthday". It should have come yesterday.

WAIF (*altered?*) So God didn't forget me!

The bird ascended. Did Death applaud mockingly?

GRANDDAD Pl... Please don't k... k... keep me here.

WAIF Oh Granddad! Don't leave me!

DEATH (*like a polite sportsman*) Mine, I think.

Death carried Granddad off-stage, the plasma bottle bumped along behind them. On the way Death said "Up!" or snapped his fingers and the corpses "zombied" after him revealing their skull masks for the first time. (Were they bowing to the audience as they exited backwards?) Jesus collected his "apparatus" and wandered glumly away.

WAIF (*to Jesus*) Thank you for trying.

She covers the teddy bear with dead leaves.

People without eyelids. Burned men who can't lie down. People who burst into flame if they lift their arms out of the water. Forests without leaves. Elephants on crutches.

Headstone was watching her from over the top of the half-curtain.

HEADSTONE You there! Don't move or you'll be blown to pieces!

WAIF No I won't. I step in other people's footprints.

HEADSTONE (*entering?*) Well you'd better step in them back the way you came!

WAIF (*shows him the feather*) We were looking for the last bird.

HEADSTONE A bird? (*Taking the feather.*) Ah yes. (*He touches himself with it – no effect.*)

WAIF You can keep it.

HEADSTONE My little girl will be as big as you one day. You like chocolate? Catch! (*He tosses her some chocolate.*) Go on home now. Your parents must be worried.

WAIF (*kneeling by Granddad?*) They bulldozed our house. Jesus was trying to raise my Granddad from the dead.

HEADSTONE It's a lot to ask. (*Galvanized.*) Jesus was here?

WAIF (*urgently*) Can I help look after your little girl?

HEADSTONE Why you?

WAIF Because I'm special.

HEADSTONE You're not special.

The Waif ran a little distance and jumped up and down, cramming chocolate into her mouth. Headstone threw himself flat.

HEADSTONE (*frightened*) What the fuck you doing! Ahhhhhhhh!

She stopped jumping and looked at him blankly.

(*Rhetorically.*) You want to kill yourself!

She nodded.

(*Pain.*) These mines won't kill you! They just rip off your foot and ruin you forever.

WAIF (*she stops jumping*) Won't that make me special?

HEADSTONE Not in this country! (*In pain.*) Auuuuggghh! (*Recovers.*) Which way did Jesus go?

WAIF That way!

245

HEADSTONE Why don't you help me look for him? He can heal my wounds and find someone to take care of you. Come on! Just the two of us? (*Waits.*) I'm not walking over there to get you. There's nothing for you here. Come on! (*Tempting her.*) I've got chewing gum.

Pause. She made no response.

Your choice then. Have a nice day! (*Uses trampoline.*) Gerrroonniimmooo!

He hurtled out on an upwards angle as in Scene 1. The Waif ran to another spot and started jumping. The Bach faded in as she jumped.

WAIF (*saying one word with each jump as if playing a game – hopscotch?*) Burning. Tearing. Clawing. Grinding. Skinning. Crushing. Suffocating. Blinding. Slashing. Piercing.

The B-minor Mass drowned out her words.

14. JESUS FISHING

Sounds of war. Jesus was fishing with a stick and a line. Klausius sat cross-legged some way away from him. He was wrapped in a blanket and covering his face. The fake Cripple entered using a crutch.

There was the sound of a bomb or shell approaching.

FAKE CRIPPLE (*throws himself flat*) Incoming!

A dummy of the Bishop (minus the wings?) fell out of the "sky". *

JESUS (*unchanged, and not looking*) It's the Bishop.

FAKE CRIPPLE (*getting up*) Must 'ave forgot his parachute! I thought we were all goners then. Oh my goodness. (*Recovers.*) Phew! (*To Jesus.*) Have you... have you seen the faith healer?

JESUS What's he look like?

---

* The "dummy" of the Bishop could have been lashed high up below the roof on a "quick release" from the start, or since the interval. Or maybe it could be thrown in over the half-curtain.

FAKE CRIPPLE   Military gentlemen, so they say. Whipped the money-lenders out of the Cathedral. I wish I'd seen that! Mind if I join? (*He makes himself comfortable beside Jesus, uninvited.*) Caught anything?

JESUS   No.

FAKE CRIPPLE (*smug*)   And you won't. Too many herbicides. If there was fish you couldn't eat them.

JESUS   There's no hook.

FAKE CRIPPLE   No hook!

JESUS   I just came here to think really.

FAKE CRIPPLE   I see. (*Sees Jesus as a "nut" and possibly a soft touch. He rattles a tin.*) You wouldn't have any loose change, would you? I come from a place where they cripple people. You reach a certain age and they have this ceremony…

JESUS   You're lucky.

FAKE CRIPPLE (*insulted*)   Lucky! You call me lucky and you sit here fishing without a hook!

JESUS   They cripple the mind here.

FAKE CRIPPLE   How so?

JESUS   Your food knows you eat it?

FAKE CRIPPLE   Yes.

JESUS   Your bed knows you lie on it?

FAKE CRIPPLE   Of course.

JESUS   Even the dust has intelligence?

FAKE CRIPPLE (*raises hat to the dust*)   Good mornin', dust! Mornin', dust!

JESUS   Everything watches us?

FAKE CRIPPLE (*confidently*)   Oh yes! We're the centre of everything!

JESUS   Well, the government wants to maroon you on a small planet, third orbit out in a insignificant solar system.

FAKE CRIPPLE (*disbelieving? sending him up?*)   You are a funny feller!

JESUS (*looking into the audience*)   These corpses… They never saw the earth, only words about the earth. They never saw the sky, only words about the sky. How can you resurrect these? They've never existed.

FAKE CRIPPLE (*amused disbelief*) So what does that make me then?

JESUS The mechanism that observes the mechanism?

FAKE CRIPPLE (*taken aback. Then laughs admiringly.*) I must say, you do know how to put a different slant on things (*Studies Jesus – sudden realization.*) You're that faith healer!

JESUS (*shows hands?*) Not me!

FAKE CRIPPLE I distinctly noticed a sort of glow there for a moment!

JESUS A trick of the light. Many have seen it.

The fake Cripple crept up to Jesus and touched his robe.

Did you touch me?

FAKE CRIPPLE Only the corner of your robe.

JESUS (*interested*) Feel anything?

FAKE CRIPPLE (*tests himself cautiously*) Not really. Well, I… perhaps… perhaps there *is* something. Definitely an improvement. My … my feet don't hurt! I can move my toes! Oh there's certainly a… a difference. Yes! Yes! I think I'm… I'm… (*leaps up, shouting and dancing.*) I'm cured! I'm cured!

Jesus took a crutch that was hidden under his robe (or was it the fake Cripple's crutch?) and pendulumed away on it at great speed. The fake Cripple, amazed, watched him as he exited through the audience.

JESUS (*shouts loudly from the audience*) Klausius!

KLAUSIUS (*looks up, uncovering his face*) Yes, Lord?

JESUS Someone needs you.

KLAUSIUS But I have a decision to make, Lord.

JESUS (*shouting from a distance? from the foyer?*) Use gasoline.

KLAUSIUS Thank you, Lord.

Was the Cripple shouting "I'm cured! I'm cured!" as the sounds of war crossfaded into the B-minor Mass.

15. WORM

The branches were swung in over the top of the half-curtain. A few apples dangled from them. Note (19). The Waif was sitting on the stage.

WAIF (*doesn't have the teddy*) Poor Teddy's gone.

A squeaky, high-pitched, not-too cute voice was heard (actually from behind the curtain but seemingly from the apple).

WORM Hello! Excuse me! Up here! That's right, you're looking right at me.

WAIF An apple?

WORM Are you stupid! Apples can't talk! Can't you see my body waving? I'm the worm!

WAIF What do you want, Worm?

WORM I want to go to that apple over there.

WAIF What's wrong with the one you're in?

WORM It's a cooker. (*If cooking apples are unknown say – "It's sour"*) You could take me on your finger.

WAIF All right. (*She moved the worm very gently to another apple.*) This apple? Does it taste better.

WORM Much better.

WAIF (*she waits. Then:*) Excuse me. Hello?

WORM (*munching?*) Yes?

WAIF Suppose a storm blew your apple into a puddle?

WORM I'd drown I suppose. Most of us don't live long enough to get our wings.

WAIF Could I look after you? Take you with me?

WORM (*appalled*) Pluck me!

WAIF I could see no one hurts you.

WORM Can I trust you?

WAIF If they spray more poison you'll be dead. But if you were in my pocket… (*She trails off.*)

WORM (*big decision?*) All right. But go careful.

The Waif plucked the apple and put it in her pocket.

Ohh! It's like a high wind.

WAIF Shout if you want something.
WORM I will.
The Waif left the stage as the lights faded.
The B-minor Mass.

16. FAMILY

Two voices commented on this scene. (I'd like one to be a woman's voice but maybe this won't be possible.) The voices were expressive when they were chatting but not when they were translating. They were unobtrusive (like golf or tennis commentators?). Joan was breast-feeding a baby. The Father, and Joan, wore half-masks. The Mother wore a full mask.

MALE VOICE (*quietly*) So this is a ruined house at the edge of the free-fire zone? Is that Joan?

FEMALE VOICE (*quietly*) Yes. She taught at the school before it was bombed.

JOAN (*to someone off-stage*) Hanga borg knagert zando?

FATHER (*answering from off-stage*) Lanto karg.

FEMALE VOICE Will the network show the breast-feeding?

MALE VOICE No problem. They'll blur out anything offensive.

Joan's Father crossed the stage brushing his teeth.

FEMALE VOICE That was Joan's father. He does the laundry for the Executioners and studies electronics by correspondence course.

MALE VOICE Extraordinary juxtapositions between the twenty-first century and a way of life that hasn't… Who's that?

Joan's Mother entered with the Waif (who was clutching the apple). The mother was played by a man in drag. He wore a full-mask. Was the father heard peeing?

FEMALE VOICE She's Joan's mother. The child's grandmother.

Joan's Mother was holding the hand of the Waif. She sat the Waif down and fed her from a bowl. The Waif wore a long white cotton nightdress. (Did a follow-spot keep a blurred circle of extra light on her?)

MALE VOICE   I wonder where they got the nightgown.
FEMALE VOICE   Joan's sister died of cholera.
MALE VOICE   So that would be the dead child's nightdress?
FEMALE VOICE   These people can't afford to discard anything.
MALE VOICE   So they were recycling before we thought of recycling.

They chuckled. The Waif took the spoon and began wolfing the food.

JOAN   Banda lorga narg.
MALE VOICE   What did she say?
FEMALE VOICE   That the porridge would stick to her ribs.
MALE VOICE (*slight chuckle*)   My mother used to say that.
FEMALE VOICE   I suppose most parents have said that one time or another.

The Mother wanted the bowl but the Waif held it and licked it.

JOAN (*to Waif*)   Would you like to stay with us? You could help with the baby.

The Waif didn't answer.

FATHER (*from off-stage?*)   Lanthar javmot. Binortarg.
FEMALE VOICE   He says that they have enough mouths to feed.
FATHER   Fango kanta harg. Ontogosa. Legin!

Was Joan tucking the Waif into blankets on the floor? Was Mum burping the baby?

MALE VOICE   Did you catch that?
FEMALE VOICE   Something about millions of homeless children.
JOAN   Canfo halarda!
FEMALE VOICE   She said "But this one's here".

The Mother leant into Joan and seemed to whisper to her.

MALE VOICE   What did Joan's mother say?
FEMALE VOICE   That she'll speak to him. I think she wears the trousers in this family.
JOAN (*to Waif*)   Would you like a story…? (*No response from Waif.*) There was a girl called Little Karen whose mummy and daddy were so poor that they had no food to share with her, so the Virgin Mary carried her up to Heaven and cooked her hot dinners. Christmas came, and the Virgin Mary had to go back to earth to give presents

to all the good Christian people, so she said: "Here are the thirteen keys of Heaven. Make sure you keep the place clean while I'm away, but promise me never to open the thirteenth door!"

Joan's Father entered.

JOAN (*to Father*) Fallan targo hajart!

FATHER (*to Waif*) Jango clant pargar? Where your house? You got big people? (*Waits for a response – to daugher?*) Kanfor wandahar!

FEMALE VOICE (*translating*) He said "perhaps she's dumb".

WAIF I'm nobody's nothing.

FATHER (*leaving?*) She can speak English then.

Joan and her Mother exchanged glances.

JOAN (*continuing the story*) Every time Little Karen finished one of her chores, she unlocked one of the doors and looked inside. One room was full of fish all leaping and splashing about; one was full of birds; one was full of animals; one was full of forests, and one had a landscape of hills rolling away into the distance – but the room that she most wanted to see was the one behind…

WAIF (*sleepily*) The thirteenth door…

Dad was setting up the room for sleep. The Mother tried to gently take the apple away from the Waif. The Waif kept hold of it.

It's mine!

MALE VOICE (*amused*) She very attached to that apple.

Joan reassured the Waif in quiet gibberish. The Mother fluffed the Waif's pillow? The Waif kept hold of the apple.

JOAN So to go on with my story – Little Karen had just scrubbed out the oven when she thought: "If I open the thirteenth door and peep in for just one second no one will ever know!" So she opened it just a crack and looked in. Then the Virgin Mary arrived and said: "Did you open the thirteenth door?" Little Karen shook her head. "And is that the truth?" Little Karen nodded her head, so the Virgin Mary kicked her over the edge of Heaven. She landed among thorns that hooked onto her so that she couldn't move. And when she tried to shout for help, no one could hear her – because she had been… struck… dumb.

The Mother murmured something.

FEMALE VOICE (*translating*)   She said, "She's asleep poor girl…'

WAIF   And is that the end?

JOAN   Oh, no. A woodcutter chopped his way into her and she bore him a beautiful baby, but one day the Virgin Mary looked in the window and said: "Did you open the thirteenth door?" Little Karen shook her head so the Virgin Mary took the child. Each time the little girl had a baby the same thing happened. The villagers said she was a monster who was eating her own children, and because she was dumb she couldn't tell them what had happened. They said that the woodcutter should chop off her head, but as he raised the axe she shouted: "Yes, I did open the thirteenth door!" And the clouds parted, and God and the Saints appeared in all their glory, and the Virgin Mary floated down with the missing children in her arms, but then Little Karen said: "And I saw God sitting on the toilet!" And God was so angry that he shat six feet deep all over the world and we've been living in it ever since.

They laughed.

The Waif was fast asleep. The Father had already hung up a sheet up by one end and now he hung up the other end, thus dividing part of the upright of the "T" lengthways. The family went to bed: the Waif, the baby, and Joan were on one side of the sheet, and Mum and Dad on the other. The family murmered in gibberish.

As we only lit the parents' side of the sheet, half of the audience only saw the shadows on the sheet (i.e. they saw a brief "shadow play")

FATHER   Chirhad lontifar.

FEMALE VOICE (*translating*)   Winter's coming.

JOAN   Jargarn.

FEMALE VOICE (*translating*)   Good night.

FATHER   Jargarn.

Blackout (had they been using fake oil lamps?). A pause during which a metal alarm clock was wound up. It ticked loudly. Then we heard some quiet gibberish.

MALE VOICE   Could you follow that?

    FEMALE VOICE   Something about getting a good price.
    JOAN (*indignant*)   We can't sell her to the brothel.
    FATHER   Wrana gatt canigart hantoy?
    FEMALE VOICE (*translating*)   "Would you rather we eat each other?"
    JOAN   She gave us Death's knife. That must be worth something.
    FATHER   Zargo narg enda lornt.
    FEMALE VOICE   He said "You can get those in any novelty store."

We listened to the ticking of the alarm-clock in darkness.

    MALE VOICE (*eventually – whispers*)   No point in both of us being awake, so why don't I…

He was interrupted by machine-gun noises plus screams far and near, plus yells, and explosions (and/or helicopter sounds). There were flashes. Did moving slits of light occasionally crawl over the stage as if headlights were penetrating through slits in the walls?

Terrified Executioners blundered onto the stage using flashlights and screaming in shrill voices.

In a smallish area flashlights can create a Rembrandtish chiaroscuro and leave lots to the imagination – the spectators only saw what we wanted them to see. Note (20).

At first the Executioners spoke in high-pitched voices.

    JAGGER (*screaming in terror*)   Caldor nargar! Caldor nargar! How many men? How many men!
    FATHER (*terrified*)   Gandorr! Gandorr rando pagora!
    FEMALE VOICE (*unemotional*)   We are friends. We are friends.
    EXECUTIONER (*screaming in terror*)   Gandorrs of the beast!
    JOAN   No terrorists here! (*Ad lib about not being terrorists?*)
    FATHER   Panga Yagoraborta! Estrag! Gandorr! Gandorr!

A struggle. We heard screams. One end of the sheet fell but the other end stayed tied to the rope that supported it. The Father was tied to this rope. Glimpses of light later on showed him standing, seemingly tied by the neck and with his hands bound behind him. He was partly draped by the sheet (perhaps a bit like the image of the teacher as a "Saint" in Vigo's Zéro de Conduite?). The Waif hid in the bedding or between the stage and the audience – she wasn't visible.

SLUD (*re: Joan*) Keep hold of the bitch!

Joan shrieked. We only heard the violence. Headstone arrived.

HEADSTONE (*shouting?*) Slud!

SLUD (*shouting*) Sah!

HEADSTONE (*shouting*) How many people?

SLUD (*shouting*) How many people!

JAGGER (*indicating with flashlight*) Just these!

JOAN (*struggling – weeping?*) We don't feed the beast!

Flashlights illuminated the Mother as Headstone yelled at her.

HEADSTONE Onto gar hyanto fangat. Fanget nort! Na ta gahr!

Joan was hurt – had been hurt? – in some unseen way. She moaned and gasped. Mum screeched and/or moaned. Someone had Joan by the hair.

EXECUTIONERS Say "We feed the beast!" Say it! Say "We feed the beast!"

HEADSTONE (*referring to Mum*) Get rid of the old bag.

JOAN (*terrified*) Garg. Jaimo! Habor nog tanta!

FEMALE VOICE (*translating with no emotion*) Don't hurt the baby!

JAGGER (*rage*) Gartar knant hargda yata! Dagh!

FEMALE VOICE (*as always, with no emotion*) I'll rip out your lungs, you… (*Embarrassed.*)… it's a bad word…

The baby is crying. We see that Joan is being held down. Mum is taken away screaming 'Tavparg! Tavparg! Tavparg!'

The baby… The baby…

HEADSTONE (*standing over Joan*) Where's the Doctor?

JAGGER Get the Doctor!

EXECUTIONERS The Doctor! The Doctor! Where's the fucking medic! (*Ad lib.*)

The Doctor from Scene 5 was shoved on-stage – the baby cried. The Executioners gradually began to create a party atmosphere.

EXECUTIONERS (*offering Doctor's bag – throwing it at him?*) Here's his fucking bag.

DOCTOR Who are these people?

GOUGER Feeders of the beast!

HEADSTONE (*impatient*) Just examine her!

DOCTOR Is she ill?

HEADSTONE Is she ill? You think we're here for the good of these people? Is she clean! What am I going to catch from her? Herpes? Syphilis? Gonorrhoea?

DOCTOR I can't examine her if she keeps moving!

JAKE (*hitting her in the darkness?*) You'll hold still for us, won't you my dear?

JAGGER (*overlapping?*) Christ! Who shat themselves?

The Doctor examined Joan who was being held down. She was screaming until someone gagged her. The Executioners began to laugh – they were starting to have a good time. Did we glimpse one or two of them whose trousers were round their ankles?

HEADSTONE (*shouting?*) Well! (*Screaming?*) Well?

DOCTOR There are some sores. They might be venereal.

EXECUTIONERS Shit! Fuck! Buggary! (*Ad lib.*)

HEADSTONE Get her the fuck out!

EXECS (*ad lib*) Slut! Whore! Stupid cunt!

She was dragged out howling in gibberish and English.

GOUGER Hey!

He pulled the Waif out from under the bedding.

See what I found!

Did the Waif yelp in pain? Were they laughing?

FATHER Devils!

JAGGER And proud of it!

He seemed to hit the Father in the stomach (with the flashlight?).

HEADSTONE (*to Doctor*) How about this one?

They pushed the frantic Waif to the floor for the medic to examine.

WAIF (*molested and protesting*) Gar don yag narbar!

JAGGER (*screeching?*) In her hand!

SLUD Grenade!

EXECUTIONERS (*shrieking*) Grenade!

They took cover, covering their ears. Over-breathing in terror. Could the audience see what was in the Waif's hand? I'm not sure.

Shit! Christ! Fuuuuuuuck!

Darkness. The baby was crying.
Did a flashlight roll across the stage and fall into the "moat"? Was Jake muttering the Lord's Prayer? Was someone gasping "Jesus-Jesus-Jesus"? Was someone chanting: "Mother! Mother! Mother!"? Was the Waif snivelling?

WAIF (*finally*) Hello? (*Pause.*) Hello?

SLUD It's a dud!

EXECS It's a dud! It's a dud!

The flashlights were all on the Waif.

EXECUTIONERS (*ad lib*) An apple! A fucking apple! It's just an apple! (*Laughing, sneering.*) Grenade!

JAGGER Grenade! Fucking lunatics we are!

Caunter wrenched the apple away from her as they pushed the Waif down for the Doctor to examine. The baby was louder.

WAIF (*protesting*) It's mine! Give me! Augh!

EXECUTIONER She knows some English then!

EXECUTIONER I bet she's a cunning little linguist!

They laugh. Had someone cuffed her? We heard Caunter bite the apple and spit a piece out. The Waif protested in gibberish.

CAUNTER Ugh! There's a worm! (*He tosses the apple away? Stamps on it?*)

WAIF Noooo!

HEADSTONE Will someone quiet that fucking baby!

The medic examined the Waif while they held her legs apart. Her nightdress was lit from inside by the flashlights. We heard the cradle being trampled. The baby was silent.

SLUD Thank Christ for small mercies!

HEADSTONE (*to Doctor – sarcastic*) Well!

JAGGER You're stopping us getting our fuck shit-head!

WAIF You're hurting me! (*Does she mumble that a few more times?*)

DOCTOR She's a virgin.

Cheers.

HEADSTONE That's good enough for me!

GOUGER I saw her!

JAKE Tough shit!

HEADSTONE (*climbing on the Waif*) Augh! Hold her down! Keep her still for me! Stop her struggling, arsehole. Spread out her legs for me! (*Cries in agony.*) Auuughh! (*Rejects help.*) I'll do it! I can do it! Auggh! (*He can't do it – his wounds hurt terribly.*) Oh fuck! Fuck! Fuck! Fuck! Christ! – don't these people have a proper bed?

SLUD There's a manger!

HEADSTONE Right then!

They carried the Waif off-stage – they were elated.

CAUNTER (*leaving*) Be like Christmas!

Laughter. We don't hear the Waif, just men shouting and celebrating.

EXECUTIONERS (*in the distance – muted*) Augh! Oh no you don't bite! Strong little bugger! Yippee! Ride her cowboy. In! In! In! In! In! In! In! In! Faster! Faster! My turn! Fuck you! Arsehole! Aughh! Bitch! Bitch! Bitch! (*Ad lib.*)

MALE VOICE (*after a while*) I… er… I think that's a wrap.

FEMALE VOICE Will they show any of this footage?

MALE VOICE Can't say. The burning orphanage was sexy. This might disturb the sponsor.

Caunter and Jake had drifted on-stage. They lit cigarettes or shared one. Note (21). *They were at the half-curtain end. Were they lit by a faint red glow that came from somewhere off-stage? Did the cheers and laughter become like bestial roarings? The pace is slow.*

JAKE My heart was about to tear its way out of my chest.

CAUNTER We'll take her with us. The company virgin.

JAKE Not any more.

They laughed. Sounds of rape continued. Were some of the rapists singing the Christmas carol "Away in the manger, no crib for a bed?"

(*Making conversation.*) Did you see the Oscars?

CAUNTER (*groans*) That fucking baby!

JAKE You know if Tom Hanks (*Name a current star.*) got the "best actor"?

CAUNTER I worked in a shipyard. I could have been a welder for a thousand years and never…

The father made strangled sounds.

JAKE What's wrong with him?

Caunter pointed a flashlight at the father for a moment.

CAUNTER (*bored*) Strangling. (*Remorse.*) It was like some force took hold of me. It was…

JAKE (*interrupting*) If that's the worst you ever do …

CAUNTER True… (*Draws on the cigarette.*) Suppose it ain't dead?

JAKE Go and look.

CAUNTER No point. I felt its ribs crack under my boot.

A pause while they smoked.

JAKE They'll all be roast meat when we light the thatch. (*Curious.*) You crying?

CAUNTER No. (*Sniffs again.*) I got an allergy.

They extinguished the cigarette/cigarettes.

JAKE She'll be all juiced up by now. Let's educate the bitch.

CAUNTER Yeah.

They exit.

MALE VOICE Hello?

He's talking to an unintelligible tinny ear-phone voice.

Er… I see… (*White noise.*) Yes… (*White noise.*) Miss World… (*White noise.*) Understood… (*White noise.*) Miss World. Roger. Over and out!

FEMALE VOICE What did they say?

MALE VOICE (*to woman*) We've been pre-empted.

If lights sometimes entered though slats – as if from vehicles moving outside – have them move across the father who hangs limply.

The B-minor Mass slams in.

17. HEADSTONE MEETS JESUS

A scarecrow stood upstage (an actor was inside it). Its sleeves were held out by a stick. Note (22).

Jesus sat cross-legged sewing up the teddy bear – unless stuff had been left on stage in error after the previous scene in which case he might tidy it before sewing – no need to hurry this opening.
Headstone entered. Jesus just kept on sewing, ignoring him.

    HEADSTONE Excuse me…

    JESUS (*not looking*)   Yes.

    HEADSTONE I wonder if I might have a word… if you have a moment? (*Loses nerve. Seems about to leave?*) If it's inconvenient I can…

    JESUS (*still concentrating on the sewing*) I know you…

    HEADSTONE (*secretly aghast*) Oh no. I'm just one of the Executioners.

    JESUS (*neutral*) Headstone.

    HEADSTONE (*tries to laugh it off*) There's a lot of Headstones: my brother works at the Palace. I got a sister in the War Room.

    JESUS (*stops sewing but doesn't look up*) Harold.

    HEADSTONE (*shocked*) People can't usually tell. (*Trying to be cheerful.*) The helmet, you see. (*Differently.*) Well, I suppose you are… er… all-knowing.

    JESUS (*still sewing – still neutral*) You cut the wings off my Angel.

    HEADSTONE (*appalled*) Well… er… it wasn't only me! Anyway… (*Laughs it off.*) … Call that an Angel! They had it chained up outside the cathedral as an advertisement and fund-raiser. It was sucking off all the… (*He pauses. Laughs?*)

He longed for a response but Jesus just kept on sewing.

    Look er… Jesus. May I call you Jesus? (*Makes a fresh start, trying to justify himself.*) It's all military necessity you see. You must know that, of all people! You sit up there in the clouds and take out a village six miles below, you cut the wings off an Angel – *c'est la guerre*! (*Encouraged because Jesus is staying calm.*) They got this computer in the basement of the palace, and if it says "Take out that city" or "Skin that child" – well if I don't do it, someone else will. (*Feels more at ease – does he remove his helmet? Or push it up to his forehead? Or does he do this later?*) I remember once we "took out" an orphanage… (*He's told this story many times before.*) Mistake actually: "You wanted a Code

Three, Lieutenant, you got it!" they said. (*Laughs. He decides to have another stab at getting Jesus to understand.*) It's... (*How to explain the obvious?*) ... It's all about... lines of demarcation – humans on one side, evil-minded scum on the other. But the lines of demarcation – they keep changing.

Jesus passed him a photograph.

(*Casually.*) Oh yeah, I gave her chocolate!

JESUS (*neutral*)   You raped her.

HEADSTONE (*not in the least guilty*)   Never entered my mind.

JESUS (*prompting him*)   In the dark, when the baby...

HEADSTONE (*shocked into interrupting*)   And that was her! I wouldn't have touched her for all the fucking world. (*Apologizes.*) Sorry about the language. (*Trying to make light of it.*) Well, I've seen worse. They was cooking sausages for her next morning down by the lake.

JESUS   She drowned herself.

HEADSTONE (*determined to defend himself*)   You're the one who goes on about "free will".

Did he stare at the photo? (*He would certainly have pushed his helmet up by now.*) *He decides that this placid Jesus is harmless.*

(*Taking the offensive.*) Anyway, what do you do?

JESUS (*neutrally*)   I go on protest marches.

HEADSTONE   But what do you *do*?

JESUS   I ... I write letters to *The Observer* (*name a respectable paper of the country you're in.*)

HEADSTONE   But what do you *do*!

JESUS (*slightly ruffled*)   I go to political Theatre.

HEADSTONE (*confident now. He changes position.*)   I have these sores.

JESUS   Yes.

HEADSTONE   The pain's unbearable.

JESUS   I know.

HEADSTONE (*suppressed rage*)   I turned some water into wine the other day! I've got lepers following me!

JESUS   I'm sorry but...

HEADSTONE (*pain. And rage?*)   Aurrggh! (*He's desperate – this is his last chance.*) That Angel was in a free-fire zone! Anything in a free-fire zone is ours to mutilate or kill! Geneva Convention, article number … number – whatever the fuck it is! (*Glancing at the photograph?*) Look! Cards on the table, Jesus. This whole country is ravaged from end to end! And you think what we did was worse because it was *personal*? Just because of a bit of male bonding that helped relax the boys before we set light to the thatch? How was I to know who she was? In the dark! In that place! I never even looked at her! She was a hole! Something to put it in! How can that be *personal*! (*He runs out of some energy. Both rows of teeth are exposed. He breathes audibly. He subdues.*) The Government wants to bring democracy to these people so what the fuck else are we supposed to do? (*He crushes the photo – the action hurts his hands.*) Mistakes were made. (*He stares at his hands, grief-stricken?*) Look at these hands! (*Rage?*) How can I rend anyone with hands like these?

JESUS (*looks at him*)   What do you want me to do?

HEADSTONE (*very deliberately*)   Take… the wounds… back.

JESUS (*neutrally*)   No.

HEADSTONE (*suppressed rage? Indicating audience.*) Look at these people! They don't have the respect for life that we have. That's why the brain's so baffled, you see. We couldn't have stood a thousandth of this in our own country. (*Perhaps he grips Jesus's arm as he points to an audience member? – not at someone in the front row.*) That peasant! That one over there! What's he worth on the scale of things! What does he know of the mysteries of this universe? Yet he's alive and free from pain. Well? (*Demands a response.*) Well? Well? (*He wills Jesus to understand, but finally shakes his head in exasperation and has to say it.*) Give… him… these… wounds!

Jesus stood up. Headstone was caught between hope and terror.

JESUS   I could give them to this scarecrow!

HEADSTONE   Anything!

JESUS   It's done!

The Scarecrow screamed. (*Did the sound slowly change to agonized groans?*)

HEADSTONE   Thank you! Thank you! (*Weeping?*) I'll worship you! I'll worship you!

He kow towed to Christ and backed off and ran out.
Jesus placed the teddy bear against the Scarecrow. The Scarecrow's concealed hands clutched the teddy bear through the clothing so that it stayed there. Teddy bear and Scarecrow made a double crucifixion image.
The B-minor Mass.

18. HEADSTONE DIES

A small sofa is on-stage. The baby is not on-stage.
Headstone stood where he was at the beginning of Scene 1. He held a remote control and pointed it at the audience as if switching off a TV. The B-minor Mass cut out abruptly as if he'd switched it off.

HEADSTONE   (*speaks to someone off-stage but still faces the audience*) And that bishop said there were no miracles. I can breathe freely now. I can grasp things! My feet aren't stabbing me any more – we could go dancing.

The Wife had entered with a bowl of water. She was as "unreadable" as Headstone was in Scene 1. She washed away the scars from his hands and feet and side (ritually?).
Two Executioners entered at the trampoline end. Did they open a trapdoor? Did strips of cloth flutter up from below to represent fire?

EXECUTIONER   (*shivering*)   Cold!

SLUD   Bitter.

EXECUTIONER   I pity those poor buggers in the cells.

SLUD   Getting soft in your old age?

EXECUTIONER   (*looking around?*)   Need some more wood.

SLUD   So let's find some.

They exited.

HEADSTONE   I brought some milk home. (*Pause?*) I remembered. (*Chastened.*) I'm sorry about… (*Why can't she understand?*) I didn't know who I was. Look – I've asked for time off – we'll take that holiday. On the archipelago. (*Laughs.*) A second honeymoon.

WIFE You'll wake the baby.

She continued washing him. Did the Scarecrow start to moan off-stage?

HEADSTONE They're good lads down at the barracks. Salt of the earth really. War heroes the lot of them. Such… (*searches for the word*) … comradeship. (*Remembers something.*) Ah yes! (*He picks up the remote control and points it at the audience.*) One of the monks set himself on fire outside the Cathedral. It'll be on television.

As he "channel-surfed" to find the burning monk we heard fragments of TV commercials, plus explosions and dialogue from earlier scenes – perhaps a bar of the "You must be, same as me" song followed by Granddad making bird noises. Then perhaps some chanting of "This is your gun, this is your cock…" ending with: "The network blurs out anything that might offend people." Anyway, keep it short.

Meanwhile the two Executioners chased the Scarecrow across the stage.

The wife wept. Headstone stopped channel-surfing and settled for one channel. We heard shouts and sirens and screams, etc. from the TV. Klausius was burning? The Executioners re-ntered carrying an identical but non-human Scarecrow.

What you crying for? (*Tries ineptly to comfort her.*) Everything will be fine from now on. Let me dry your eyes. (*Points at "TV".*) Look – there's that monk! What an idiot. Must be out of his mind. Burning himself alive and not moving a muscle! They're not human, some of these people. (*Irritation.*) For Christ's sake, Thelma! What's past can't hurt us.

The Executioners broke up the Scarecrow and used it to feed the fire. Note (23)At this moment Headstone writhed in agony as if having a heart attack. Synchronize the breaking with Headstone's cries of agony? (If you're using a "Keith" sofa he could fall onto it and vanish partly masked by his wife as she struggles to revive him).

WIFE Harold! What's happening Harold! What's happening! Harold! Harold! What's happening? Harold! Harold!

Was the baby screaming?

If Headstone goes through the hidden slit in the sofa, the Wife can mime shaking and trying to revive an invisible Headstone for a moment and could run around the sofa, unable to find him. Note (24).
B-minor Mass.

19. EPILOGUE

A smell of incense (lit a little earlier) began to permeate the auditorium. The lighting became coloured (rotate the colour-wheels if you have some). The branches of the orchard swung forwards to project over the half-curtain (were there some leaves and some more apples now?). Those small thick little metal "cymbals" from India were being struck all around the auditorium and behind the curtains.
Jesus and the Waif were in front of the half-curtain. They were playing animal snap. The Angel stood behind them. It had spread its wings and was fluttering them.
Beside Jesus was the tin can that the Cripple had begged with in Scene 14.

    WAIF (*for example*)   Horse, Eagle, Penguin, Aardvark, Sparrow, Mole, Elephant, Pack-Rat, Kangaroo, Polar Bear, Ostrich, Dolphin … (*triumphant*) Dolphin!

She took the cards she'd won. The Angel stopped vibrating its wings and lowered them.

    JESUS (*dealing the cards again*)   You're good at this game.

Two Executioners entered. Did they crawl on-stage as if in battle? Or were they clambering out of the "moat"? Or did they come crouching through the audience? Jesus and the Waif played cards silently.

    JAKE   Hay, Slud! I can't hear the guns.
    SLUD   So?
    JAKE   There's a sweet smell in the air.
    SLUD (*sniffs*)   Corpses!
    JAKE (*points at the ground*)   No! There's little flowers! (*Looking around.*) And – and animals! Look! There's butterflies!

We hear a "dawn chorus" of small birds.

    SLUD (*looking up*)   Birds! Impossible!

    WAIF (*winning again*)   Snap!

The Executioners realize they're not alone.

    SLUD   It's the girl.

    JAKE   Nah! She drowned herself!

    SLUD   Must have swum away under the water.

Jesus had stood up somewhere about here. He held the Cripple's begging-tin in his hand.

    (*To Jesus.*) Hey, you! Where is this place?

    JESUS   My orchard.

    SLUD   This ain't no fucking orchard! Arsehole! Augh!

Slud had grabbed him (intending to hit him?) and had staggered back staring at his burned hand.

    It burned where I touched him! Kill the hippy bastard!

Jake "shot" Jesus by honking a bicycle horn at him. Did the stuffed animals take cover? Was there a huge cawing of startled crows?

Jesus mimed catching the bullets in his teeth. He "spat" them into the can and we heard them clang against the metal – an easy magic trick. Note (25). We repeated this effect a few times.

    What's wrong with you! Can't you shoot straight?

He shot Jesus. Same gag. He shrinks back.

    Oh, shit!

    JESUS (*calmly*)   I'm sorry. It's just a reflex. I used to work in a circus.

Everyone who was back-stage and who had their hands free, operated at least two stuffed toy or glove-puppet animals. These were looking over the top of the half curtain and through slits in the half-curtain. Note (26).

Granddad was tearing through the paper of Jesus's portrait (the one on the papered hoop that was set above the centre opening of the half-curtain). He was beaming happily and waving at the spectators.

The Angel had spread her wings and was vibrating them again. A mirror-ball cast moving lights over both the stage and the audience. As many puppet animals as possible began to wave to the Executioners and to the audience through gaps in the curtains. Little animals on springs – dozens of them – could be fastened to long narrow boards and placed so that their vibrating upper bodies projected over the top of the half-curtain.

   GOUGER (*terror*)   What's happening?

   SLUD (*to Jesus – trying to hide terror*)   What are the coordinates of this place?

   GOUGER (*rage*)   Where the fuck are we!

   SLUD (*rage*)   What's happening to us!

They were on the floor, crouched back to back, terrified of an attack that they expected to come from all directions. Did Jesus raise a hand to quieten them?

   JESUS (*calmly*)   Don't you like it here?

The Angel and Jesus and the Waif were a tableau facing front. The Executioners clutched each other. The B-minor Mass rose to a climax, swamping out all other sounds as the lights slowly faded. Did Jesus and the Waif have very slight smiles as if they were trying not to smile?

I don't think we ever did a curtain call. A massive chorus from the B-minor Mass kept playing as the audience left the theatre.

If this last scene seems underwritten it's probably because you haven't imagined the "effects" – the smells and colours, the glorious music, the host of little animals, etc.

SOME NOTES (Best not to trust them)

DOUBLING AND ALLOCATION OF ROLES

(Although maybe I'm wrong?)

I wrote this play for a class of seven or eight students at the Copenhagen State Theatre School – I can't remember the exact number. Each student played at least two characters, one masked and one unmasked. There were more than twenty roles to play, so most of the students played several people.

   These students were young and fit, perhaps an important requirement, especially if you are doubling the roles. Since then I've usually cast seven players plus an "Acting Assistant-Stage-Manager". It needs an acting A.S.M. so as not to weaken the "chorus" of Executioners. In Brazil the company used at least twice that number of actors.

I haven't directed this latest version of the text, so there may be problems that I haven't foreseen, and maybe you can find a better "doubling" so check it out for yourself.

ALLOCATING THE ROLES BETWEEN SIX MEN AND TWO WOMEN
THE WAIF – Has played an Executioner in Scene 3 and Scene 8.
THE WIFE – Plays the Double Figure. The Angel. And Joan.
HEADSTONE – Played Death in all the productions that I've seen. He's available for "Media" and – surprisingly – for the voice of the male commentator in Scene 16. He could play Bart.
GRANDDAD – Plays the Bishop. A Cripple? And an Executioner in Scenes 8, 11, 16, and 18.
KLAUSIUS – Plays a Cripple, The Mother (in drag), and probably the Voice of the Worm? He plays an Executioner (Jagger?) and "Media".
JESUS – Plays the Doctor. Plays a Cripple? Plays an Executioner? Plays one of the "Media" at the end of Scene 9?
JAKE – Plays the Cripple (who we see broken). Could play Death.
VOICES – Headstone can do the man's voice in Scene 16 because he's never on-stage at that time, but I can't find a way to allow one of the two women to do the woman's voice – so I guess that it might have to be played by a man.
An Acting Stage manager plays the Legs? An Executioner? A "Media" person? Dad, etc.

QUICK CHANGES
The change into Scene 3 – The Executioner (who probably also plays Jesus) enters holding one end of the "sheet" while the Executioner who holds the other end is still changing from being a Cripple.

The change into Scene 4 – The Bishop became Granddad while the Executioners were playing music to entertain the audience.

The Angel entered by herself in Scene 7 to give time for the Monks to change into Executioners (it's not necessary for the Executioners to arrive simultaneously).

Scene 13 – The most difficult costume change was from the Bishop in Scene 12 to Granddad in Scene 13 because he had to get out of the harness that flew him. Granddad wasn't lying on the stage when Scene 13 started. But in this version, Jesus talks to the Waif after the Bishop has flown up to Heaven. This gives a more time for the costume change so maybe he can be there when the scene starts.

Of course, if you've oodles of money you can have lots of actors, but some of the power of the first production was the realization that the roles were played by a small class of young drama students.

PHYSICAL CHARACTERISTICS – as I see them.
Man 1. Headstone/Death – Athletic?
Man 2. Granddad/Bishop – Plump (pad him?)
Man 3. Jesus/Jake – Normal size?
Man 4. Bart – Plumper than Klausius.
Man 5. Klausius – Short. Slight.
Wife/Double Figure – Not fat.
Waif – Not tall. Slight.

Whenever it's truthful the Executioners should be together (except for Headstone), standing and moving as a "clump". They should tend to expose both sets of teeth – especially the bottom teeth – and often breath, audibly. Exposing your teeth and breathing audibly can make you feel like slowly scanning left and right in search of possible victims to rip to pieces.

Headstone – Number 1 in the pecking order. Normal intelligence. Can't be short if he is also to play Death.

MENTAL CHARACTERISTICS – as I see them
Slud – Number 2. Big, stupid, brutal, and ungraceful.
Jagger – Number 3. Nasty and bright. Ferret-like. Slim.
Jake – Number 4. Ebullient if he likes you. Brutal otherwise.

CAUNTER – Number 5. Enjoys life? Positive attitude?
GOUGER – Too stupid to be Number 5? Has a grudge?
Any other executioners that you can add would be fives or sixes.

STATUS
In this play one person is usually superior to another.
HEADSTONE is superior to his Wife.
GRANDDAD is superior to the Waif.
THE BISHOP is superior to Bartholomeus who is superior to Klausius.
THE DOCTOR believes himself superior to Headstone (until he becomes afraid of him) and to Jake. He'd like to be equal to the Bishop.
JESUS starts off superior to everyone but doesn't insist on it – even when they nail him back he's calm, unaffected.
THE BISHOP believes that he should be superior to everyone, but he's is often flustered because he knows that he's a fake, that it's all a performance. He's more confident in Scene 12 because God has spoken to him.
DEATH is superior to mortals, and believes that he should be superior to Jesus (it's important that he likes the Waif).

***

"TECK"; NOTES
(1) We borrowed a small trampoline, about a metre square, from the gymnastics classes. The height could be adjusted to be the same height as the rostra that formed the stage. It was useful for super-hero exits, but it was also nice at other times – as when Monks who entered from the full-curtain did a three-inch bounce on it and crossed themselves. Have someone ready to part the curtain as Headstone soars through. Forbid cast members from resting on the "soft-landing".
(2) There is a description of how to use half-masks in the last chapter of my book *Impro*. It's not important that these cripple masks are "deep masks" but Granddad and the Waif who we meet later on should be. In my productions Granddad has always worn a half-mask but in a version we took to New York the Waif was played by Veena Sood without a mask – this worked okay because of the actress but a half-mask would probably have been more "universal".
(3) This fire is not necessary for the scene, and would be pointless unless it were also used in Scene 18.

(4) An actor who had not played a Cripple was always the Executioner who entered first with the edge of the sheet. This gave us another few seconds – if necessary – for the costume change. The sheet was extended and moved along in front of the half-curtain to stop centre – in front of and below the papered hula-hoop that had the face of Jesus drawn on it. A bench was then inserted (secretly) halfway through the centre of the half-curtain. A man with bare legs lay on this bench with his head behind the half-curtain and with his legs in front of the half curtain.

A woman (referred to as the Double Figure) entered secretly behind the sheet (unless there was some hitch in the set-change in which case she looked over the sheet as it entered and hurled abuse at the Executioners and/or at the audience). She stood over the man who lay face-up on the bench while the Executioners wrapped the sheet around her neck so that it became part of her costume. Her own legs were hidden inside "pillow-cases" that were made of the same material as the sheet, so that the man's legs seemed to be her legs. The effect was of a grotesque giantess who was sitting down (see diagrams opposite). If she crossed her arms, the legs would usually cross – and vice versa. We usually asked her to seem a little "unstable" – if she swayed to one side the legs would move towards the other side and if she leaned back the legs would go up. Sometimes an Executioner might have to steady her, but we played the scene for grotesqueness rather than for comedy.

When a rather short woman played the speaking part of the Double Figure a small platform was slid under the bench so that it projected to each side for her to stand on. The Double Figure's rages are an opportunity for the legs to be very expressive.

(5) BALLOONS: We used "airship" balloons – I've written about these in my book *Impro for Storytellers*. Sometimes they burst and if you tie them by just tucking the end of a balloon into the loop of the knot (instead of pulling it right through the loop) the balloon may deflate at unpredictable moments – when beating an audience member perhaps. Have someone paint them black with a quick drying paint about an hour before the performance – this gives them a nasty wrinkled look. The person who paints them should have a plastic screen or a plastic face mask for protection because sometimes they burst and spray paint droplets in all directions.

(6) Agree beforehand which parts of the audience each actor will choose to relate to. In one performance almost every actor accidentally chose the same audience member to relate to – make sure that you avoid this. Try to choose audience members who will hold eye-contact with you.

(7) Applause boards should be oblong and much wider horizontally than vertically. They should be painted yellow and the writing should be printed in black.

(8) We saw this "cross" earlier in Scene 3. It's as tall as a bishop's crook would have been, and it has to be strong enough to be used as a weapon later in this scene.

(9) Onward, Christian soldiers, marching as to war,
With the cross of Jesus going on before.

Christ, the royal Master, leads against the foe;
Forward into battle see His banners go!
Onward, Christian soldiers, marching as to war,
With the cross of Jesus going on before.
At the sign of triumph Satan's host doth flee;
On then, Christian soldiers, on to victory!
Long as earth endureth, men the faith will hold,
Kingdoms, nations, empires, in destruction rolled.
Onward, Christian soldiers, marching as to war,
With the cross of Jesus going on before.

(10) This trick proved far easier than it looked, but if you've no trampoline (or if your actors just aren't up to it physically) have Klausius run out through the gap in the half-curtain, and have Death stab through with the scythe. Death then looks through the curtain to see what damage he did, while holding his scythe in a vertical position. As his head pushes through the curtains, Klausius re-enters by jumping in over top of the half-curtain, grasping onto the scythe to break his fall, and retaining hold of it automatically – and being amazed to find himself in possession of it.

(11) Full masks, tragic and neutral masks, and paper masks are described in my book *impro*. To make a paper mask, cut a beautiful life-sized face of a model from a fashion magazine, stick it on a plastic backing, and fasten elastic to the sides so that can it can be worn as a section of a cylinder held against the face – i.e. the plastic must only bend in one dimension at a time – the mask will be ineffective if it conforms to the contours of the face.

The photo will be beautiful to start with – or why did you choose it? – but the face will narrow it because of the curve, and it will have its own "lighting" (i.e. the lighting provided by the photographer).

If someone faces you, wearing such a mask, and makes no movement of any kind you feel that you are in the presence of something supernatural because of the absence of "human" signals – e.g. the eyes won't blink). Therefore the Angel should often be motionless with the paper mask facing to the audience – it follows that on a "T"-shaped stage her natural place is in front of the hula-hoop where both audiences have a good view of her. If the wearer moves in a clumsy way, or an uncontrolled way, we'll stop looking at the mask and will look at the body. This will weaken the effect. Therefore the Angel should be "choreographed" so that it is usually still, or moving very simply and never unnecessarily. The mask can slowly turn from left to right as if surveying the audience, but it takes a very skilled performer to keep the mask as powerful in movement as when it's motionless. To learn to move such a mask extensively while maintaining its power can take a lot of training, and anyway it's not practical with paper masks – because the wearer is blind or is allowed just fragments of vision through pin-holes that are made in the mascara that surrounds the photo-model's eyes, but the

EXECUTIONER HELMETS

way the scene is written means that you don't need a great mask-expert – where would you find one anyway? The important thing is to allow for stillness and simplified movement except when it's struggling or trying to break free – and even then keep the mask facing front. Even when she's pressed into a kneeling position to have her wing cut off the face should still be "flat on" to the spectators

Make lots of paper masks so you can choose the one that works the best. Some faces are wonderful but others don't have the same magic. Don't make the mask bigger than head size or the angle will look stunted.

(12) The wings have a strong wire-frame with loops to push the upper arms through and handles for the hands to grip.

(13) Someone will always agree to take notes, but in a proscenium production this may need to be cut (or add a Nurse?).

(14) The Angel's torso and arms (and perhaps her legs) are inside the rostrum but this shouldn't be obvious at first glance. Maybe her own feet are showing? If it's obvious that she's become much shorter, try fake legs and feet that the Angel can move. Or maybe there are two people inside the rostrum so that we see the Angel's head but someone else's feet. Try a "mock-up" to find the best method.

Why not use short elasticized "bungee cords" to hold the Angel's slit torso open? The kind that are used to strap cases, skis etc. onto the top of cars? The other ends of these cords could be fixed permanently to the platform.

The torso is packed with fake internal organs. Don't make them look real – they should look obviously fake.

(15) FLYING THE BISHOP: In the first production the Bishop was standing in front of the full-curtain (at the edge of the trampoline). On the other side of the split in the curtain was a block and tackle which he was hooked secretly too. We lit him from the sides and hoisted him up about four feet into the air flapping vigorously as the lights faded. With more time and resources the Bishop could "fly" our like Peter Pan or Liberace, so I've placed a short interlude with Jesus and the Waif after the Bishop flies out. This helps the change of costume from the Bishop to Granddad.

If you can't get the Bishop to "fly by wire" (because of the architecture of the building, or because you lack the resources, he could flap and be lifted up by extra "monks" who could lift him and rush him off-stage while pretending to hold him down as he flaps. Bartholomeus could be shouting "Not yet! Not yet, my lord!" and the Bishop could be shouting "Hold me down! Hold me down till we get outside". Or perhaps you could find some other method – a crane from behind the half-curtain perhaps.

(16) If you need more time for the change – although I don't imagine that it will be necessary in this version – please try letting the Waif pull Jesus down as a helicopter is heard passing over. This wins time for the costume change. If you still need more time, try adding this dialogue:

    WAIF Keep down. They kill anything that moves.
    JESUS (*indignant*) What about the animals!
    WAIF They used the elephants for target practice.
    JESUS (*indignant*) My elephants!
    WAIF (*reproving Jesus*) Keep in my footsteps!

(17) I'd see what possibilities are available. I could have had him come up from under the stage, or be discovered in a seat at the back of the audience, or enter dressed as a cowboy with two "six shooters" and then as a ballerina in a tutu, or restraining a slavering dog (add the slaver!). I'd check out the prop department – perhaps they have a wheelchair, or a sedan chair or a "boat" that he could row on stage. But keep it simple and neat – don't hold up the play just because you have an interesting effect.

(18) The string that lowers the bird could have been used to lower the "crisps" in the first Cathedral scene (unless they just fell from above).

(19) We hung branches behind the half-curtain. We pulled them backwards and tied them in position before the play started. We kept the lights off of them but they could be glimpsed in the gloom – which was fine because they were in no way distracting (the apples weren't visible). We swung the branches forwards and retied them so that they projected over the top of the half-curtain (for this worm scene and for the Epilogue). This was an efficient and simple way to establish the orchard.

(20) The movie *Alien* was far more terrifying that the later *Alien* movies that followed it, because it hardly ever showed the alien. Use the same principle here.

(21) Maybe fake the cigarette – they're in the dark after all and why let the smell torment the tobacco addicts? All you'd need is a electrical device that glows red and that can glower redder when you're pretending to suck on it.

(22) A handkerchief fixed to a fedora hat hung in front of its face. This handkerchief had two black dots for eyes and a black slash for a mouth. Fake straw stuck out of the sleeves.

(23) Until this re-write we've always mimed the fire, but cloth-fires are easy to make. Down in the "hole" would be an electric fan with yellow ribbons tied to the finger-guard. Add power (slowly?) and these would flutter upwards into view. If you have lights pointing up through the fan these ribbons will make excellent fake flames. They could push bits of the Scarecrow into the "hole" and/or lie the rest of the Scarecrow across the opening. (This fire could also be used by the Cripples in Scene 2.)

(24) HEADSTONE'S DISAPPEARANCE: If the sofa is "rigged" (as described in Scene 10) Headstone could collapse on the sofa and his Wife could try and revive him, partly masking him as he disappears through the sofa. She could then react as if he had vanished into thin air or mime still trying to revive him as if he hadn't vanished at all.

(25) To "catch bullets in his teeth" Jesus had some metal balls or marbles concealed in the hand that held the container. He pretended to spit into the container and released a metal ball at the same time. Try spitting into the air and stretching out the container to catch the "bullet".

(26) PUPPETS: Buy these from toy-shops, they don't even have to be glove puppets – it's okay to glimpse fingers manipulating soft toy animals. Dozens of tiny animals – baby animals – could appear along the top of the half-curtain if these were fastened to poles by springs (so that they vibrated). These poles could be placed into "slots" at the back of the top of the curtain so that the poles and the springs are invisible. Vibration of the curtain from the movements of the other "animals" should be enough to keep them alive – although I've never tried this effect.

MOBY DICK

This play has been successful when played in other languages, but it's important for the translator to be aware of the strong rhythms in the dialogue.

The placing of the "Sirs" and the "Perkinses" should be learned exactly. If you play this play with truthful feeling we'll pity the characters and then it won't work. Remember, nothing in this play is real – it's all the characters fantasy. They should be elated, and enjoying the ideas and the dialogue.

The first two actors used to toss a coin in front of the audience before each performance to see who would play which role.

This play was written to be performed with no scenography. Use dark curtains to seal off the back-stage area?

Sir and Perkins are wearing sou'westers. Perkins mimes wrestling with a ship's wheel. They sway from side to side making the sounds of a storm at sea (waves hissing, sea gulls screaming). Perhaps Sir has a long "airship" balloon to hit Perkins with. (If so keep a supply of balloons in boxes at the side of the stage so that Perkins can replace the ones that burst or fizzle down. Tie the balloons so that they may deflate at any moment, i.e., only push the neck a tiny distance into the loop.)

SCENE ONE

    PERKINS (*runs to side. Ventriloquizing seagulls?*) Land hoooooo! Land on the port bow.

    SIR (*firmly*) Keep the course nor-nor-west, Bosun.

    PERKINS But Sir! That's away from the island!

    SIR Of course it's away from the island, Mr. Perkins.

    PERKINS But Sir, we haven't set foot on land for five months.

SIR Nor shall we, nor shall we, Mr. Perkins, except, God willing, we may sight and utterly destroy – the White Whale.

PERKINS But Sir – what chance that in all these millions of square miles of ocean…?

SIR I do not care to be instructed by my juniors, Mr. Perkins. Tell me rather, whether my daughter Dorothea is still lashed stark naked to the bowsprit?

PERKINS She is indeed, Sir! But half dead from the severe cold of these latitudes.

SIR Are the men still forcing hot rum into her?

PERKINS Oh yes, Sir. And they're giving her constant massage, but I can't think she'll survive much longer! Oh Sir, it's upsetting the crew having her tied stark naked to the bowsprit like that. The men are getting very roused. At least let me cover her Sir.

SIR Cover her, Mr. Perkins! Never!

PERKINS But she goes under every other wave.

SIR Exactly! Exactly! And one day the White Whale will sniff her out, and then, and then, only let my brave harpooners sink their darts deep into his muscle and there'll be no saving him. While this creature roams the seven seas which of us is safe, Mr. Perkins? Even at the sacrifice of my daughter, Dorothea, who, God knows, I love more than any other living creature – the White Whale must be destroyed!

PERKINS (*kneeling before Sir?*) But I love her too, Sir.

SIR (*clutching him?*) Love! What can lesser mortals know of that celestial passion that welds two natures into one enduring flux!

PERKINS (*ventriloquizes?*) Thar she blows!

SIR The telescope! The telescope, man!

Perkins hands him long balloon to use as telescope.

There! You see it, Mr. Perkins! The colour, the colour!

PERKINS White, Sir! (*Ventriloquizes?*) The White Whaaaalle!

SIR Hard a starboard! Unfurl all canvas!

PERKINS But you'll run us under, Sir.

SIR   Stick to your post, Mr. Perkins! Bosun! Prepare a harpoon for me! I shall climb out along the bowsprit and make the first thrust myself! Faster! Faster!

Sir stops his frenzy. He removes his hat, calms down, and begins to take off the sou'wester.

PERKINS (*still building climax*)   Sir! Thrust with your harpoon!

SIR (*unperturbed*)   Perkins!

PERKINS (*still excited*)   For the love of God, thrust, Sir.

SIR   Perkins!

PERKINS (*taken aback*)   Sir?

SIR   It's no use, Perkins.

PERKINS   What, Sir!

SIR   All these fantasies.

PERKINS (*deflating?*)   Fantasies, Sir?

SIR   Yes, Perkins. These games we play to excite each other.

PERKINS   Oh Sir!

SIR   Nothing works any more!

PERKINS (*trying a new tack*)   But Sir, I thought the sauna and the birch twigs had you properly roused.

SIR   That was all show, Perkins. All pretene. (*Tapping his own chest.*) Inside here, it's all dead wood – yes, Perkins, the sap's dried up at the source. Your poor old master's impotent at last.

PERKINS   Are you sure, Sir?

SIR (*flaring up*)   Sure! Of course I'm sure! How could I be mistaken about a thing like that?

PERKINS (*tentative*)   Couldn't I read you a selection from your erotica, Sir?

SIR   No, Perkins.

PERKINS (*more enthusiastic*)   What about the vibratory apparatus ,Sir? Or what about the stuff we inject into the bull?

SIR   Do you think I haven't tried, Perkins!

PERKINS (*really enthusiastic*)   But the bull!

SIR   That too, Perkins! Useless! Useless! I admit I felt a little restive towards evening, but...

PERKINS   What about a bit of humiliation then, Sir? I could make you clean out the lavatories and then walk all over you with the gardening boots.

SIR   No, no, Perkins, I don't want to be *cured*!

PERKINS   (*taken aback*)   But Sir! You've always depended on me before.

SIR   Perkins, Perkins, can't you understand that the end, when it comes, comes as a blessed release?

PERKINS   Does it, Sir?

SIR   Yes, yes, at last I am free, Perkins. Why, impotence is a great boon to a man. Would to God my peasants were all impotent, then we wouldn't be so over-populated. Yes, yes, Perkins! I look forwards to a long period of tranquillity untroubled by the storms of the flesh.

PERKINS   Er, well, Sir.

SIR   Perkins?

PERKINS   Your daughter, Sir.

SIR   (*revelling in the sound*)   Dorotheaaaaa…

PERKINS   Yes Sir – er – when I took her breakfast down I noticed that the chains were beginning to fray her wrists and ankles.

SIR   As is only natural, Perkins.

PERKINS   They might leave permanent scars, Sir.

SIR   You think I don't have permanent scars?

PERKINS   Where, Sir?

SIR   On the heart, on the heart, man.

PERKINS   But it's making her ill, Sir.

SIR   She has only herself to blame! Night after night she crept down to that shed with Jake the woodsman.

PERKINS   She was so young, Sir.

SIR   Orgies, Perkins. Stark naked in the lily pond with the American airman.

PERKINS   That was…

SIR   Hysterical laughter in the rhubarb patch in the early hours.

PERKINS   I know, Sir, but…

SIR The mechanical mower in the orchard still clogged with old contraceptives. Oh I know how she used to suffer. "I'm evil, Father," she would say as I tied her to the bedposts. "I want you to beat the devil out of me, Father," she would cry, harder, harder, her breasts squirming against the bed-knobs.

PERKINS (*distraught*) Oh Sir, Sir, I can't stand the description.

SIR But it was all useless. (*Anti-climax?*) She takes after her mother, you see.

PERKINS Don't you think she's suffered enough!

SIR (*provoked*) Suffered? Deliberately to bereft me of the affection which is a father's right!

PERKINS But you were trying to seduce her, Sir.

SIR (*reasonable*) Seduce? Seduce? I merely wanted to pat her bosoms. Should a father be entitled to less? I'm not a lustful man, Perkins, but when those bosoms are there, all day, at my elbow as it were, with an ever present danger of their pressing into me… Am I not flesh and blood, Perkins?

PERKINS But you climbed on top of her, Sir.

SIR Can you blame a man for a momentary impulse?

PERKINS She could have broken your back on that fender, Sir.

SIR True.

Pause.

PERKINS Sir… (*Tentative.*) Er… Wouldn't you like her taken off your hands?

SIR What?

PERKINS Well, you know, married, Sir.

SIR Fine chance she has of marriage after her behaviour in the coronation procession.

PERKINS I thought, perhaps, married to me, Sir.

SIR Married!

PERKINS Well, since you're impotent…

SIR (*aghast*) To my servant!

PERKINS Well you can't have much use for her, Sir.

SIR Use! It's knowing she's there, that's the use, Perkins. I could hardly marry my daughter to my servant, well could I?

PERKINS It's just I feel so sorry for her, locked up in that dungeon among the spiders and the breadcrumbs. Oh Sir, now that you're impotent, couldn't I at least take her down a blanket? I mean, do we have to keep her down there anyway? I could get a ball-and-chain from the armoury…

SIR (*expansive*) No, no, Perkins, my life can't change as rapidly as that. I must wean myself psychologically. Ah, but I can't tell you the relief. I thought that I would become one of those frustrated old men who expose themselves in the park and then rush home to eat their sandwiches, instead of which I shall reside here, having child after child among the villagers, without any of the emotional disturbance that has so plagued me in the past!

PERKINS Children, Sir?

SIR Why, yes, Perkins. I can still have children after all.

PERKINS (*apprehensive*) Er, Sir.

SIR Yes Perkins?

PERKINS Those bottles of sperm in the refrigerator, Sir.

SIR (*with pride*) My sperm!

PERKINS Well, the power-failure, Sir. All the ice melted and everything went sour.

SIR Sour!

PERKINS Solid in the bottles.

SIR Solid! Tell me it's not true, Perkins!

PERKINS Oh Sir, I thought we could always replace it.

SIR Perkins!

PERKINS I didn't anticipate that there was any hurry.

SIR It – it – oh don't speak to me Perkins! Augh! Silence! Silence! Solid in the – auggh! Augh! Ohhhh!

PERKINS Don't hit me, Sir!

SIR Hit you! I'll…

PERKINS Oh Sir, there is just one left, Sir.

SIR (*taken aback*) What!

PERKINS (*stress each word?*)   One sperm left, Sir.
SIR (*grasping at straws?*)   One left.
PERKINS   Yes, Sir.
SIR   One, Perkins.
PERKINS   One, Sir.
SIR   Where? Tell me where!
PERKINS   In the goldfish bowl in the kitchen.
(*Keep the pace up.*)
SIR   In the fish bowl!
PERKINS   Well, I been feeding it.
SIR   Feeding it, Perkins! What on?
PERKINS   Fish-food.
SIR   Feeding my sperm on, on, Fish-Food!
PERKINS   Oh, he liked it, Sir. You see, Sir, after Charlie my shubunkin died, you know, the one what panicked during the thunderstorm, well it was lonely in the kitchen and…
SIR   Say no more! (*Dramatic*) One sperm surviving out of all that multitude! I had million upon million in old United Dairy milk bottles! *Whole quarts*!
PERKINS   *Oh Sir*!
"*Whole quarts*" *and* "*Oh Sir*" *are said in the same rhythm, each word emphasized.*
SIR   But *one* still alive!
PERKINS   It was only my fondness for animals made me keep it, Sir.
SIR   Don't reproach yourself on that score, Perkins. Tell me, tell me, is it thriving?
PERKINS   Oh yes, Sir.
SIR   And it's eating plenty of ant's eggs, eh?
PERKINS   Oh it snaps them up, Sir.
SIR   Indeed… it… it must be quite large!
PERKINS   Oh a good six inches.
SIR   Six inches!
PERKINS   And fat with it, Sir.
SIR   It's quite active though?

PERKINS   Active! It snatches flies out of the air.

SIR   It's not possible, Perkins.

PERKINS   It's quite muscular, Sir.

SIR (*dramatic*)   So! Thanks to the strange workings of providence, I still have a chance of a male heir! But – I doubt anyone ever encountered a six-inch sperm. I mean we can hardly slip it into the pool when Miss Hershaw is bathing.

PERKINS   I don't see why not, Sir.

SIR   No?

PERKINS (*sudden idea!*)   Oh Sir, what about Betty, the harelip girl I bring up from the village every Saturday?

SIR   What of it?

PERKINS   Well, I scrub her down in the bath, like I always do, and then, when she's soaking in the bath water, I just slip it in, unobserved.

SIR   Unobserved?

PERKINS   Into the bath water.

SIR   But the heat and the soapy water!

PERKINS   It'll only be there a second. It'll be off like a little torpedo.

SIR   Well… I… I… I'd better see this little pet of yours.

PERKINS   I'll get it for you, Sir. (*Going to exit.*) I… I'm sure you'll have every reason to be proud of it, Sir.

There's a moment when Sir might get enraged again but he doesn't. Perkins leaves the stage. Nothing happens until we hear a glass crash.

SIR   Perkins?

Pause.

What is it, Perkins?

Enter Perkins, holding his finger.

PERKINS   It bit me, Sir.

SIR   Bit you?

PERKINS   I think the daylight scared it, Sir.

SIR   You didn't drop the bowl!

PERKINS   Oh Sir.

SIR   Well.

PERKINS Sir.
SIR Where is it? Where is it, man!
PERKINS Oh Sir! It's in the moat! It's in the moat!

SCENE TWO

Perkins is trying to entice the sperm from the moat (miming that the water is between the stage and the audience).
PERKINS Bessie! Bessie! Come on, Bessie!
Enter Sir.
SIR Well, Perkins?
PERKINS No luck I'm afraid, Sir.
SIR We must find it, Perkins.
PERKINS But I've been trying for days, Sir. Oh Sir, it's been eating the ducks.
SIR Eating my ducks!
PERKINS Yes, Sir. It swims up from underneath and seizes them by the ankles.
SIR Are you sure?
PERKINS I think it drags them under for spite as much as anything. It can't eat that many!
SIR That many! But I've already spoken to the Vicar about the water carnival.
PERKINS Water carnival!
SIR For the girls in the village. The Vicar was most enthusiastic. It seemed to me that if we could get the girls from the village up here the thing could take its choice.
PERKINS It could strip a bullock in three minutes!
SIR You exaggerate, Perkins.
PERKINS No, Sir! You see – all those months I was feeding it in the goldfish bowl, well Sir, it's not natural for a sperm! It wants to get – you know – it was desperate for an egg, not just stale old ant's eggs,

but an egg to unite with. And what with the desperation and the loneliness, well, I think it's turned its chromosomes!

SIR What!

PERKINS Yes, Sir! What we are confronted with here is a mad sperm of abnormal muscularity and perverted appetite.

SIR A mad sperm gone berserk in my moat!

PERKINS It attacked a swan this morning, Sir!

SIR (*taken aback, but determined*) Well, we shall just have to pacify it. When we get the bunting up, and the flags flying…

PERKINS Look, Sir!

SIR Great heavens!

They pretend to be watching the sperm swim past (between them and the audience).

PERKINS Careful, Sir!

SIR But what a hideous creature!

PERKINS I think it's seen us, Sir. There it goes. (*They watch it vanishing into the depths.*) Never comes close enough to get a real swipe at it.

SIR (*horrified*) This – this is unprecedented, Perkins. Fence off the moat. Don't let the animals near. It's not just a question of capture – this creature must be destroyed!

PERKINS Not kill it, Sir!

SIR Tell me, man – when I was potent, what was the desire that obsessed me?

PERKINS (*sheepishly*) Oh Sir…

SIR (*cutting in*) The overriding desire, Perkins.

PERKINS (*brightening up*) Oh you mean…

SIR No! No! I mean my incestuous desire for my daughter, Dorothea. I am well aware that an actual carnal relationship would be wickedness, sheer wickedness, but just as she obsessed me, so may she obsess my sperm!

PERKINS I don't think she's in any fit state to cooperate, Sir.

SIR No?

PERKINS Kept naked in that dungeon all these months. In the dark, and nothing but bread and water. I always said it was cruel, Sir.

SIR Cruel! Cruel, Perkins!

PERKINS (*utterly tormented*) You know I love her, Sir!

SIR Be silent! Be silent!

PERKINS (*weeping?*) Oh Sir, won't you reconsider?

SIR Never!

PERKINS (*clutching Sir's knees*) Let me marry her, Sir.

SIR Silence! Silence! Now then! I want her taken out and chained to the drawbridge!

PERKINS Not naked, Sir!

SIR Of course! We want the bait to be effective, don't we? And I want a guard round her, day and night with, with harpoons. (*Agony/grief.*) And when, when this thing comes up to her I want it, I want it… impaled… impaled, do you hear!

PERKINS But Sir! Your son!

SIR (*bravely*) I have no son! (*Stiff upper lip.*) Raise and lower the drawbridge all night until this … this (*utter revulsion*) thing… comes up to her.

PERKINS Look out, Sir!

Sir mimes an attack by the sperm on his leg.

SIR Arruugghh!

PERKINS Oh Sir, are you all right, Sir?

SIR My leg! My Leg! Perkins! I'm injured Perkins! (*Secretly liking the idea?*) Unnatural creature, to dare attack it's own, it's own… (*Can't find the word.*) Help me into the Castle! (*Limps off assisted by Perkins.*)

SCENE THREE

Sir has a long "airship" balloon to beat Perkins with? Try adding a reluctance to use it.

SIR All right, Perkins! Tell your story!

PERKINS Oh Sir, we spent all night dangling Dorothea over the water like you said, and we could see the sperm lurking in the shadows, but it was too crafty for us, Sir! So I decided to drain the moat – as seemed reasonable, Sir – but it burrowed down into the mud, so I had all the men down there, probing vigorously, when we heard the uproar.

SIR   Uproar?

PERKINS   From the village, Sir! Lights, and shouting. So we ran across the fields, carrying Dorothea with us, Sir, in case the sperm took advantage of her in our absence.

SIR (*outraged*)   So you took her down to the village, did you, Perkins!

PERKINS   Oh Sir, the sperm had worked its way down to the bridge and had bitten old Grampher Pomeroy. (*Urgently – to stop Sir hitting him.*) Sir, Sir, they were trying to club it to death!

SIR   Kill my sperm!

PERKINS   They weren't to know that were they, Sir? But our men fought them off. And seeing it was your last chance of a son, I called it by name, and… and it came squirming over the grass towards me like a resilient slug. And as we got away from the lights it started overtaking me Sir, always keeping between me and the lights. And I didn't know what it would do, it having mixed feelings, what with me feeding it the same time as I was frustrating it, Sir.

SIR   Get on! Get on!

PERKINS   Oh Sir, and then I saw something else, white, jerking towards me across the heath. Oh Sir, it was Dorothea, her blanket torn off by the gorse, and her body all bleeding. And she was holding a dish of sausages from the Inn. "This way," she said, "Fritz," she called me Fritz, Sir, and she was throwing sausages so it would pause to snap them up. Then it followed us back to the Inn where the men captured it with nets and put it in a tin trunk with plenty of water, but it was making a terrible noise drumming its tail against the metal until we thought of putting a live goose in with it. Oh Sir, don't hit me, Sir!

SIR   Get to the point!

PERKINS   I was about to take it back to the castle when Dorothea began, you know, making up to me, Sir, and telling me how attractive I was, and never taking her eyes off me. Well, how could I refuse her, Sir?

SIR   Refuse her what, Perkins!

PERKINS   She said run off with her, Sir – oh Sir, she said "Take it to London and sell it to the zoological society..."

SIR   Sell my sperm!

PERKINS   We needed the money, Sir. (*Sir about to kill him.*) Oh Sir, Sir, no, Sir!

SIR   My servant run away with my daughter to the metropolis! With my one remaining sperm shut up in a tin trunk!

PERKINS   She used to visit him every day at the exhibition.

SIR   Exhibition!

PERKINS   At the aquarium.

SIR   (*total outrage*) You put my sperm on exhibition in an aquarium!

PERKINS   Well, he got too big for the bath, Sir, and when the ship sunk ...

SIR   Ship sunk!

PERKINS   ...On the way to America...

SIR   I can't bear it! I can't bear it!

PERKINS   And when they landed us at Bridport, the bailiff recognized us and...

SIR   Be silent! Be silent! (*Heroic.*) Between us we have released a monster into this world, but I shall not rest until this creature is destroyed and the wound inflicted by it on my leg – revenged!

They suddenly realize that they can segue back to the beginning of the play. They struggle eagerly into their sou'westers. Perkins has a spray bottle and he sprays a fine mist over them.

PERKINS   (*runs to side, does seagull sounds etc.*)   Land ho! Land on the port bow.

SIR   (*firmly*)   Keep the course nor-nor-west, Bosun.

PERKINS   But Sir! That's away from the island!

SIR   Of course it's away from the island, Mr. Perkins.

PERKINS   But Sir, we haven't set foot on land for five months.

SIR   Nor shall we, nor shall we, Mr. Perkins, except, God willing, we may sight and utterly destroy the White Whale.

PERKINS   But Sir – what chance that in all these millions of square miles of ocean …?

SIR   I do not care to be instructed by my juniors, Mr. Perkins. Tell me rather, whether my daughter Dorothea is still lashed stark naked to the bowsprit?

PERKINS   She is indeed, Sir! But half dead from the severe cold at these latitudes!

SIR   Are the men still forcing hot rum into her?

PERKINS   Oh yes, Sir – and they're giving her constant massage but I can't think she'll survive much longer! Oh Sir, it's upsetting the crew having her tied stark naked to the bowsprit. The men are getting very roused. At least let me cover her, Sir.

SIR   Cover her, Mr. Perkins! Never!

PERKINS   But she goes under every other wave.

SIR   Exactly! Exactly! And one day the White Whale will sniff her out, and then, and then, only let my brave harpooners sink their darts deep into his muscle and there'll be no saving him. While this creature roams the seven seas which of us is safe, Mr. Perkins? Even at the sacrifice of my daughter, Dorothea, who, God knows, I love more than any other living creature – the White Whale must be destroyed!

PERKINS   But I love her too, Sir.

SIR (*clutching him*)   Love! What can less mortals know of that celestial passion that welds two natures into one enduring flux!

PERKINS (*ventriloquizing*)   Thar she blows!

SIR   The telescope! The telescope, man! There! You see it, Mr. Perkins! The colour, the colour!

PERKINS   White, Sir! (*Ventriloquizes?*) The White Whaaaalle!

SIR   Hard a starboard! Unfurl all canvas!

PERKINS   But you'll run us under, Sir!

SIR   Stick to your post, Mr. Perkins! Bosun! Prepare a harpoon for me! I shall climb out along the bowsprit and make the first thrust myself! Faster! Faster! Throw the cannon overboard. Jettison the stores. Twenty crowns a head if we capture her.

PERKINS (*rushes about ventriloquizing for crew?*) Hurrah! Hurrah! Thar she blows! The White Whaaaale!

SIR   You see it, Mr. Perkins. The stumps of old harpoons sticking out all over her. Look at her roll there! Look at her great underbelly! Come Bessie! Don't you recognize your old progenitor!

PERKINS   Oh don't enrage it, Sir!

SIR (*amazed and delighted*)   Perkins! Perkins! After all these years!

PERKINS   What ever is it, Sir?

SIR   I become, yes, yes…

Perkins wrestling with Sir, trying to repel him.

PERKINS   Let me go, Sir!

SIR   I feel, I feel, Yes… I'm…

PERKINS   Oh, Sir! It's attacking the ship, Sir.

SIR   I'm regaining my potency!

Perkins is still making the noises of the storm?

PERKINS (*point*)   Sir! Thrust with your harpoon!

SIR   I'm cured! I'm cured!

PERKINS   It's going to ram us, Sir! Sir, the men are waiting for you to make the first thrust! Augghh!

Crashing sounds, tearing of timbers, etc. They stagger about.

Swim, Sir. Swim!

Then everything is calm. They stand side by side, gently bobbing in a pool of red light. Take your time.

PERKINS   Swim for your life, Sir.

SIR   The ship?

PERKINS   Sunk with all hands. Keep your arms moving, Sir. Don't lose heart.

SIR   But I'm touching bottom, Perkins.

PERKINS (*likes the idea but mystified*)   In these waters, Sir?

SIR   It's warm.

PERKINS   And throbbing.

SIR   Great heavens, Mr. Perkins. Swallowed alive by the White Whale!

PERKINS (*doing echo*)   Whale… ale… ale…

SIR I can't bear it!

PERKINS (*doing echo*) Bear it… air it… air it…

SIR My mind's going…

PERKINS (*doing echo*) Goinggg… owinggg… owinggg… You must cling on to reality, Sir … (*Doing echo.*) irrr… irrr…

SIR (*hallucinating that Perkins is Dorothea*) Dorothea!… (*Doing echo.*) eeaa… eaaaa

PERKINS (*realizing*)   No! No! It's me, Perkins Sir! Help! Help! Let me out! Noooooo! Help!

Sir chases Perkins around the stage.
Exit.

CRUSOE

The play was first performed by Louie Mahoney and Roddy Maude Roxby at the Mercury Theatre, Notting Hill, London, in 1969 (four years before a very similar play that it has often been compared to).

In Scenes 1, 2, and 4, the action takes place in front of the closed curtains of an inner false proscenium, (Maybe write the name CRUSOE across the top in big "cut-out" letters). In Scenes 3 and 5 the curtains open to show "Crusoe's Cave". This has a perch for the parrot.
The effect should be naive, as if Crusoe had built the false proscenium, and had painted it and assembled the props himself.
The lines should be spoken with an awareness of their strong rhythm. This play has often been performed with live music playing between each scene. Please don't do this.
Crusoe can be hysterically funny with the right audience (e. g., an audience who identify with Friday. I'm thinking of Inuit, Lapps, Somalis etc.). It should be played by happy and "detached" comedians. If you use actors who "identify" with their roles there won't be much laughter.

SCENE ONE

Crusoe has a fake parrot on his shoulder (a cross-eyed parrot capable of standing by itself?).
He carries a horn with a rubber bulb on the end (a bicycle horn will do, but one of those early carriage horns might be better, because larger). He's dressed in some appropriate way – a "solar topee" perhaps, plus bits of fur and odds and ends of clothing.
He has a beard (straggly?).
Don't rush this opening section.

CRUSOE (*pleased with himself*) My name is Crusoe – Robinson Crusoe – and this is the island on which I was shipwrecked by Mr. Daniel Defoe in the book which is a landmark in the history of the English Novel.

I'm quite self-supporting here. I grow my own food, and I dress myself in the skins of the animals that I kill. And of course I fish in the sea surrounding the island – (*Gestures.*) that's where you are!

This is my parrot that I have taught to speak: (*Talks like bad ventriloquist.*) "Polly wants a cracker! Polly wants a cracker!" – and you see me now on the famous day when I discover the footprint in the sand. (*Peeved.*) I should be seeing it any moment now in fact!

Friday runs in, happy and positive, sees audience, plonks foot down in front of Crusoe, and runs off.

Great heavens! There it is! The water still oozing into it! Am I dreaming? Can it be my own? (*Checks size against own.*). No... I hear a cry!

FRIDAY (*off-stage*) Ahhh!

CRUSOE Stealthily I crawl to the top of a dune and part the branches of a small bush. (*Mime this? Or maybe he picks up a branch to peer through?*) Oh! Dreadful sight! A pack of cannibals have put a prisoner in a pot and a cook is seasoning him! Seized by an overwhelming revulsion, I sight my musket, and fire! (*Honks horn as if it were a gun.*) Reloading with extraordinary rapidity...

He cleans the "gun", pours in powder from a baby-powder tin, mimes inserting the bullet, uses a ram-rod to press it home, etc. (He does this as quickly as possible but it'll take a while.)

... I discharge again. And by exposing myself on the skyline... (*thrusts pelvis forwards?*) ... put them to flight. They rush to their canoes and paddle away across the horizon. (*Crusoe feels that this is a job well done.*) I run forwards to release their prisoner.

Exit Crusoe around one side of curtain (Or false pros.) as Friday enters around the other. Friday is very positive. Big eyes. Wide smile. Lots of teeth.

FRIDAY My name is Friday. Mr. Crusoe call me Friday because dat was de day on which he rescue me! Who would have dreamed that anyone would be living alone on dis island? And with such an amazing weapon! Truly dis is a man I should be proud to serve! He teach me his language, and he read to me from a book he calls de Bible. It say I must work for him, and follow the teachings of Jesus. He says that below ground is a place called Hell where sinners burn in everlasting fire. But if I be good and do all that Mr. Crusoe tell me, I will go to a place called Heaven, where God will let me clean up after de Angels!

Friday is happy and respectful, but during the play he realizes that Crusoe is an idiot. Enter Crusoe.

CRUSOE Friday!

FRIDAY Oh Sah! Is something de matter, Sah!

CRUSOE You know perfectly well what's the matter, Friday!

FRIDAY Oh Sah! Friday only take small small snooze, Sah!

CRUSOE (*This wasn't what he had in mind.*) Snooze! Falling asleep when I put you on look-out duty! Supposing some Great White Ship should have sailed by!

FRIDAY Oh Sah! Friday only close one eye at a time so as to rest then Sah! Please forgive dis one indiscretion!

CRUSOE Forgive you! That isn't even what I wanted to see you about!

FRIDAY Oh Sah! Not de telescope, Sah!

CRUSOE The telescope!

FRIDAY Oh Sah, he tumble down on de rock and smash himself, Sah!

CRUSOE (*rage*) You... You smashed my telescope?

FRIDAY Oh no, Sah! Only de glass in de end, Sah!

CRUSOE Oh... Augh! ... I... That's not what I...

FRIDAY Oh Sah! Not de peach, Sah!

CRUSOE (*disbelief*) What about my peach?

FRIDAY Friday ate him, Sah...

CRUSOE (*berserk*) You ate my peach! Five years I spent growing that peach!

FRIDAY (*producing stone*) Oh Sah, Friday keep de stone so you can grow him again, Sah!

CRUSOE   I… I… Whoooo… Augh!…(*Throws it away and then picks it up?*) Sometimes! Sometimes I… Aughhh!

FRIDAY (*interrupting for his own survival but blandly*)   What you want see Friday 'bout anyway, Sah?

CRUSOE (*taken aback*)   Don't you know!

FRIDAY   Friday's mind a blank, Sah!

CRUSOE (*discomfited*)   Well, it's about your trousers. You've been removing them!

FRIDAY   Oh no, Sah!

CRUSOE   Don't lie to me! I saw you standing up against the skyline. You were most conspicuous!

FRIDAY   Oh Sah, deese trousers are a torment to me, Sah!

CRUSOE (*trying to master his anger*)   Did I not teach you that your body was shameful? Have I not read you the story of Adam and Eve from the good book? Well then, I won't have you flaunting yourself about the island! What would happen if the Lord Jesus should float down and see you without your trousers?

FRIDAY   Oh Sah! Friday not be allowed into Heaven to clean up after de Angels, Sah!

CRUSOE   Exactly! (*Steaming up again.*) Falling asleep at your post. Smashing my telescope. Eating my peach!

FRIDAY   Oh Sah! You forgive Friday like it say in de good book, Sah! And he be new man from today.

CRUSOE   Huff!

FRIDAY   Alone together amid all de prodigality of Nature – should we not live in peace and mutual cooperation, Sah?

CRUSOE   Well… Live and let live, I suppose, Friday.

FRIDAY   Friday love you, Sah!

CRUSOE   No, Friday, you mean you like me.

FRIDAY   Den Friday like you, Sah!

CRUSOE   Yes, and I like you, Friday. (*Suppressing his rage.*) Well, I think I shall garden a little!

FRIDAY   Yes, Sah!

Crusoe goes to where vegetables and a trowel are lying. (He tries to make the carrots stand upright?)
Pause.

All the same it not Friday's fault if telescope want to smash himself, Sah!

CRUSOE *(angry?)* I don't want excuses, Friday.

FRIDAY Oh, Sah! The spirits on de island are angry because you do not thank them.

CRUSOE This is rank superstition, Friday.

FRIDAY No, Sah! Every time you go to the beach you throw a pebble in the water and annoy the sea-god, Sah! And Sah! That peach was crying out to be eaten by me because he know I will thank him, Sah. Oh, Sah! Oh Sah! Can you not hear the spirits crying out all over the island – eat us, sit on us, drink us, lie on us, but thank us, thank us! Oh listen, Sah!

Voices like a chorus of tiny birds cheep "Eat us!", "Suck us!", "Drink us!", "Nibble us!" "Fuck us!", "But thank us!", "Thank us!" etc.

CRUSOE *(having listened)* I don't hear a thing, Friday. Spirits do not exist!

The voices stop instantly.

FRIDAY No spirits, Sah?

CRUSOE The universe is one vast clockwork, Friday, and it has been explained by an Englishman!

Crusoe walks off, followed by Friday.

FRIDAY Oh Sah! you forgive Friday. Friday poor ignorant savage man, Sah!

SCENE TWO

Crusoe enters, hangs up "Whites Only" notices on the false proscenium. Then he strips to his old-fashioned (Union Jack?) bathing costume. He deep-breathes? Does exercises? (If in an intimate theatre he throws a pebble into the audience where an assistant catches it and plops it into a bucket of water making a splash.) Enter Friday in modish bathing-costume and carrying a surf-board.

CRUSOE Friday!

FRIDAY Sah!

CRUSOE Just what do you think you're doing?

FRIDAY Bathing, Sah! Very good day, Sah, for a most refreshing swim. Good for de limb, for de complexion, and for de regulation of de bowel, as you have taught me, Sah!

CRUSOE Don't you know what beach this is?

FRIDAY Yes, Sah! This am de sandy beach, Sah!

CRUSOE This is my beach, Friday, this is the beach I swim on!

FRIDAY (*friendly*) Oh Sah! You not really serious about dat Whites Only stuff! Friday am really to swim on the rocky shore where de stones cut the feet?

CRUSOE Separate but equal, Friday!

FRIDAY But how will we romp and frisk together if we on opposite sides of island, Sah!

CRUSOE Englishmen do not romp, Friday!

FRIDAY Not jump up and down and splash de water, Sah?

CRUSOE You may hold my towel to stop the sand getting on it.

FRIDAY (*amazement*) Friday am not to go in de water, Sah?

CRUSOE (*trying to contain his anger?*) Any free time you have you are of course at liberty to climb over to the native beach.

FRIDAY (*outraged*) Dis am an inhumanity, Sah!

CRUSOE I am the dominant species on this island, Friday! With my superior brain and advanced sensibilities, I am your natural superior! You are an untutored savage. Friday!

FRIDAY (*very clearly*) Then *tutor* me, Sah!

CRUSOE (*ignoring him*) Well I'm glad we have that settled. I… er … I'll just wade out until the audience deepens a little. You can act as lifeguard.

FRIDAY (*bitterly?*) Very well, Sah!

Crusoe climbs into audience and pretends to swim and splash about. Meanwhile the assistant (assistants) gives some large triangular soft-edged shark-fins (marked "shark-fin – pass it on") to people sitting at the ends of the rows. Four to six should be enough. The audience will automatically begin to pass these towards Crusoe who will panic. It's wonderful to see these shark-fins moving towards Crusoe through the audience.

CRUSOE   Help! Help!

FRIDAY   (*interested*)   Oh Sah! The shark want you for dinner, Sah!

CRUSOE   I know that Friday, do something!

FRIDAY   Friday come to de rescue Sah!

CRUSOE   Help! Help! *Au secours! Hilfe!*

FRIDAY   Swim, Sah! Swim!

Friday tickles girls in audience, etc. and mimes killing the sharks – throwing the fins onto the stage. This distracts our attention from Crusoe who takes a secret mouthful of water. Friday drags him back to the stage and lies him down and tries to revive him. He presses Crusoe's stomach several times and spurts of water come from Crusoe's mouth.

CRUSOE   Ugh! Oooff! Splutter!

FRIDAY   Oh Sah! You all intact, Sah!

CRUSOE   (*embracing Friday*)   Ah Friday, my dear fellow! (*Remembers shark. Shrinks away from shark fins?*) Auggghhhhhh! The sharks!

FRIDAY   (*throws fins off-stage?*)   Oh, Friday slit them from mouth to belly, Sah!

CRUSOE   Good Lord! You… you saved my life, Friday.

FRIDAY   (*still cheerful*)   Thank you, Sah!

CRUSOE   I… I shall remember this. I… I might even give you a day off. God, but what a fiendish creature! When I saw its great jaws open, and those teeth…

FRIDAY   Oh, we kill them for sport! Sah! (*The thought horrifies Crusoe.*) You strong enough to hold my towel now?

CRUSOE   Certainly, Friday, but… What are you doing?

FRIDAY   Friday go bathing, Sah!

CRUSOE   On the Whites-Only beach!

FRIDAY   You not complain when I save you from de shark, Sah!

CRUSOE That was work, Friday: this is recreation.

FRIDAY Be reasonable, Sah! You say Friday work for you because you save him from de Cook-Pot, Sah! Now Friday save you from de shark belly – surely we are equal, Sah!

CRUSOE Nothing you do or say can ever make you the equal of me!

FRIDAY (*baffled*) Oh Sah! How can that be, Sah!

CRUSOE (*exasperated*) Because of your skin, Friday.

Friday looks at himself? Follows Crusoe off.

FRIDAY Oh Sah! Is Friday on the black list forever?

SCENE THREE

Friday opens the curtain to show Crusoe sitting on a wooden chair, brooding over a chessboard which is set up on a box or packing case. Friday sits opposite him (on the floor?). They play chess. This scene begins very slowly.

FRIDAY Sah...

CRUSOE Ummm?

FRIDAY You are not a magical creature, Sah!

CRUSOE Magical creature? You didn't really think that, did you?

FRIDAY Not for long Sah! But at first encounter... your red and pink blotchy skin, Sah!

CRUSOE Er... my white skin, Friday.

FRIDAY Yes Sah! And a face like an armpit, Sah!

CRUSOE My... My beard, Friday.

FRIDAY Well you are not very like a man, Sah!

Friday takes a chess piece.

CRUSOE Ah now you shouldn't have done that, Friday, because now I take you.

FRIDAY And Friday take you, Sah!

CRUSOE Good Lord! I couldn't have been concentrating. Hummmm

Pause.

FRIDAY   How you come to be on dis island, Sah!

CRUSOE (*pondering the board?*)   Ship blown off course: ripped her bottom out on the reef. Dead slaves washed up all round the island.

FRIDAY (*mildly*)   Black men, Sah?

CRUSOE   Slaves, all in irons, of course. Terrible screaming. Still hear it, every time the wind howls round the island. Managed to swim out and rescue a few things: gunpowder, iron nails, golf clubs. (*Peruses board*) Tell me, Friday, why were your compatriots going to eat you?

FRIDAY   Oh, Sah! I would become part of de whole tribe, Sah!

CRUSOE (*anger? Contempt?*)   I've never heard of such revolting behaviour. The sooner we send a few gun-boats in…

FRIDAY   Check, Sah!

CRUSOE   Check!

FRIDAY   Check, Sah!

CRUSOE   But I'm just teaching you the game!

FRIDAY   Yes Sah! It is check though, Sah!

CRUSOE   Well, you pick up the rules very quickly. (*He moves.*) There!

FRIDAY   Check, Sah!

Crusoe moves.

Double check, Sah!

CRUSOE   What!

FRIDAY   And now your king must go there.

CRUSOE (*angry*)   Don't tell me where I have to move, Friday.

FRIDAY   Well you are check in every other position, Sah!

Crusoe moves.

FRIDAY   Check, Sah. Two more moves and den mate, Sah!

CRUSOE   Impossible!

FRIDAY   Friday has already won in simple logic, Sah!

CRUSOE   Well you can just take back that move and let me have another move!

FRIDAY   Is dat permitted, Sah?

CRUSOE   It's one of the rules I hadn't told you about!

FRIDAY   Very well. Checkmate, Sah!

CRUSOE Mate! I… I shall put my bishop in the way.

FRIDAY But dere am a "discovered" check here, Sah!

CRUSOE Well, we'll just have to go back a few moves.

FRIDAY No Sah! Else Friday can never win, Sah!

CRUSOE Now your queen was here, and my rook was there …

FRIDAY Admit Friday has won, Sah!

They are both moving pieces about the board.

Dis am stupidity, Sah!

CRUSOE I'm not going to argue!

FRIDAY Put it back, Sah!

A scuffle over the board.

CRUSOE (*shouting*) Stop it, Friday! Right! Give me your queen!

*He throws the queen to assistant in audience (*splash!*).*

There! Let that be an end to it!

FRIDAY Brilliant, Sah! Just one moment, Sah!

Friday exits.

CRUSOE Hah! Ignorant savages!

*Friday enters with flaming blow-torch. He sets Crusoe's half of the board alight (*see notes*).*

Friday! Have you taken leave of your senses?

FRIDAY Friday play to de new rules, Sah!

The flames excite Friday. He rubs against walls, etc.

CRUSOE Why I… I… Stop it, Friday!

FRIDAY Friday has de itch, Sah. Friday has de itch for a woman, Sah!

CRUSOE Well, how do you think I feel, cooped up here year after year!

FRIDAY Exactly, Sah! It am no wonder you are acting so strangely Sah.

CRUSOE Acting strangely!

FRIDAY All dese "Whites Only" notices everywhere! And getting angry, bout a little child game! But now dere are two of us and Friday has the itch terrible, Sah!

CRUSOE Well you'll just have to do what I do: stiff upper lip, cold baths, vigorous exercise...
FRIDAY Friday be gentle, Sah!
CRUSOE Are you making an indecent proposal?
FRIDAY (*starting to undress*) All the woman find Friday most attractive! Friday have very big repertoire, Sah!
CRUSOE Stop it, Friday. Don't you dare remove your trousers! (*He pulls Friday's trousers back up.*) Get back to your quarters!
FRIDAY No, Sah!
CRUSOE (*disbelief*) No!
FRIDAY I offer to help you as am only common sense, and you act as if I shit on you! It is not as if you were so attractive in your pinkness and prickliness! (*Pulls elastic top of his trousers forwards and looks down.*) You already made me lose my erection, Sah!
CRUSOE I suppose you want to spend the time lying about in the sun having homosexual orgies!
FRIDAY (*seemingly shocked*) Oh Sah! No, no, Sah! (*Crusoe relieved.*) Not if dere were women about Sah! (*Crusoe appalled.*) Oh Sah! What are our bodies for if not to give pleasure, Sah?
CRUSOE (*kneeling to pray*) Get thee behind me, Satan!
FRIDAY (*moving behind Crusoe*) Very well, Sah!
CRUSOE (*at bay*) Nooooooooo!
FRIDAY Let me tell you something, Mr. Crusoe! All this story about Adam and Eve and the Serpent, Sah! My people also have this story about the first man and the first woman, and I can tell you that that snake was the best thing that ever happened to them. Why the first man had testicles the size of footballs until the snake showed them the way.
CRUSOE Blasphemy!
FRIDAY Friday love you, Sah!
CRUSOE Like! Like!
FRIDAY No Sah! Friday love you, Sah! But Friday not like you very much at all!

Friday chases Crusoe. (*Friday closes the inner curtain.*)

SCENE FOUR

Inner stage closed.
    CRUSOE (*off-stage*) Forrrrrre!
Golf ball comes over top of curtain and rolls to a halt (we used a homemade one made of white tape so that it wouldn't roll far). Enter Crusoe with golf club and with a disgruntled Friday as his caddie. There is a Union Jack among the golf clubs. Maybe he moves the ball to a better position before Friday can get on stage?
    A number five iron I think.
Friday gives him a number five club.
    Wind direction?
    FRIDAY (*testing with wet finger*) North by north-east, Sah! Humidity sixty per cent, ozone content...
    CRUSOE (*shutting him up*) All right! All right! Forrrre!
Friday interrupts before Crusoe can hit the ball.
    FRIDAY Sah!
    CRUSOE Do not address me when I am addressing the ball!
    FRIDAY Beg pardon, Sah!
    CRUSOE Actually I think a number three.
Change of clubs.
    Wind direction?
    FRIDAY North by north-west now, Sah! Humidity...
    CRUSOE (*shutting him up*) All right! Foooorrrree!
Friday interrupts him before he can hit the ball.
    FRIDAY Sah! What has this ball done that you hit him all round de island, Sah?
    CRUSOE This is golf, Friday. Now that I have you working for me I have more time for recreation. And frankly, I'm beginning to need the exercise.
    FRIDAY Then why you not carry de bag, Sah?
    CRUSOE I do not work, Friday. Have I not shown you the good book where it says that God created you to work for me?
    FRIDAY I think a white man wrote that book, Sah!

CRUSOE (*restraining his temper*)　Now stand clear! Wind direction?

FRIDAY　Friday has no spit left, Sah! One moment, Sah!

Crusoe watches Friday pick up the ball and polish it. Friday then throws it to the assistant in the audience who drops it in bucket with a splash. (See notes.)

CRUSOE (*enraged*)　My last ball!

FRIDAY　You knock all de others into de sea, Sah! Why shouldn't I do one?

CRUSOE　I've had just about enough of your impudence, Friday!

FRIDAY (*proud*)　My name not Friday, Sah. My name Obongobo, son of a king! This my people's island, Sah!

CRUSOE　Oh don't be so… (*Dumbfounded.*) Your island! Oh no! This is my island, Friday.

FRIDAY　No Sah! This where we come for our picnics, Sah!

CRUSOE (*at wits' end*)　Er… er… (*Inspiration.*) Pass me that Union Jack.

Friday gives him flag from golf bag.

Now! All I have to do is stick this flag upright in the sand (*gives it to audience member at end of front row*), salute it, cry in a loud voice – "I claim this land in the name of King George the Third, or whoever it is," and there you are – part and parcel of the British Empire. (*He takes back the flag?*)

FRIDAY (*to audience*)　What mumbo-jumbo is this, Sah?

CRUSOE　This is diplomacy, Friday! Oh, we may have to hang a few of the malcontents, but those who survive can work on the plantations …

FRIDAY (*appalled*)　Plantations!

CRUSOE　For the export trade.

FRIDAY　One moment, Sah!

Friday hangs his shirt on a golf club and gives it to someone at the opposite end of the front row. Then he does a parody of Crusoe's ceremony using gibberish.

FRIDAY　This now my island again!

CRUSOE I'm sorry, Friday, but I was first by about one minute and fifteen seconds! (*Self pity?*) Well now, you've completely ruined my game of golf! (*Determination?*) Just for that I shall declare Martial Law. Curfew half an hour before sunset. Possessions of arms a criminal offense. And I forbid you to assemble in groups of more than two! (*Starts to get weepy.*) When you came here I offered you the hand of friendship. I thought I would have a companion to share my loneliness. You don't know what it's like not to have… oh…expensive clothes… and linen bed-sheets… and… and people to admire you and say what a fine fellow you are… Ohhhhhhhhhh!

He weeps on knee of audience member – if the architecture of the theatre permits (see notes). Friday, a little embarrassed, pulls him back on stage.

FRIDAY There, Sir, there…

CRUSOE (*uncontrollable weeping*) Cast up here, a poor Philoctetes … If only I could see a chequebook again, or a daffodil!

He looks at his hands, aghast.

Is… is this shit, Friday?

FRIDAY Oh Sah! Very likely, Sah!

CRUSOE Have you been shitting on my vegetable patch?

FRIDAY Oh Sah! The plants were crying out for it, Sah! Shit on me! Shit on me!

Little voices saying 'Shit on me!'?

CRUSOE (*berserk*) After I take years constructing a viable sewage system I expect you to use it!

Crusoe mimes slipping about on the shit. Friday helps him up. Crusoe mimes wiping shit on Friday, on the curtains, etc.

FRIDAY But Sah! Your shit so strong all the fish die where it come out in de sea!

CRUSOE (*disbelief*) Is… Is that my Bible?

FRIDAY Oh Sah! Friday had no leaves on which to wipe himself, Sah!

CRUSOE You tore the pages from my Bible to use as toilet paper!

FRIDAY Oh dere plenty left, Sah!

CRUSOE (*in extremity – picking up pages*) Genesis! Moses! Isaiah!

FRIDAY Oh Sah! You no hit poor Friday, Sah!
CRUSOE (*furious*) Give me one good reason!
FRIDAY (*with car horn*) Because Friday has the car horn, Sah!
CRUSOE Auggghhh! Don't... don't point that thing at me...
FRIDAY Oh Sah! Do not make Friday nervous, Sah!
CRUSOE Don't shoot! Please... Augh!
FRIDAY (*indicating bag*) I think it your turn to carry de bag, Sah! A number five iron I think.
CRUSOE As you wish Friday.
FRIDAY Mr. Obongobo!

Friday conjures golf ball from the air, or out of his mouth or in some other magical way.

CRUSOE Mr. Obongobo.
FRIDAY (*prompting him*) Sah!
CRUSOE Mr. Obongobo, Sah.
FRIDAY (*hitting ball*) Foooorrrrrree!

SCENE FIVE

Friday opens the inner stage to show a disgruntled Crusoe in a wooden bath (see notes). Give the audience time to relish this image.

CRUSOE (*to audience*) I save his life! I let him share my cave! I give him his own beach! I... I give him simple instructions as befitting his station, yet he remains oblivious of his cultural and biological inferiority. Could he build the Parthenon? Write the *Divine Comedy*? Could three of him typing for all eternity ever produce the complete works of Shakespeare? (*Glancing round.*) Can he even make a quick costume-change without leaving me here with egg on my face?

Friday enters in savage regalia, shocking Crusoe.

CRUSOE Augh! Very commendable this attempt to keep up your native customs, Friday...
FRIDAY Mr. Obongobo!

CRUSOE   Mr. Obongobo! (*Shocked.*) But... but where did you get those feathers!

FRIDAY   The parrot, Sah!

CRUSOE (*distraught*)   My parrot!

FRIDAY   He was calling me stupid nigger so I ate him, Sah!

CRUSOE   You ate poor Polly?

FRIDAY   Oh, Sah! It is time for the ceremony! Can you not hear the voices of the spirits!

Voices as before but saying "Dance, Friday! Dance, Friday!"?

FRIDAY   Friday must dance, Sah!

Friday does spectacular "native dance" – lots of foot stamping. He becomes "possessed". Crusoe gets alarmed.

CRUSOE   Friday – Mr. Obongobo – that's enough of this hockus pockus!

FRIDAY (*as a God and seizing Crusoe*)   White mannnnnn!

CRUSOE   Auuughh!

FRIDAY   Why do you abuse my servant and claim him as your own?

Friday plunges Crusoe's head into bucket of water concealed in the bath (between Crusoe's legs). Crusoe mimes drowning, splutters, gasps etc. Friday pulls him out.

CRUSOE   Stop it, now stop...

Friday plunges Crusoe's head into the bucket again.

FRIDAY   You treat my servant like those black men who lie around the island, still in their chains and encrusted with coral!

CRUSOE   Augh! Help! Help!

A phone rings (Crusoe is "saved by the bell").

FRIDAY (*normal*)   Oh Sah!

CRUSOE   What... what's that noise?

Friday hands Crusoe phone from behind bath.

FRIDAY   Oh Sah! Friday invent the telephone, Sah! Listen, Sah!

CRUSOE   Augh! Spirits!

Crusoe drops the receiver – Friday catches it.

FRIDAY Not to drop de receiver in the water, Sah! Hello? Hello? (*Speaks in educated voice.*) Most gratifying. (*Hangs up. Usual voice.*) Friday use dis machine to call his relatives on the other island, Sah!
CRUSOE (*to audience.*) Is it possible?
FRIDAY Friday would invent de speedboat, Sah, but has no petrol for the outboard motor!
CRUSOE Most ingenious, Friday.
FRIDAY We have big celebration for you, Sah! It will be a surprise party!
CRUSOE But look here… if it's a surprise party, surely you shouldn't be telling me about it?
FRIDAY Oh, Friday kick himself, Sah!

Friday kicks himself. He holds a large towel to hide Crusoe climbing out of bath. Crusoe sits on chair wrapped in the towel.

CRUSOE You're sure your people will welcome me!
FRIDAY My people will love you, Sah!
CRUSOE Like! Like, Friday.
FRIDAY My people will relish you, Sah.

He dries Crusoe's head with second towel. Perhaps leave a pause to let audience contemplate the implications.

CRUSOE Yes, but… er… (*New thought.*) Why… Why have you built that great fire on the beach?
FRIDAY To guide my people to the island, Sir!
CRUSOE But they must see the smoke of the volcano from a hundred miles away!
FRIDAY Oh Friday one stupid nigger, Sir.

Friday is acquiring an educated accent.

CRUSOE Will there be a meat dish?
FRIDAY (*sharpening huge knife*) Very sweet, and with a nutty flavour, Sir.
CRUSOE Er… Friday…
FRIDAY (*sadly*) Oh, Sir! How could you live among my people, Sir! You are such a torment to the spirits, Sir.
CRUSOE Couldn't you just leave me here like I was before?

Distant chanting ("ah-ee-ya-ohhh" – or similar "Sanders of the river" stuff). The chanting gets louder.

> FRIDAY   Oh Sah! Can you not hear my people approaching the island, and singing your praises! (*Uses his earlier voice.*) Oh Sah! Friday must dance, Sah.

He dances again – a knife-sharpening dance?

Crusoe appeals to members of the audience. He runs about the stage, talking to them?

> CRUSOE   Why can't he understand that it was all legal? A slave eats! He sleeps in a dry bed! My own crew used to beg the slaves for food on the way over from Africa! A slave is far better off than the average Englishman! Why! I've dragged half-dead wretches out of the poor house to labour in my fields! Half of my crew were captured in the streets and dragged aboard. When I was a magistrate I used to hang men for chipping the balustrade of Westminster Bridge!

> FRIDAY   (*brandishing the knife and becoming the "God"*)   White man!

Friday chases Crusoe.

> CRUSOE   (*terrified*)   All right! You can have the cave! You can swim on the white beach. Take everything! Democracy! That's the answer! One man one vote! And I vote for… Augh!

> FRIDAY   (*stabbing Crusoe*)   Too late, Mr. Crusoe!

Or – they run off, with Crusoe yelling "Democracy" as their voices fade into the distance.

Or – Crusoe can say "Finish me!" and Friday can reply "Oh no, Sah, you must bleed to make the meat white!"

Now that it's calm we realize that little voices have been saying (and are still saying): "Eat us!", "Suck us!", "Drink us!", "Nibble us!" "Fuck us!", "But thank us, thank us", etc.

Blackout. Crusoe and Friday take bows, receive flowers from the assistants (like at the ballet or the opera or at some grand gala performance). They shake hands, embrace each other, shake hands with the audience, and are best friends.

NOTES

The "Friday!"s and "Sah!"s are used through the play for rhythm, and to show dominance and submission (or fake submission). When they are absent, it's because something personal is being said, or at the end of the play where Crusoe doesn't want to be to be totally submissive and yet daren't anger Friday. An understanding of why „Sah!"s and „Fridays!" come where they come will be a help to learning this text correctly. The text is rhythmical and the percussive effect of the "Friday!"s and "Sah!"s is important.

The blow-torch is readied back-stage. The old-fashioned kind are best, because they roar. We put salt on Crusoe's side of the board, and poured spirit on just before the scene began so that only his side of the board ever caught fire. If the fire regulations don't allow this in indoor-performances (even though you could have the Assistants enter with fire extinguishers), you may have to settle for an explosion. Have Friday mime attaching a cable to the board and then have him mime pumping a handle as the board explodes. Or have him enter with a chainsaw and saw up the prepared board and the box it's standing on. Or have him attack it with a axe. But the fire is best because Friday can dance around the flames, getting roused. If you have an explosion, why not find a way to substitute a blackened and battered parrot for the green one.

Perhaps create a fake fire using a fan with fluttering strips of ribbon lit from below with a powerful light, both items being hidden in the box – the effect of this can be very convincing.

Our golf ball was uneven to prevent it from rolling into the audience. Try a ping-pong ball half filled with sand.

Crusoe should choose some hopefully sympathetic woman's knee to weep on during the daffodil speech. Usually they pat Crusoe gently on the head.

In my productions the play usually lasts about forty minutes.

OLIVER

Oliver lived in a cottage near the beach. He had such hopes when he was younger, but nothing he touched had ever prospered. Even worse, he had been unable to establish a mature relationship with a woman.

One day he wrote a note that expressed his frustration and loneliness. He added his address (plus a photograph of himself), sealed it into a bottle, and threw it into the sea.

Every morning he waited for the post to arrive, eagerly at first, and then with resignation. Years passed before he received a reply. It enclosed a photograph of a woman who had been sitting on the shore when a wave had deposited the bottle at her feet. She wrote that she understood him, that he was her true soul mate, and that God had meant them for each other.

Overjoyed, Oliver poured his heart out in a second letter, ending with "… I have been waiting for you for the whole of my wasted life, and I feel sure we will find true happiness together." And then he sealed it into a bottle, and hurled it into the sea.

But the bitch never replied.

Printed in Poland
by Amazon Fulfillment
Poland Sp. z o.o., Wrocław